Mental Illness

OPPOSING VIEWPOINTS®

Other Books of Related Interest in the Opposing
Viewpoints Series:

AIDS
America's Cities
America's Prisons
Chemical Dependency
Child Abuse
Crime and Criminals
Drug Abuse
Health Care in America
The Homeless
Poverty
Social Justice
Suicide
Violence in America
War on Drugs

Mental Illness

OPPOSING VIEWPOINTS®

David Bender & Bruno Leone, *Series Editors*

William Barbour, *Book Editor*

OPPOSING
VIEWPOINTS
SERIES®

Greenhaven Press, Inc., San Diego, CA

Greenhaven Press, Inc.
PO Box 289009
San Diego, CA 92198-9009

Library of Congress Cataloging-in-Publication Data

Mental illness : opposing viewpoints / William Barbour.
    p.   cm. — (Opposing viewpoints series)
  Includes bibliographical references and index.
  ISBN 1-56510-209-6 (acid-free paper : lib.) — ISBN 1-56510-208-8 (acid-free paper : pbk.)
  1. Mental illness—Juvenile literature. I. Barbour, William, 1963–   . II. Series: Opposing viewpoints series (Unnumbered)
RC460.2.M47   1995
362.2—dc20   94-4977
                                                              CIP0
                                                              AC

"Congress shall make no law . . .
abridging the freedom of speech,
or of the press."

First Amendment to the U.S. Constitution

The basic foundation of our democracy is the First Amendment guarantee of freedom of expression. The Opposing Viewpoints Series is dedicated to the concept of this basic freedom and the idea that it is more important to practice it than to enshrine it.

Contents

Chapter 6: What Policies Would Benefit the Mentally Ill?

Why Consider Opposing Viewpoints?

"The only way in which a human being can make some approach to knowing the whole of a subject is by hearing what can be said about it by persons of every variety of opinion and studying all modes in which it can be looked at by every character of mind. No wise man ever acquired his wisdom in any mode but this."

John Stuart Mill

In our media-intensive culture it is not difficult to find differing opinions. Thousands of newspapers and magazines and dozens of radio and television talk shows resound with differing points of view. The difficulty lies in deciding which opinion to agree with and which "experts" seem the most credible. The more inundated we become with differing opinions and claims, the more essential it is to hone critical reading and thinking skills to evaluate these ideas. Opposing Viewpoints books address this problem directly by presenting stimulating debates that can be used to enhance and teach these skills. The varied opinions contained in each book examine many different aspects of a single issue. While examining these conveniently edited opposing views, readers can develop critical thinking skills such as the ability to compare and contrast authors' credibility, facts, argumentation styles, use of persuasive techniques, and other stylistic tools. In short, the Opposing Viewpoints Series is an ideal way to attain the higher-level thinking and reading skills so essential in a culture of diverse and contradictory opinions.

In addition to providing a tool for critical thinking, Opposing Viewpoints books challenge readers to question their own strongly held opinions and assumptions. Most people form their opinions on the basis of upbringing, peer pressure, and personal, cultural, or professional bias. By reading carefully balanced opposing views, readers must directly confront new ideas as well as the opinions of those with whom they disagree. This is not to simplistically argue that everyone who reads opposing views will—or should—change his or her opinion. Instead, the series enhances readers' depth of understanding of their own views by encouraging confrontation with opposing ideas. Careful examination of others' views can lead to the readers' understanding of the logical inconsistencies in their own opinions, perspective on why they hold an opinion, and the consideration of the possibility that their opinion requires further evaluation.

Evaluating Other Opinions

To ensure that this type of examination occurs, Opposing Viewpoints books present all types of opinions. Prominent spokespeople on different sides of each issue as well as well-known professionals from many disciplines challenge the reader. An additional goal of the series is to provide a forum for other, less known, or even unpopular viewpoints. The opinion of an ordinary person who has had to make the decision to cut off life support from a terminally ill relative, for example, may be just as valuable and provide just as much insight as a medical ethicist's professional opinion. The editors have two additional purposes in including these less known views. One, the editors encourage readers to respect others' opinions—even when not enhanced by professional credibility. It is only by reading or listening to and objectively evaluating others' ideas that one can determine whether they are worthy of consideration. Two, the inclusion of such viewpoints encourages the important critical thinking skill of objectively evaluating an author's credentials and bias. This evaluation will illuminate an author's reasons for taking a particular stance on an issue and will aid in readers' evaluation of the author's ideas.

As series editors of the Opposing Viewpoints Series, it is our hope that these books will give readers a deeper understanding of the issues debated and an appreciation of the complexity of even seemingly simple issues when good and honest people disagree. This awareness is particularly important in a democratic society such as ours in which people enter into public debate to determine the common good. Those with whom one disagrees should not be regarded as enemies but rather as people whose views deserve careful examination and may shed light on one's own.

Thomas Jefferson once said that "difference of opinion leads to inquiry, and inquiry to truth." Jefferson, a broadly educated man, argued that "if a nation expects to be ignorant and free . . . it expects what never was and never will be." As individuals and as a nation, it is imperative that we consider the opinions of others and examine them with skill and discernment. The Opposing Viewpoints Series is intended to help readers achieve this goal.

David L. Bender & Bruno Leone,
Series Editors

Introduction

"The deinstitutionalized mentally ill have too often faced a future of abandonment, hopelessness and despair."

U.S. senator Edward M. Kennedy

Society has not always treated its mentally ill citizens well. In seventeenth-century America, people with mental illnesses were thought to be possessed by demons and were severely punished. Later, according to David A. Rochefort, author of *From Poorhouses to Homelessness*, they were placed in almshouses where "living conditions were ghastly, and little if any medical care was provided." Conditions for the mentally ill improved somewhat in the late 1700s and early 1800s, when the concept of "moral treatment"—the idea that mental illnesses could be cured through humane treatment in stress-free settings—led to the creation of numerous asylums. By the late nineteenth century, however, these asylums, which were initially uncrowded, well staffed, and pleasantly maintained, had devolved into large public institutions—state hospitals—that housed the mentally ill but offered little psychiatric treatment or medical care.

Conditions for the mentally ill remained relatively unchanged until the mid-1950s, when various social, political, and economic forces culminated in a policy of "deinstitutionalization"—a massive emptying of state mental hospitals that continued into the 1980s. In general, deinstitutionalization reflected the belief among professionals and the public that people with mental illnesses could be treated more humanely and effectively in communities than in institutions. This belief was spurred in part by the publication of numerous media exposés that portrayed state hospitals as overcrowded and poorly run "warehouses" for the mentally ill. These exposés prompted a movement among social reformers and civil libertarians to secure legal rights for mental patients—including the right to refuse treatment under most conditions. Deinstitutionalization was also stimulated by the development in the 1950s of new antipsychotic drugs to control the symptoms of many mental illnesses, offering hope that the mentally ill could lead relatively normal lives outside institutions. Due to these and other factors, the number of public mental health patients declined from 559,000 in 1955 to 101,402 in 1989, according to Rochefort.

Many critics argue that deinstitutionalization has created several serious problems in the way the mentally ill are treated. To encourage deinstitutionalization, the federal government authorized, under the Community Mental Health Centers Act of 1963, a network of 2,000 Community Mental Health Centers (CMHCs) nationwide to treat the mentally ill; but fewer than 800 CMHCs were actually created, leaving many of the released mental patients without the community supports they needed to function outside institutions. Moreover, due to the prevailing belief at the time that mental illnesses were preventable through early psychotherapeutic intervention, the CMHCs that were established became counseling centers for people with relatively minor problems while ignoring the severely mentally ill, according to psychiatrist E. Fuller Torrey. Others contend that the new antipsychotic drugs, while effective, did not live up to their promise because mental patients often refused or forgot to take them. Consequently, critics charge, deinstitutionalization left large numbers of mentally ill people homeless. According to Torrey, "A study in Massachusetts showed that 27 per cent of those discharged from state psychiatric hospitals became homeless within six months; a similar study in Ohio found the figure to be 36 per cent."

In response, many propose aggressive measures to get the mentally ill more psychiatric care. They argue that the symptoms of mental illness often leave people too disoriented to know they need help and make them distrustful and resistant toward medical personnel. Also, due to the efforts of civil libertarians in the 1960s and 1970s, current laws in every state grant patients the right to refuse treatment unless they pose an immediate threat to themselves or others. Because of these factors, critics argue, too many mentally ill people go untreated: Families must often wait until a mentally ill spouse or child becomes violent or self-destructive before professionals can legally intervene, and many mentally ill citizens are left homeless because they refuse the housing and treatment services offered to them. Consequently, commentators such as Rael Jean Isaac and Virginia C. Armat, authors of *Madness in the Streets*, favor changing the laws to make it easier to forcibly hospitalize mentally ill people who need, but refuse, attention.

Others contend that while deinstitutionalization has led to problems, it remains a favorable alternative to the state hospital system. These advocates maintain that most of the mentally ill are better off in community settings than permanently housed in institutions. They argue that the idea behind deinstitutionalization is a good one, but that its implementation was flawed. "Deinstitu-tionalization was, in itself, not a mistake," according to Torrey. "We know now that opening the gates [of the mental hospitals] is not enough." Ann Braden Johnson, author of *Out of Bedlam*, agrees: "Deinstitutionalization was a great step forward. . . . Our mistake was in thinking that to initiate the process was to com-plete it. Simply discharging patients to community life was not, as we have seen, the whole of the exercise. First we had to find out what they would need to survive—who knew?"

Johnson and others argue that rather than assertive psychiatric treatments, the mentally ill need services and programs de-signed to help them function in the community. According to Torrey, "Most of these patients need continuing medication, so-cial support, rehabilitation, job training, and housing." Experts agree that services for the mentally ill should be tailored to meet individual needs. For example, housing arrangements should include a degree of supervision appropriate for the indi-vidual, and case managers should be assigned to each patient to coordinate various services and treatments. Many commenta-tors also advocate programs that encourage and enable mentally ill people to become autonomous and integral members of soci-ety. For example, Johnson stresses the importance of occupa-tional programs for the mentally ill: "We cannot seriously expect the mentally ill to live out their whole lives wasting time—no one, perceiving that to be his future, could seriously want to go on with it."

Whether it represents a failure or a good idea still in progress, deinstitutionalization has radically altered America's mental health landscape. People who, prior to 1950, would have been permanently housed in state institutions, now occupy various community settings—from independent housing to halfway houses to cardboard boxes. The impact of deinstitutionalization is a theme that emerges repeatedly in *Mental Illness: Opposing View-points*, which contains the following chapters: How Should Men-tal Illness Be Defined? What Causes Mental Illness? Are Mental Health Treatments Beneficial? How Should Society Respond to the Homeless Mentally Ill? How Should the Legal System Deal with Mental Illness? What Policies Would Benefit the Mentally Ill? In these chapters, the social, political, legal, and medical is-sues associated with mental illness are discussed and debated.

How Should Mental Illness Be Defined?

Mental Illness

Chapter Preface

The number of conditions defined as "mental illness" has increased dramatically since the 1950s. For example, Erica E. Goode reports in *U.S. News & World Report* magazine that the number of possible diagnoses included in the American Psychiatric Association's *Diagnostic and Statistical Manual of Mental Disorders* (DSM), the nation's definitive diagnostic handbook, increased from 106 in 1952 to 292 in 1992.

Some people oppose this proliferation of diagnoses. They complain that psychiatrists are redefining relatively normal personality traits as illnesses. According to Goode, these critics contend that "the realm of the abnormal [is] encroaching on areas that were once the province of individual choice, habit, eccentricity or lifestyle." Some believe this intrusion of the medical establishment into people's personal lives promotes a limited view of human existence. Goode writes that "the advent of more and more psychiatric pigeonholes, some critics feel, reflects a broader trend toward turning any behavior that departs from the ideal into a medical condition. The splendor of human diversity thus runs the risk of becoming simply a collection of syndromes and disorders."

Others argue that broad definitions of mental illness are beneficial. They contend that mental illnesses manifest themselves in varying degrees of severity. According to commentators Denis J. Prager and Leslie J. Scallet, "We should conceive of mental health as a continuum of well-being from good health at one end to catastrophic dysfunction and suffering at the other." Robert Sapolsky, a neuroendocrinologist at Stanford University, agrees. He argues that mental conditions of varying severity result from the same biological underpinnings. For example, he writes, "If you have a certain genetic makeup, you're predisposed to schizophrenia. Have a milder version of this genetic makeup, and you may be predisposed to placing a strong faith in magical ideas." According to Sapolsky, a broad view of mental illness breeds compassion and tolerance by "recognizing the continuity between the workings of our benign little personality quirks and the versions that might qualify as diseases."

The line between mental illness and mental health is often indistinct. Some argue that only severe disorders such as schizophrenia, clinical depression, and manic-depressive illness should be classified as mental illnesses. Others maintain that mental illnesses include a broad spectrum of conditions, from relatively mild to catastrophic. In the following chapter, the authors debate where this elusive line should be drawn.

> *"Being healthy . . . really consists of having the same disease as everyone else."*

Broad Definitions of Mental Illness Are Beneficial

Robert Sapolsky

In the following viewpoint, Robert Sapolsky argues that because mental disorders are caused by the same neurological and genetic factors that influence all human behavior, borders separating normal and abnormal behavior are artificial. According to Sapolsky, definitions of mental illness should be broad enough to reflect the varying degrees of abnormal behavior common to both mildly eccentric and severely ill individuals. Sapolsky is a neuroendocrinologist at Stanford University in California.

As you read, consider the following questions:

1. What is "schizotypal personality disorder," according to Sapolsky?
2. According to the author, why is obsessive-compulsive disorder harmful? Why is a lesser degree of obsessive behavior beneficial?

From Robert Sapolsky, "How Big Is Yours?" *Discover*, March 1992, ©1992 The Walt Disney Co. Reprinted with permission of *Discover* magazine.

Contemplating the treatment of an insane person from a century ago is something of a Rorschach test for us. Do we focus on the vast progress that has been made in psychiatry? Or do we see no difference at all from our own miserably inadequate treatment of the mentally ill?

Some things remain depressingly the same across the centuries: in so many times and places, the mentally ill give the rest of us the willies, and they are carefully isolated and ostracized. Yet many other things have changed. When we discuss treatments now, we think of drugs to manipulate brain chemicals such as neurotransmitters, while in earlier times it was lobotomies and insulin-induced comas, and still earlier, restraint and ice baths. Our notions of causes have changed as well. Now we discuss receptor regulation and genes, while earlier we would have blamed mothers sending conflicting signals of love and hate to impressionable young children.

What has changed most palpably, however, is our attitude toward abnormal behavior. We have become far more subtle when we consider the thorny issues of blame for disturbed actions. Centuries ago epileptics were persecuted for their presumed bewitchment. We no longer do that, nor would any rational person prosecute an epileptic for assault and battery should that epileptic injure someone while flailing during a seizure. We have been trained to think: "This is not a violent person. This is a person whose arms swing uncontrollably at times because of a disease." We have drawn a line between the essence of a person and the neuropsychiatric disorder that distorts that essence.

But precisely where this line is drawn is still shifting. And some astonishing new trends in neuropsychiatry and behavioral biology indicate that the line is going to have to shift in directions we never would have guessed. This shift affects much more than our understanding of the biological imperatives that drive a small group of us to monstrous behavior. It also affects how we view the quirks and idiosyncrasies that make each of us a healthy individual.

Degrees of Schizophrenia

To me, one of the most intriguing changes has occurred in the way we see "schizotypal" individuals. A few decades ago a team headed by psychiatrist Seymour Kety of Massachusetts General Hospital initiated studies that demonstrated a genetic component to the disordered jumble of thoughts known as schizophrenia. The scientists examined adoption records meticulously maintained in Denmark, reviewing the cases of children adopted from their biological parents very early in life. If a child of a schizophrenic parent was adopted by healthy parents, Kety wanted to know, was the child at greater than average risk for schizophrenia? Conversely, did any child of healthy biological parents raised in a household with a schizophrenic adoptive parent have an increased risk for the illness?

Kety's work showed that genetics does in fact increase the likelihood of the disorder. But to get that answer, doctors had to conduct intensive psychiatric interviews with the various biological and adoptive parents. This involved thousands of people and years of work. No one had ever studied the relatives of schizophrenics in such numbers before. And along the way someone noticed something: a lot of these folks were quirky. These relatives were not themselves schizophrenic—just a bit socially detached and with a train of thought that was sometimes a little hard to follow when they spoke. It was something subtle, and not the sort of thing you'd note in talking to the family members of a few schizophrenics, but it suddenly stuck out when you dealt with thousands of them. They believed in strange things and were often overly concerned with magical or fantasy thinking. Oh, nothing certifiably crazy—maybe a heavy interest in science fiction and fantasy, or a firm belief in some New Age mumbo jumbo or astrology, or maybe a very literal, fundamentalist belief in biblical miracles.

Schizophrenics Are People

Schizophrenics are people. This may seem self-evident, but the twentieth-century history of the hundreds of thousands of schizophrenics in the public care of the United States provides little evidence to suggest that they are indeed considered to be fully human. . . .

If schizophrenia can be discussed and regarded in a more humanistic, more reasoned, and less superstitious manner, then the sense of otherness surrounding schizophrenics will necessarily decrease. With this, hopefully, will come some sympathy and empathy and a desire to help those truly incapable of helping themselves.

John S. Allen, *The Humanist*, May/June 1991.

None of these are illnesses. Many adults go to Star Trek conventions, presidents' wives consult astrologers, and others believe that Jesus literally brought people back to life. But today psychiatrists call the collection of traits seen by Kety "schizotypal personality disorder," especially the emphasis on magical thinking and the loosely connected thoughts. Apparently, if you have a certain genetic makeup, you're predisposed to schizophrenia. Have a milder version of this genetic makeup, and you may be predisposed to placing a strong faith in magical ideas that are not particularly based on fact. Is there a gene for believing in the Force and Obi-Wan Kenobi? Certainly not, but perhaps there's something closer to it than we ever would have imagined.

A Little Bit "Frontal"

Behavioral biology is also revealing the workings of our normal inhibitions. Over the course of an average day there must be a dozen times in which you have a thought—perhaps lustful or angry or petulant or self-pitying—that you would *never, ever* say. Damage a certain part of your brain's frontal cortex and you now *say* those things. Phineas Gage, a nineteenth-century railroad worker, became a celebrated neurological patient and fairground exhibit after his left frontal cortex was destroyed in a freak accident. He was transformed from a taciturn man to a pugnacious loudmouth who told everyone just what he thought.

Some neuroscientists even use the word *frontal* in a sardonic sense: A terrified student gives a quavering lecture to his elders, and some insensitive big shot gets up and savages the kid over some minor point, taking the opportunity to toot his own horn while he's at it. "Christ," someone will mutter in the back of the lecture hall, "he's getting more frontal all the time."

Blow away that part of the brain and you can still remember the name of your kindergarten teacher, still do a polka, still feel what all of us feel. You just let other people know about it far more often than do most of us. Is it absurd to hypothesize that there is something a *little* bit wrong with the frontal cortex of the insensitive big shot in the lecture hall?

Relatively Obsessive

Some epileptics undergo a shift toward the opposite behavioral extreme: inhibition and embarrassment. Roughly defined, an epileptic seizure is an abnormal electrical discharge in the brain. Neurologists have known for a long time that just before the onset of a seizure there will often be a strange sensation, or "aura," and the location of the seizure in the brain can influence the type of aura—for example, epileptics will typically have a sensory aura, perhaps imagining a particular smell. But auras can be far odder than that, and documented cases of them include feeling an intense sense of embarrassment, a surge of religious conviction, or in one case, always hearing the same few bars of Beethoven's Fifth Symphony. The existence of auras demonstrates the not very surprising fact that sudden bursts of electrical activity in different parts of the brain will influence thought and sensation. Now neurologists are coming to recognize that different types of epilepsy also affect personalities—influencing the person all the time, not merely seconds before a seizure.

People with a type of temporal lobe epilepsy, for example, tend to be extraordinarily serious, humorless, and rigid in their ways. They tend to be phobic about doing new things, and instead perseverate [repeat to an exceptional degree] on old behaviors and tastes. Such people also tend to be especially interested in religion or philosophy. And, characteristically, they not only think obsessively about their problems, they write about them—endlessly. Temporal lobe epileptics are renowned among neurologists for this "hypergraphia." In a typical scenario, someone first seeing a new neurologist will present the doctor with a carefully handwritten 80-page diary, insisting that reading it will give the doctor vital insight into the patient. At the next visit the epileptic will return with a new, 50-page addendum.

There's another version of a constrained life that is being defined biologically. At some time each of us has, to our irritation, left on a trip and felt such nagging doubt as to whether or not we locked the door that we returned home to check. Or after dropping a letter into a mailbox, we have peeked in a second time just to make sure it went down. This is normal and common. But among people with obsessive-compulsive disorder, these thoughts dominate and ruin their lives. They miss vacations because they return home repeatedly to check if the oven was turned off. They lose their jobs because they are late each day, spending hours each morning washing their hands. They torture themselves by obsessively counting numbers in their heads. For most of us, little rituals of thought or behavior can calm us and provide structure at an anxious time. For someone with obsessive-compulsive disorder—now thought to be caused by an imbalance of brain chemicals, possibly serotonin and dopamine—there are no limits, and the person becomes a creature of these rituals.

Extending the Definition of Illness

What does this tour of neuropsychiatric oddities mean? We are beginning to learn what certain parts of the brain, what specific genes, or what our early development has to do with some of the odder corners of human behavior and thought. In the process we are extending our definition of illness. For some time we have generally accepted that people who rave and gibber are ill, that they cannot control these things, are made miserable by them, and deserve care, protection, and forgiveness. Slowly we are coming to recognize that you can also be made miserable by a ceaseless march of number counting in your head, or by paralyzing fears of anything new, and that these too can be uncontrollable illnesses that demand understanding and treatment.

As we gain more labels and explain more biology, eventually we might be able to cure some of these maladies. But something

21

else is going to happen: we will find we have moved far beyond the realm of disease and mental illness. Things will have gotten closer to home—and as we all know, even if everyone else is crazy, me and thee are just fine.

I recognize facets of myself in these pages. At times when I am overworked and anxious, I develop a facial tic and I count stairs as I climb them. I tend to wear flannel shirts all the time. In Chinese restaurants I always order broccoli with garlic sauce. Invariably I think, "I'll get broccoli and garlic sauce," then I think, "Nah, order something different," then I think, "Why? I enjoyed broccoli last time, why get something different?" and then I think, "Careful, I'm becoming a perseverating drudge," and then the waiter is standing there and I get flustered and order broccoli with garlic sauce.

I do not have temporal lobe epilepsy, obsessive-compulsive disorder, or any of the other problems I have discussed. Yet it is reasonable to assume that there is some sort of continuum of underlying biology here—whatever it is about the temporal lobe of some epileptics that makes them perseverate may share some similarity with my own temporal lobe, at least when it is menaced with options like Buddha's Delight or General Po's Szechuan Chicken. Perhaps whatever neurochemical abnormality makes a schizophrenic believe that voices are proclaiming her the empress of California is the same abnormality that, in a milder form, leads a schizotypal person to believe that Jesus literally walked on water. In an even milder form it may allow us to pass a few minutes daydreaming that we are close friends with some appealing movie character.

Kinship in Neurochemistry

What if we eventually understand the genetics, the neurochemistry, and the hormonal bases of clothing preference, of who votes Democratic, of religiosity, or of why some worry too much about money and others too little? Some of these are irritating traits or, at worst, character weaknesses, but nothing more pathological. Slowly we will be leaving the realm of disorders and disabilities. We will be defining instead a biology of our strengths and weaknesses, of our potentials and constraints. We will be approaching the reductionist basis of our individuality. . . .

This new world of understanding will be rife with old dangers. With scientific understanding comes the potential for manipulation, and the temptation to judge and "correct" is never far behind. Those who would use behavioral biology in the future to rid us of whatever facets of individuality are deemed unacceptable will probably be as common as were the brownshirts of the past, whose biological template was an Aryan profile.

But this new knowledge would be rife with promise as well.

Recognizing the continuity between the workings of our benign little personality quirks and the versions that might qualify as disease would benefit those with the latter. When science teaches us repeatedly that there but for the grace of God go I, when we learn to recognize kinship in neurochemistry, we will have to become compassionate and tolerant, whether looking at an illness, a quirk, or a mere difference. And when this recognition becomes commonplace, we will have learned that drawing a boundary between "the essence of a person" and "the biological distortion of that essence" is artificial. It is simply a convenient way to classify the biological limitations common to most of us and other, rarer limitations. Being healthy, it has been said, really consists of having the same disease as everyone else.

"The splendor of human diversity . . . runs the risk of becoming simply a collection of syndromes and disorders."

Broad Definitions of Mental Illness May Be Harmful

Erica E. Goode

The number of disorders classified as mental illnesses has expanded from 59 in 1917 to 292 in 1992, according to Erica E. Goode, a reporter for *U.S. News & World Report*, a national weekly newsmagazine. In the following viewpoint, Goode writes that this expanding definition of mental illness may be harmful. For example, it may cause people to think that any minor deviation from normalcy is a serious problem. Furthermore, labeling their problems "diseases" may enable people to evade responsibility for their condition.

As you read, consider the following questions:

1. Why is it more difficult to diagnose mental disorders than physical ailments, according to the author?
2. What three diagnoses does Goode cite to substantiate her assertion that decisions about the definitions of mental illnesses are not based on science?

Ever since certain ancient Greek kings went around killing their fathers and marrying their mothers, people have argued over which peculiarities of human behavior should be considered normal and which aberrant. Is Jane's sister Edwina, who organizes her clothes alphabetically according to fabric, normal? What about her Aunt Rose, who goes home at night and gorges herself on chocolate until she feels sick? Or cousin Ethel, who always gets involved with men who treat her badly? And how is one to view Jane's next-door neighbor, George, who at times is depressed enough to make life difficult but never plunges into despair?

Traditionally, the task of mapping abnormality has fallen to psychiatrists and others who treat psychic ills. And in their hands, the formally appointed categories of mental disorder have been multiplying: In 1917, for example, the classification system used by the American Psychiatric Association included only 59 forms of mental complaint. By 1952, when the first APA *Diagnostic and Statistical Manual of Mental Disorders* (DSM) appeared, there were 106. The latest version of the manual, which is employed widely by mental-health professionals, insurance companies and the courts, lists 292 possible diagnoses, from "Major Depression" and "Schizophrenia" to more arcane designations like "Hypoactive Sexual Desire Disorder."

This proliferation of labels is causing some dismay. Indeed, some critics wonder if the multiplication of mental disorders has gone too far, with the realm of the abnormal encroaching on areas that were once the province of individual choice, habit, eccentricity or lifestyle. Few people would question calling the hallucinations of schizophrenia or the violent mood swings of manic-depression "illnesses." Research suggests they have biological roots. But what are we to make of "binge eating disorder," "negativistic personality disorder" or "minor" depression? . . .

Political Diseases

The propagation of diagnoses is not, of course, unique to psychiatry. What was once simply called "fever" is now known as hundreds of distinct diseases. Yet human behavior is in many ways less quantifiable and more subject to debate than lungs, arteries or gall bladders. There are no chromosomes or viruses for psychiatrists to point to as the cause of their patients' ills. No blood tests or X-rays as yet can determine if someone is mentally disturbed. As a result, psychiatric diagnoses rest mostly on description of symptoms. And deciding which diagnoses to include, and how to define them, has historically been a judgment call. Cynics question how heavily such decisions are influenced by factors that have nothing to do with science—for example, social mores, psychiatrists' wish to be seen as "hard" scientists, economic motives or the idiosyncratic views of prominent experts. As one psychologist says, "It's a very political process."

Happiness Is a Psychiatric Disorder

Happiness meets all reasonable criteria for a psychiatric disorder. It is statistically abnormal, consists of a discrete cluster of symptoms, there is at least some evidence that it reflects the abnormal functioning of the central nervous system, and it is associated with various cognitive abnormalities—in particular, a lack of contact with reality. Acceptance of these arguments leads to the obvious conclusion that happiness should be included in future taxonomies of mental illness, probably as a form of affective [mood] disorder. This would place it on Axis I of the American Psychiatric Association's *Diagnostic and Statistical Manual*. With this prospect in mind, I humbly suggest that the ordinary language term 'happiness' be replaced by the more formal description *major affective disorder, pleasant type*, in the interests of scientific precision and in the hope of reducing any possible diagnostic ambiguities. . . .

Once the debilitating consequences of happiness become widely recognised it is likely that psychiatrists will begin to devise treatments for the condition and we can expect the emergence of happiness clinics and anti-happiness medications in the not too distant future.

Richard P. Bentall, *Journal of Medical Ethics*, June 1992.

Critics point to the rare diagnostic categories that have been retired over the years, either for lack of evidence or because society's attitudes changed. In the classic example, homosexuality was removed from the psychiatric manual in 1973. And while 50 years ago no one considered smoking cigarettes abnormal, by the time DSM III was published, "Nicotine Dependence" had found its way in. Controversy also erupted a few years ago over a proposed new diagnosis—"Self-Defeating Personality Disorder"—defined in part as affecting someone who "enters into relationships with persons or places himself or herself in situations that are self-defeating and have painful consequences." When critics objected that the category could be stigmatizing to women, it was relegated to the manual's appendix.

Labeling Unhappiness

The cultural "wiggle" of specific diagnoses, however, is in some ways just a straw man for larger concerns. The advent of more and more psychiatric pigeonholes, some critics feel, reflects a broader trend toward turning any behavior that departs from the ideal into a medical condition. The splendor of human diversity thus runs the risk of becoming simply a collection of syndromes and disorders. "Life is so puzzling and mystifying and obscure," says Herbert Fingarette, University of California philosophy professor emeritus, "that giving something a name seems to give it clarity and power."

Take the case of "minor depressive disorder.". . . [Some] psychiatrists who want the diagnosis included [in the DSM] argue that many people seek treatment for bouts of melancholy that don't meet the current criteria for major or chronic depression. And though such complaints may be very common, they say, so is obesity—a condition medicine has long considered to be officially unhealthy. Yet to call what some might term "the blues" a medical problem, Fingarette and others counter, has tricky consequences. Not only does it suggest that any departure from happiness is abnormal, it also shifts responsibility away from the individual, encouraging people in the questionable belief that life's difficulties are readily fixed by experts. And, of course, creating a new diagnosis gives doctors one more condition to treat.

In a similar vein, some mental-health professionals wonder if the present system of psychiatric diagnosis at times does more to obscure patients' problems than it does to clarify them. The danger, they say, is that taking the diagnostic categories too literally may lead clinicians to focus more on symptoms than on the person behind them. What takes place inside a person and how it appears externally, "though related, are not identical. Psychiatric nosology does not always seem to keep this in mind," write San Francisco psychoanalysts Dr. Edward Weinshel and Dr. Owen Renik, in the journal *Psychoanalytic Inquiry*. . . .

Standards Have Been Tightened

Aware that adding a diagnosis to [DSM] is far easier than getting it out again, the standards for proposed new categories of mental disorder have been tightened: Researchers' desire for government funding to study a given mental condition will no longer be deemed sufficient to include it in the manual. Nor will categories be added when they are backed by no evidence other than psychiatrists' conviction that they exist. "For a diagnosis to be included, it should have proven its utility," says Dr. Allen Frances, professor of psychiatry at Columbia University, chairman of the task force [charged with evaluating new diagnoses].

Raising the bar for new diagnoses is part of a larger effort by Frances and his colleagues to increase the scientific rigor of the diagnostic process. . . . The hope, says Frances, is that what today remains an imperfect system will be steadily refined and improved by research—in particular the explosion of scientific work in neuroscience and genetics. Eventually, he believes, today's descriptive categories will be tied to solid evidence about the causes of mental disorders.

Well, maybe. Or maybe not. In the meantime, the arguments about normality and abnormality will inevitably continue. Nearly everyone agrees that some method of classifying the ills of the psyche is essential. It allows clinicians to compare notes, guides treatment and ensures that researchers are all studying the same thing. But producing such a system is a thankless task, with no shortage of kibitzers and little chance of pleasing everyone. [The] DSM should be taken "with an educated grain of salt," says Frances. University of California at San Francisco psychologist Bryna Siegel puts it more bluntly: "People need to realize that these categories are not given by God."

"Many, if not most, of the serious psychiatric illnesses probably have an organic basis in terms of disturbed brain function."

Mental Disorders Are Medical Diseases

Sheldon H. Preskorn

Sheldon H. Preskorn argues that mental illnesses should be seen as medical diseases because they are linked to biological factors. In the following viewpoint, he advocates applying the "medical model"—a scientific approach to diagnosing, treating, and researching illnesses—to psychiatric disorders. Preskorn is vice chairman of the department of psychiatry at the University of Kansas School of Medicine and director of the Psychiatry Research Institute, both of which are located in Wichita.

As you read, consider the following questions:

1. What two developments led to the "quiet revolution" in psychiatry, according to Preskorn?
2. According to the author, what are the four levels of diagnosis under the medical model?
3. Does the "biological imbalance" theory of mental disorder relieve patients of responsibility for their illnesses, according to Preskorn?

From Sheldon H. Preskorn, "The Revolution in Psychiatry." Reprinted from *National Forum: The Phi Kappa Phi Journal*, vol. 73, no. 1 (Winter 1993). Copyright ©1993 by Sheldon H. Preskorn. By permission of the publishers.

For the general public, no other area of medicine is shrouded in more mystery than psychiatry. It is often viewed with an admixture of fascination and concern. This ambivalence is reflected in the public's contradictory beliefs that psychiatry is, on the one hand, therapeutically without substance and, on the other, virtually omnipotent and able to deal with such diverse subjects as the effects of poverty and holiday mood swings.

The profession itself has contributed to these misconceptions. In the 1950s and 1960s, leading psychiatrists suggested that adherence to psychoanalytically derived principles could virtually free human beings from their restrictions and allow them to realize their "full potential." Yet psychiatry did not fulfill its promise to cure serious mental illness by redefining the meaning of psychosis as simply "being sane in insane places." Nor was psychiatry able to ensure that the chronically mentally ill, released from state hospitals under the therapeutic optimism of the 1960s, would not suffer a much more dehumanizing and terrifying existence on the streets of large U.S. cities.

The Detour

What may be difficult for many Americans to understand is that American psychiatry took a significant detour from the rest of world psychiatry and is only now regaining its medical roots. Because of the right constellation of forces, American psychiatry became dominated by psychoanalysis for much of the first half of this century and still feels the effects today. The foothold of classic psychoanalysis and its derivatives extends into many parts of American life, including the arts (e.g., Freudian themes in books, plays, and movies), the popular press (e.g., "holiday blues," "stress-induced mental illness"), and even business with the popularity of motivational speakers and programs.

The factors that made the United States a good medium for the growth of the psychoanalytic movement were varied and included the movement's promise of being able to cure psychiatric illness through personal reflection, which resonated with the basic philosophies of the country, especially those formalized and popularized by John Dewey and William James at the end of the nineteenth century; the reliance of a young country on imported knowledge from Europe, perhaps particularly in medicine, following the Flexner report [an evaluation of medical education in the U.S. by Abraham Flexner] in the early twentieth century; and the fact that large numbers of psychoanalysts emigrated from central Europe to escape religious and cultural prejudice and eventually overt persecution under the Nazis. All of these forces promoted the growth of psychoanalysis in this country in the first half of the century to the virtual exclusion of a more medically oriented approach to psychiatry. Interestingly, the converse was true in much of the rest of the world, with the result that after World War II, American psychiatry had little similarity to its European progenitor.

The Quiet Revolution

Psychoanalysis and its derivatives are not without merit but have not proved to be effective as primary treatment for serious psychiatric illness (e.g., schizophrenia and manic-depressive illness). That fact, coupled with the discovery of medications that are effective in treatments of these disorders, led to a quiet revolution within American psychiatry and a return to its medical roots. That revolution has been and continues realigning American psychiatry with the rest of the world's psychiatry and with medicine in general. Without fanfare, psychiatry has changed so that today it bears little resemblance to the popular image of the field. The gap between that image (e.g., the couch and talking as the exclusive mode of treatment) and reality is growing. This viewpoint will present a view of the current status of the field and the further changes that are expected with increased knowledge from basic and clinical neuroscience [the study of the relationship between biology and behavior], research concerning basic brain mechanisms relevant to psychiatric illness.

Psychiatry and the Medical Model

The medical model refers to the approach to illness uniformly adopted in all medical specialties. The model emphasizes the role of diagnosis with regard to both the treatment of patients and research into the fundamental nature of their complaints. There are four levels of diagnosis: symptomatic, syndromic, pathophysiological, and etiological. (See Table 1.) Patients typically present symptoms to physicians. Physicians attempt to further understand the patient's complaints at a level beyond simply a symptom-based diagnosis (e.g., headache). That process is accomplished by eliciting details concerning the nature of the patient's problem (e.g., when the symptom occurs, what other symptoms occur with it, what relieves or aggravates the symptom?), through physical examination, and finally by way of laboratory tests. The rationale for this approach is that the more specific the diagnosis, the more appropriate and effective the treatment.

Scientific validation is the hallmark of the model. Although theories are generated about the pathophysiology [the organic processes] and etiology [the causes] underlying a given diagnosis, this model is not wedded to any single philosophy of the causation of illness. Any potential etiology warrants consideration. For example, genetics, pathogens (e.g., viruses), or environmental exposures either singly or in combination may be responsible for a given disorder. The determination requires empirical proof.

The same approach is now the rule in psychiatry whether the

illness be schizophrenia, manic-depressive disorder, major depressive disorder, or an anxiety disorder. Although such an approach may seem axiomatic, it was not the case in American psychiatry for a long time. The reason is that the field thought that it understood the causation of psychiatric disturbance: unconscious conflicts arising from the patient's psychosexual development. The pervasiveness of this theory in American society leads patients to frequently come with explanations for their problems. Patients with the first onset of major depression in their mid-forties will suggest that their symptoms must be due to some conflict arising from the way they were raised, although even they are perplexed as to why it took so long for their troubles to become apparent.

Table 1: Levels of Diagnostic Sophistication

Level	Descriptive Basis	Example
Symptomatic	*a single symptom*	Ordinary Headache
Syndromic	*a cluster of symptoms and/or signs*	Migraine Headache
Pathophysiologic	*knowledge of physiological disturbance*	Vasospasm [spasms in a blood vessel]
Etiologic	*knowledge of causative agent*	Viral-induced Arteritis [inflammation of arteries]

Sheldon H. Preskorn, *Phi Kappa Phi Journal*, Winter 1993.

An agonistic approach to psychiatry and neuroscience research has found that many, if not most, of the serious psychiatric illnesses probably have an organic basis in terms of disturbed brain function. The evidence includes studies on twins showing higher concordance rates even in those reared apart; brain-imaging studies demonstrating disturbances in brain structure and/or function; biochemical changes in affected versus nonaffected individuals; and responsiveness to medication. As with other medical diseases, different psychiatric illnesses appear to have different causes, so that any single theory of causation is not likely to be universally applicable. Leading candidates as etiologically important variables are the same as those for other medical conditions, including genetic susceptibility, pathogens [specific agents, such as bacteria or viruses], and environmental exposures. Progress in understanding the fundamental nature of psychiatric illnesses comes through the same slow and often painstaking research that is needed in every field of medicine. . . .

Chemical Imbalances and Responsibility

The concept of psychiatric disorders due to a "chemical imbalance" has gained considerable popularity. However, there are several limitations to this concept. The medical model does not assume that all psychiatric disorders are due to disturbances in brain function, but rather that such a possibility must be considered along with other possibilities until research demonstrates the critical factors in the pathogenesis [origin and development] of a specific illness. Undoubtedly, some psychiatric disturbances occur for reasons other than "chemical imbalances." To use computer language, we will likely find that some psychiatric disorders are fundamentally "hardware" problems, others "software," and still others a combination of the two.

There is also the concern that overemphasis on the "chemical imbalance" hypothesis makes the patient merely a passive recipient of care rather than an active participant and that it promotes the idea that the patient has no responsibility with regard to his or her illness. Neither is correct. An analogy with juvenile-onset diabetes mellitus may help to clarify this matter. The assumption with nonpsychiatric medical illnesses is that patients do not set out to become ill. Patients with psychiatric illnesses are no different in this regard. Even though a patient does not make a conscious decision to become ill with diabetes, that does not mean that he or she is not responsible for managing the illness to the best of his or her ability. The physician owes the patient a full explanation of the condition within the confines that current knowledge permits. The patient can then make informed decisions on his or her own behalf and be an active participant in becoming and remaining well. The diabetic patient has responsibilities: monitoring blood sugar and diet, taking insulin and other medications as instructed, keeping weight within reasonable limits, and maintaining an appropriate program of exercise. The patient with a psychiatric illness has similar responsibilities, the specifics being dependent upon which illness he or she has. For some, the illness may affect their judgment or comprehension, which in turn may compromise their ability to perform these tasks. Nonetheless, the goal is that they be active participants in their treatment to the fullest extent of their abilities. Such an expectation values the patient and may in itself help to restore some of the self-esteem that he or she may have lost due to the illness. It may also aid with compliance, because the plan of treatment is the result of the patient's choice rather than the physician's dictates.

When applied to psychiatry, the medical model does not "blame" the patient for becoming ill. Nor does it assume that the rearing practices of the family are necessarily etiologically important in the pathogenesis of the condition. If there is evidence to support such a role, then those practices must be addressed and, it is hoped, corrected through education—ideally, before the illness becomes apparent. Unfortunately, psychological explanations for psychiatric illnesses can have a suggestion of blaming either the patient (i.e., "not thinking positively") or the family (e.g., "schizophrenogenic mothers"). Such concepts have been advanced as fact without having first been submitted to rigorous scientific testing.

The medical model of psychiatry is thus an integrative approach rather than either solely "biological" or slavishly adherent to the concept that all patients need the same type of treatment regardless of their problems or circumstances.

What Next?

The quiet revolution has occurred. Now an explosion is set to follow. The revolution was the movement from an exclusive dependence on psychoanalytic theory for the conceptualization and treatment of psychiatric disorders to the medical-model approach. That revolution occurred over a period from the late 1960s to the 1980s. During those years, psychiatry changed more fundamentally than did any other area of medicine.

The revolution prepared the field for an explosion in our fundamental knowledge about the nature of psychiatric disorders and our ability to treat them. This explosion is the result of neuroscience's providing a much better understanding of the structure and function of the brain on a microscopic and macrosystemic level. The brain, after all, is the organ of the soul and the proper target for research into the pathophysiology responsible for serious psychiatric illness.

Understanding the structure and functioning of the brain has been difficult for a multitude of reasons. It is the most complicated organ in the body. For example, more than 65 percent of the human genome codes [genetic instructions] are for brain-specific components. Its systems have evolved over eons and are hierarchically organized and yet interdependent. Its output is more varied and complex than that of other organs and includes behavior, circadian [daily] cycles, special senses, thinking, language, and the regulation of other organs, to name only a few of its functions. Compare the task of understanding its function with understanding the function of an organ whose sole task is pumping fluid throughout the body. This investigation is made even more daunting by the fact that the organ, sealed within a protective bony vault, is hard to inspect. Its subsystems are also harder to study in isolation in the laboratory than are those of other organs.

Nonetheless, the relentless and imaginative efforts of countless scientists from many disciplines have yielded results. Sixty neurotransmitters [substances that transmit nerve impulses across synapses, or gaps between nerve-tissue cells] have been identified, and more than 200 more have been postulated. The means by which those first sixty neurotransmitters are formed, transported along the neurons [nerve cells] to their terminals, stored, then released, and finally broken down have been identified. The receptors for the neurotransmitters on the target cells have been identified too, as have the processes that occur within the target cell when the receptor is activated. Through the use of the techniques of molecular biology, the chemical structure of these components can be elucidated by localizing and cloning the gene that codes for the component. Knowing the structure of the components is analogous to knowing the arrangement of the tumblers when trying to open a lock.

Mental Illnesses Are Brain Diseases

Prevailing scientific judgment [holds] that severe mental illnesses are brain diseases, which at the present time are neither preventable nor curable, but are treatable and manageable with combinations of medication, supportive counseling, and community support services, including appropriate education and vocational training. The causes of severe mental illnesses are complex, and they are not understood thoroughly. There is a genetic predisposition to some mental illnesses. Although stress or drug and alcohol abuse can precipitate or aggravate episodes of an illness, these are not primary causes.

National Alliance for the Mentally Ill, *Public Policy Platform*, December 1992.

Armed with such knowledge, basic and clinical neuroscientists can develop new drugs to unlock the mysteries of the brain. Each new agent will serve as a tool both to treat patients and to further our understanding of normal brain function—and by extension, disturbances in brain function—that underlie serious psychiatric illness. Coupling this knowledge with advances in brain-imaging technology, such as positron emission tomography [a technique that allows scientists to study the brain at work], researchers have begun visualizing both normal and abnormal brain physiology in human beings.

Challenges

The potential for advancing our ability to treat brain diseases is astounding. With that potential comes responsibility. These advances could retard the progression of such devastating conditions as schizophrenia and Alzheimer's disease. Someday these diseases may even be prevented.

Advances may also alter the way in which we think about such a fundamental human characteristic as personality. We may be able to show that traits of personality have a biological predisposition and that these traits are pharmacologically responsive. Such discoveries would raise important ethical questions relating to the use of these treatments and to the impact on the Western concept of free will. Similar issues are, of course, also being raised in other areas of science, particularly those involving so-called genetic engineering. Still, perhaps none have more potential to fundamentally affect the way we conceptualize ourselves than the advances that are likely to come from neuroscience as it relates to psychiatry. The fact that psychiatry has adopted the medical model is critical to its ability to adapt to such potential discoveries and to utilize them to their maximum advantage in the care of patients.

4 VIEWPOINT

"I took up the profession of psychiatry in part to debunk the biological-reductionist impulse that has motivated its very origin."

Mental Disorders Are Not Medical Diseases

Thomas Szasz

Thomas Szasz has been a leading critic of the psychiatric profession since the 1960s. He believes that the concept of mental illness is a "myth" that enables people to evade responsibility for their problems and allows psychiatrists to justify their questionable practices. In the following viewpoint, Szasz counters the increasingly popular belief that mental disorders are brain diseases. Rather than reflecting genuine diseases, he contends, diagnoses of mental illness are determined by social, political, economic, and personal factors. Szasz is the author of numerous books, including *The Myth of Mental Illness, Insanity: The Idea and Its Consequences*, and *A Lexicon of Lunacy*, from which this viewpoint is excerpted.

As you read, consider the following questions:

1. According to Szasz, what motivates individuals to "medicalize life and entrust its management to health professionals"?
2. How does the idea of mental illness alter the concept of motivation, according to Szasz?
3. According to the author, what was the aim of the nineteenth-century model of diagnosis?

Intrigued by the patently metaphoric character of the psychiatric vocabulary—which, nevertheless, is widely recognized as a legitimate medical idiom—I decided, at the beginning of my professional career, to explore the nature and function of these literalized metaphors, and to expose them to public scrutiny. I thus set in motion a controversy about mental illness which is still raging, and whose essence is still often misunderstood. Many scientists, physicians, jurists, and lay persons believe that the demonstration of a genetic defect or a brain lesion in so-called mental patients would prove that mental illnesses exist and are like any other disease. This is not so. If mental illnesses are diseases of the central nervous system, then they are diseases of the brain, not the mind. And if mental illnesses are the names of (mis)behaviors, then they are behaviors, not diseases. A screwdriver may be a drink or an implement. No amount of research on orange juice and vodka can establish that it is a hitherto unrecognized form of a carpenter's tool.

The Religious Nature of the Belief in Mental Illness

Although linguistic clarification is valuable for individuals who want to think clearly, it is not useful for people whose social institutions rest on the unexamined, literal use of language. Accordingly, I have long maintained that psychiatric metaphors have the same role in our Therapeutic Society that religious metaphors have in Theological Societies. For example, there is consensus among Mohammedans that their God wants them to worship on Friday, among Jews that theirs wants them to worship on Saturday, and among Christians that theirs wants them to worship on Sunday. Similarly, the various versions of the American Psychiatric Association's *Diagnostic and Statistical Manual* rest only on consensus. Let me illustrate this contention with a simple, syllogistic example.

> How does a dead person become a saint? By the Vatican's declaring him to be a saint. Thereafter, say, Peter and Paul are called "saints," and Catholics (and perhaps others as well) believe that Saint Peter and Saint Paul *are* saints.

> How does the behavior of a living person become an illness? By the American Psychiatric Association's declaring it to be an illness. Thereafter, say, gambling or smoking are called "diseases," and psychiatrists and their followers (and perhaps others as well) believe that Pathological Gambling and Nicotine Dependence *are* diseases.

Still, if a person believes that mental illnesses are illnesses, his conviction is not likely to be dispelled by my argument. The religious character of the belief in mental illness manifests itself in another way as well. Religion is, among other things, the institutionalized denial of the human foundations of meaning and of the inevitable finiteness of life; the person who seeks transcendental meaning and rejects the reality of death can thus theologize life and entrust its management to clerical professionals. Likewise, psychiatry is, among other things, the institutionalized denial of the reality of free will and of the tragic nature of life; individuals who seek impersonal explanations of horrifying human action and reject the inevitability of personal responsibility can thus medicalize life and entrust its management to health professionals. Karl Marx was close to the mark when he asserted that "Religion is the opiate of the people." But religion is not the opiate of the people; the human mind is. After all, religion is a product of our own minds, and so, too, is psychiatry. In short, the mind is its own opiate. And its ultimate drug is the Word.

Literal Diseases?

Indeed, Sigmund Freud himself flirted with such a formulation, but backed away from its implications, preferring instead to believe that "neuroses" are literal diseases, and that "psychoanalysis" is a literal treatment—in fact, the best treatment for these ostensibly genuine maladies. In his essay "Psychical (or Mental) Treatment," Freud wrote:

> Foremost among such measures [which operate upon the human mind] is the use of words; and words are the essential tool of mental treatment. A layman will no doubt find it hard to understand how pathological disorders of the body and mind can be eliminated by "mere" words. He will feel that he is being asked to believe in magic. And he will not be so very wrong. . . . But we shall have to follow a roundabout path in order to explain how science sets about restoring to words a part at least of their former magical power.

Despite this historical background and these epistemological considerations, an editorial in the prestigious British medical magazine *The Lancet* remains fixated on the mirage of finding the cause of schizophrenia in the brain. Lamenting the state of psychiatry 150 years after the founding of the (British) Association of Medical Officers of Asylums and Hospitals for the Insane—today, the Royal College of Psychiatrists—the editorial writer commented:

> What about psychiatric research? We seem to be no closer to finding the real, presumed biological, causes of the major psychiatric illnesses. This is not to decry the value of such research—if the causes of conditions such as . . . schizophrenia are found it will be an advance of the same magnitude as the identification of the syphilis spirochaete in the brains of patients with general paralysis of the insane.

I took up the profession of psychiatry in part to debunk the biological-reductionist impulse that has motivated its very origin and that continues to fuel its engines; in other words, to combat the contention that abnormal behaviors must be understood as the products of abnormal brains. Ironically, it was easier to do this nearly half a century ago than today. For three centuries, the idea that every "mental illness" will prove to be a bona fide brain disease was a hypothesis that could be supported or opposed. However, after the 1960s, this hypothesis became increasingly accepted as a scientific fact. Of course, it is still possible to say that mental illnesses do not exist. But since only a charlatan, a fool, or a fanatic disputes facts or opposes science, such a critic is likely to be dismissed as irrational, or worse.

The Social Function of Psychiatry

I think [psychiatric] disease categories disempower people and prevent people from understanding themselves and taking responsibility for themselves. Rather, the concept of mental illness promotes the power of an elite few who profess to have secret or esoteric knowledge, and their relationship to society is unclear and unspoken. Their function is to manage people. Nobody dares speak about it; that's forbidden. That's the relationship between psychiatry and society, and the social function of psychiatry.

Ron Leifer, quoted by Seth Farber in *Madness, Heresy, and the Rumor of Angels*, 1993.

Thus, for the time being at least, psychiatrists and their powerful allies have succeeded in persuading the scientific community, the courts, the media, and the general public that the conditions they call "mental disorders" are diseases—that is, phenomena independent of human motivation or will. This is a curious development, for, until recently, only psychiatrists—who know little about medicine and less about science—embraced such blind physical reductionism. Most scientists knew better. . . .

I will not discuss here what is meant by the word *disease*. Suffice it to say that we do not attribute motives to diseases, and do not call motivated actions (bodily) "diseases." For instance, we attribute no motive to a person for having leukemia; it would be foolish to say that a particular motive led to a person's having glaucoma; and it would be absurd to assert that an illness (say, diabetes) caused a person to become a senator. In short, one of the most important political-philosophical features of the concept of mental illness is that, at one fell swoop, it removes motivation from action, adds it to illness, and thus destroys the very possibility of distinguishing disease from nondisease. This crucial function of the idea of mental illness is illustrated by the psychiatrists' classifying certain cases of theft as a disease (kleptomania), by the media's acceptance of this behavior as a disease, and by the mental health professionals' accounts of its alleged causes.

In a newspaper report [by C. Miller] on shoplifting, the director of Onondaga (New York) County's Drinking and Driving Program explains: "Syracuse needs Shoplifters Anonymous. . . . There are more than 3,000 arrests for shoplifting in Onondaga County. It's costing everyone a fortune." Although the program is described as "voluntary," it is a substitute for a criminal penalty: "If the thief completes the course, the arrest vanishes from his or her record." The report shows that both so-called experts and the media treat shoplifting as a disease, to which they then nevertheless attribute various motives. In the treatment program, the shoplifters "learn *why* they steal . . . there are several reasons why people shoplift. They feel entitled. Perhaps they feel prices are too high; they are angry at authority. . . . It's a mental health problem.". . .

Why Do We Make Diagnoses?

I want to say a few words about the differences between diseases and diagnoses. Diseases (in the literal sense of the term), like avalanches or earthquakes, occur naturally; whereas diagnoses, like books or bridges, are artifacts. Which raises the question: Why do we make diagnoses? There are several reasons:

1. Scientific—to identify the organs or tissues affected and perhaps the cause of the illness.

2. Professional—to enlarge the scope, and thus the power and prestige, of a state-protected medical monopoly and the income of its practitioners.

3. Legal—to justify state-sanctioned coercive interventions outside of the criminal justice system.

4. Social-economic—to authenticate persons as legitimate occupants of the sick role: for example, to secure drugs, compensation payments, etc., available only to bona fide sick (diagnosed) patients.

5. Political-economic—to justify enacting and enforcing measures aimed at promoting public health and providing funds for research and treatment on projects classified as medical.

6. Personal—to enlist the support of public opinion, the media, and the legal system for bestowing special privileges (and impose special penalties) on persons diagnosed as (mentally) ill.

It is not coincidence that most psychiatric diagnoses are twentieth-century inventions. The aim of the classic, nineteenth-century model of diagnosis was to identify bodily lesions (diseases) and their material causes (etiology). For example, the term *pneumococcal pneumonia*—a paradigm of a pathology-driven diagnosis—identifies the organ affected, the lungs, and the cause of the illness, infection with the pneumococcus. Diagnoses driven by other motives—such as the desire to coerce the patient or to secure government funding for the treatment of his (alleged) illness—generate different diagnostic constructions, and lead to different conceptions of disease.

Diagnoses vs. Diseases

Today, even diagnoses of what were strictly medical diseases are no longer pathology-driven. The diagnoses of patients with illnesses such as asthma or arthritis, and of those requiring surgical interventions, are distorted by economic factors (especially third-party funding of hospital costs and physicians' fees). Final diagnoses on the discharge summaries of hospitalized patients are often no longer made by physicians, but by bureaucrats skilled in the ways of Medicare, Medicaid, and private health insurance reimbursement (based partly on what ails the patient, and partly on which medical terms for his ailment and treatment ensure the most generous compensation for the services rendered).

In short, no psychiatric diagnosis is, or can be, pathology-driven; instead, all such diagnoses are driven by nonmedical (economic, personal, legal, political, and social) factors or incentives. Accordingly, psychiatric diagnoses do not point to pathoanatomic or pathophysiological lesions and do not identify causative agents—but refer rather to *human behaviors*. Moreover, the psychiatric terms used to refer to such behaviors allude to the plight of the denominated patient, hint at the dilemmas with which patient and psychiatrist alike try to cope as well as exploit, and mirror the beliefs and values of the society that both inhabit.

Despite their misleading—indeed, mendacious—titles, the various versions of the APA's *Diagnostic and Statistical Manual of Mental Disorders* are not classifications of mental disorders (or diseases or conditions of any kind) that "patients have." Instead, they are rosters of psychiatric diagnoses officially accredited as mental diseases by the APA. This is why in psychiatry, unlike in the rest of medicine, the members of "consensus groups" and "task forces," appointed by officers of the association, make and unmake psychiatric diagnoses; and sometimes the entire membership votes on whether a controversial diagnosis is or is not a disease. For more than a century, psychiatrists created diagnoses and pretended they were diseases—and no one in authority challenged their deception. It is not surprising, then, that few people now realize that diagnoses are not diseases.

Periodical Bibliography

The following articles have been selected to supplement the diverse views presented in this chapter.

Joseph Adelson	"The Ideology of Homelessness," *Commentary*, March 1991.
Nancy C. Andreasen	"Brave New Brain," *National Forum*, Winter 1993. Available from the Honor Society of Phi Kappa Phi, PO Box 16000, Louisiana State University, Baton Rouge, LA 70893.
Michael J. Bader	"Is Psychiatry Going Out of Its Mind?" *Tikkun*, July/August 1989.
Richard P. Bentall	"A Proposal to Classify Happiness as a Psychiatric Disorder," *Journal of Medical Ethics*, June 1992.
T.J. Collier	"The Stigma of Mental Illness," *Newsweek*, April 26, 1993.
Glen O. Gabbard	"Psychodynamic Psychiatry in the 'Decade of the Brain,'" *American Journal of Psychiatry*, August 1992. Available from the American Psychiatric Association, 1400 K St. NW, Washington, DC 20005.
Sally George	"Learning to Label," *American Health*, January/February 1993.
Elliot S. Gershon and Ronald O. Rieder	"Major Disorders of Mind and Brain," *Scientific American*, September 1992.
Jean Seligmann with David Gelman	"Is It Sadness or Madness? Psychiatrists Clash over How to Classify PMS," *Newsweek*, March 15, 1993.
Mary Suh	"Severe PMS: Is It Mental Illness or Just Normal Behavior?" *Ms.*, May/June 1993.
Thomas Szasz	"Psychiatry and Social Control," *The Humanist*, January/February 1991.
Richard E. Vatz and Lee S. Weinberg	"Is Mental Illness a Myth?" *USA Today*, July 1993.
Jerome C. Wakefield	"The Concept of Mental Disorder: On the Boundary Between Biological Facts and Social Values," *American Psychologist*, March 1992. Available from the American Psychological Association, 750 First St. NE, Washington, DC 20002-4242.
James Willwerth	"It Hurts Like Crazy," *Time*, February 15, 1993.
Reginald E. Zelnik	"On Schizophrenia, Reductionism, and Family Responsibility," *Tikkun*, January/February 1990.

What Causes
Mental Illness?

Mental Illness

Chapter Preface

Many studies have reached different conclusions about the causes of mental illness. For example, some experts have concluded that schizophrenia is a biologically based, genetically determined brain disease. Others, however, think environmental factors such as family experiences and social class are responsible for the condition. Still another theory holds that the disorder is the result of exposure to viral agents.

Some researchers contend that a person exposed to an influenza virus while in the womb has an increased risk of developing schizophrenia later in life. For example, British researcher Eadbhard O'Callaghan and others compared the rates of schizophrenia among individuals conceived and born during an influenza epidemic in England and Wales in 1957 with those of people born within two years before and after the epidemic. Because a disproportionately large number of schizophrenics were in their fifth month of gestation during the epidemic's peak, the authors conclude, "Exposure to the A2 influenza virus during the second trimester [of fetal development] increases the risk of later schizophrenia."

Others reject the theory that exposure to influenza during gestation causes schizophrenia later in life. Responding to the O'Callaghan study, British researchers Timothy J. Crow and D. John Done reviewed the rates of schizophrenia among the children of women who contracted influenza while pregnant during the 1957 epidemic. They conclude that "prenatal exposure to influenza and schizophrenia are unrelated." Moreover, they contend that for schizophrenia "no [causal] factor other than a genetic one has been established."

Researchers continue to search for the mysterious origins of schizophrenia. In the following chapter, various theories about the causes of mental illness are presented and debated.

"The tendency of schizophrenia to run in families
. . . [is] due largely to the sharing of genes."

Genetic Factors Contribute to Schizophrenia

Irving I. Gottesman

In the following viewpoint, Irving I. Gottesman argues that
genes play a major role in the cause of schizophrenia. To support
this assertion, he presents evidence that the risk of developing
schizophrenia is greater among close relatives of schizophrenics
than among distant relatives and the general population. While
environmental factors are also important, says Gottesman, a genetic "predisposition" is an essential condition for the disease to
occur. Gottesman is a professor of psychology at the University
of Virginia in Charlottesville.

As you read, consider the following questions:

1. How does Gottesman account for the different risks for
   developing schizophrenia among children and siblings of
   schizophrenics?
2. Why can the phrase "schizophrenic mother" be "expunged
   from the scientific literature," according to Gottesman?
3. According to the author, what percentage of children born to
   two schizophrenics is normal?

In this viewpoint, we shall attempt to show that genetic factors are essential as a *diathesis* (predisposition) but that they are not sufficient, by themselves, for the development of schizophrenia. Within a broad framework known as *diathesis-stressor* theory, the vast array of facts gathered by both those scientist-clinicians typecast as hereditarians and those typecast as environmentalists can be reconciled without appeasement on either side. At a landmark conference organized by David Rosenthal and Seymour Kety and held at Dorado Beach, Puerto Rico, in 1967, the sage Harvard psychiatrist, Leon Eisenberg, mediating the unique confrontation between the world-class players who preferred biological/genetic explanations and those who preferred experiential/family explanations for the transmission of schizophrenia, concluded, "These findings [adoption and twin studies] persuade me—and I trust most of you—not only that there is a genetic component in the transmission of schizophrenia (a position no more controversial than the defense of motherhood) but that it is a *significant* determinant of the occurrence of the disease." Elsewhere, he speaks of the dangers of both a *mindless* (i.e., ignoring higher order psychological functions) and of a *brainless* (i.e., ignoring biological functions) agenda for studying mental illness. . . .

An Interactionist Stance

Largely as a consequence of the Dorado Beach conference, the entire field of schizophreniology was converted, at least in public pronouncements, to some kind of interactionist stance for advancing against the common enemy—ignorance about the true causes of schizophrenia.

The development of all human characteristics requires contributions from both genes and environments; in this sense, all characteristics are "acquired" rather than simply inherited or written on a blank slate. For schizophrenia, the unresolved problems are to identify the specific genes, together with their importance as causal factors in the disease, their chemical products, and their mechanisms for modulating behaviors, and to identify the specific environments (physical and psychosocial), together with their contributions to the disease and their mechanisms for modulating behaviors.

The basic evidence for the importance of genetic factors in the etiology of schizophrenia comes from the simultaneous considerations of the results of family, twin, and adoption studies conducted from 1916 to 1989. We shall show how familiality—the tendency of schizophrenia to run in families—once demonstrated, can be interpreted as due largely to the sharing of genes rather than to the sharing of environments and experiences. Our thesis is that schizophrenia is the same kind of common genetic disorder as coronary heart disease, mental retardation, or diabetes [multifactorial-polygenetic conditions requiring an accumulation of more than two relevant genes, as well as relevant environmental contributors], and thus is not like such rare genetic diseases as Huntington's disease (HD) or phenylketonuria (PKU), a form of mental retardation, each with clear, simple Mendelian inheritance patterns [and predictable rates of heredity] associated with dominant (HD) or recessive (PKU) modes of inheritance from parents to children. . . .

Foundations for a Genetic Position

Our case for the role of genetic inheritance as a major source of schizophrenia is circumstantial, but may well be sufficient to "convict the culprit." It is based on clinical population genetics [which focuses on whole humans and their observable characteristics, or *phenotypes*, and the degree of familiality of those characteristics] and it implies, but does not prove, that there is a neurochemical and/or neuroanatomical cause for the pattern of behavioral aberration. While research on the biology of schizophrenia goes on, scientists continue to study schizophrenia to uncover the mechanisms of inheritance with clinical analyses and with DNA probes, to look for environmental influences, and to predict outcomes or levels of risk. Early research going back to 1916 laid a foundation for our knowledge; today's research continues to build understanding.

Family, twin, and adoption studies of schizophrenia provide the grist for our mill. Each contributes to the genetic argument, complementing the others. No one method alone yields conclusive proof or disproof. For some psychiatric conditions, such as bipolar affective disorder (manic-depressive illness), linkage studies [that map genes and genetic markers linked together on the same chromosome] with DNA probes within a few rare families heavily loaded with one or two forms of the disorder suggested that a dominant gene on chromosome 11 in some Pennsylvania Amish families and a different dominant gene on the X chromosome in some Israeli families cause bipolar disorder. The Amish-based claims about chromosome 11 reported in 1988 were withdrawn as nonreplicable in 1989 after diagnostic criteria were refined and new cases fell ill. If such linkage results do get replicated, they will shed enormous light on the genetic aspects of mental illness, because they will turn the circumstantial evidence of genetic involvement gained from population genetic strategies into hard, physical evidence. For schizophrenia, devoting too many resources to a similar kind of random, long-shot search for genetic markers, absent some candidate genetic marker that is logically related to the neurochemical and pathophysiological [physiological processes of abnormal states] facts established by research, would be like investing in penny stocks on the Denver Stock Exchange. However, once in a while someone makes a fortune by just such speculation. . . .

The Risks to Relatives

If transmissible genetic factors contribute to developing schizophrenia, the disorder should cluster in affected families at a higher rate than the 1 percent affected in the general population. That a disease is familial, however, does not necessarily mean that it is genetic. . . . It may be transmitted through families not by genes but through some cultural practice, some infectious source, or some kind of learning by imitation. When we look at family studies to decide whether the variable is something genetic, we want to ask if the pattern of risks rises and falls as a function of the genetic overlap rather than as a consequence of shared experience. Do closer relatives, who have more genes in common, have a higher risk, and does that risk diminish as family relatedness diminishes? Furthermore, if the relatives are not overtly affected with schizophrenia, do they have something specifically odd or different about them that might provide clues to their having inherited a "diluted" form of schizophrenia; that is, schizophrenia spectrum disorder? . . .

Figure 1 summarizes the lifetime risks of being affected with schizophrenia for the various kinds of relatives of a schizophrenic. The figure shows the degree of genetic relationship for different groupings of relatives. . . . The data come from pooling information from about 40 reliable studies conducted in western Europe from 1920 to 1987. There is some danger in pooling such information, because the study designs are not exactly alike, but pooling after the judicious removal of the poorest data gives a clear and stable summary pattern not obtainable from any one or two studies.

We have used studies from Germany, Switzerland, the Scandinavian countries, and the United Kingdom in generating Figure 1, because these countries have similarly conservative diagnostic standards. Included are a modern replication of the Franz J. Kallmann family study completed in Sweden in 1970 by David Kay and Rolf Lindelius and involving 4,000 relatives and a Swiss family study completed by Manfred Bleuler (1978) involving 3,000 relatives; the orientation of these investigators was clearly "interactional" and they had no genetic axe to grind. The European researchers, unlike those in the United States, have better access to relatively stable populations and often can use the national psychiatric registers generated by systems of national health insurance. Such factors, together with relative (compared to the United States) homogeneity for race, religion, and social class and a high degree of cooperativeness from relatives, lead us to empha-

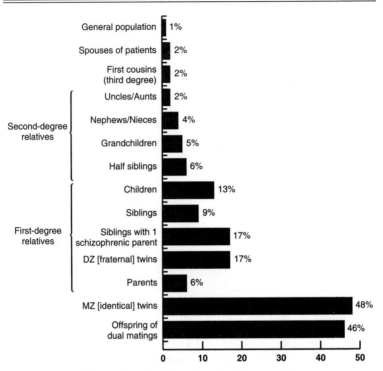

Figure 1. Grand average risks for developing schizophrenia compiled from the family and twin studies conducted in European populations between 1920 and 1987; the degree of risk correlates highly with the degree of genetic relatedness.

Irving I. Gottesman, *Schizophrenia Genesis: The Origins of Madness*, 1991.

size European data for obtaining meaningful pooled results.

Figure 1 presents the risks of developing schizophrenia for first-degree (parents, sibs, children), second-degree (uncles, nephews, grandchildren, half sibs), and third-degree (first cousins) relatives of schizophrenics. It also gives the risks for fraternal [DZ] twins, who are also first-degree relatives, and for identical [MZ] twins, who could be called zero-degree relatives because they are really genetic clones of one another. Risks for spouses, who are highly unlikely to be related genetically, are presented to test the idea of being able to induce schizophrenia in someone simply by sharing an intimate physical and psychological relationship. It also includes the risks of schizophrenia for the children of two schizophrenics, showing them to be nowhere near the 100 percent or 75 percent risks . . . for recessive and dominant genetic disorders [that fit the Mendelian model]. Except for this category, which we'll get back to later, the pooled studies represent large enough samples to be quite reliable. An enormous amount of information is summarized in the figure, and it deserves careful study.

Interpreting the Pattern of Familial Risks

Overall, the pattern of risk figures in the relatives of schizophrenics strongly supports the conclusion that the magnitude of the increased risk varies with the amount of gene sharing and not with the amount of experience sharing. Identical twins and offspring of dual matings have higher risks than do first-degree relatives, who have higher risks than do second-degree relatives, who have higher risks than do third-degree relatives, who have higher risks than do spouses and the basic risk of 1 percent in the general population.

Concern has been raised that the earlier overwhelming data showing the familial clustering of schizophrenia could have been falsely generated by unblindfolded, genetically biased psychiatrists using unreliable clinical judgments. Impetus was added to these concerns when two family studies from the United States with large numbers of first-degree relatives of schizophrenics were evaluated using the "objective" criteria of DSM-III [the third edition of the American Psychiatric Association's *Diagnostic and Statistical Manual of Mental Disorders*]. One study found no schizophrenics among 199 relatives, and the other found 2 among 128 first-degree relatives; based on Figure 1, we would expect about 10 percent from each sample to be affected. Have these modern researchers uncovered a cover-up? Not really. The negative studies had not bothered to reduce the sample sizes by using an appropriate age correction [to compensate for the variable age of onset of schizophrenia], they did not apply their criteria to a normal control sample to obtain a comparison figure, and they relied too much on secondhand information. Other family and twin studies quickly followed using the *same* objective, criteria-based diagnostic schemes and found rates in first-degree relatives some 9 to 18 times higher than in control groups *evaluated with the same standard*, thus confirming the pattern of familial risks shown in Figure 1.

The risk figures within first-degree relatives (parents, sibs, and children), all of whom have the possibility of a 50 percent gene overlap, is not uniform, and we need to look at what this might mean. Let's start with the small variation between the children of schizophrenics, 13 percent, and the brothers and sisters of schizophrenics, 9 percent. The higher risk in children may well be associated with the exposure to noxious environmental stressors or triggers provided unintentionally and haplessly by schizophrenic parenting; being a sister or a brother to a schizophrenic is likely to be less stressful than being the child of one. However, studies have reported equal risks in siblings and in children of schizophrenics. Adoption studies are needed to further our understanding here.

Within the class of first-degree relatives, parent-child pairs share *exactly* 50 percent of their genes, but pairs of siblings have *on average* 50 percent of their genes in common. Thus, it is possible for some sibling pairs to have considerably more or fewer than half their genes in common, with obvious consequences for their similarity or dissimilarity in polygenically influenced characteristics (such as height, blood pressure, and the liability for developing schizophrenia).

Parents of Schizophrenics

The observed 6 percent risk to the parents of schizophrenics is only half the risk observed for other first-degree relatives; this is an important fact that appears to conflict with either a dominant gene or a polygenic theory prediction of equal risks in parents, siblings, and children. The vast majority of schizophrenics do not have conspicuously abnormal parents, as anyone attending an annual meeting of the National Alliance for the Mentally Ill will have noted. The best explanations for the lower risk in parents of schizophrenics center about the processes of social selection for marriage and parenthood. Schizophrenics and preschizophrenics are less likely to marry than are nonschizophrenics; those schizophrenics who do marry tend to have the least severe cases of schizophrenia and/or have a later age of onset for their first serious symptoms. A post–World War II Swiss study conducted by Manfred Bleuler (1978) found that of 28 schizophrenic parents of schizophrenics, 23 had their onset after age 30 and 19 had mild cases or very good recoveries from an episode of illness. These and other selective forces explain not only the lower rate of schizophrenia in the parents of schizophrenics compared to the other first-degree relatives, but also the considerably lower rate for parents in general—it is half the usual 1 percent rate observed in the general population unselected for parenthood.

Among schizophrenics who do become parents, the ratio of mothers to fathers is two to one. This striking fact, coupled with the high risk for schizophrenia among the children of schizophrenics, has led some partisans to proclaim confirmation of the notion that pathogenic mothering causes schizophrenia. The term *schizophrenogenic mother* was coined by the psychoanalyst Frieda Fromm-Reichmann in 1948 during the heyday of explanations favoring child-rearing attitudes as the central cause of schizophrenia, with no reference whatsoever to genes. The more neutral and, we believe, valid explanation is that age of onset is earlier in males, thus reducing the likelihood of their finding a mate, and that marriage and procreation occur earlier in females, thus allowing the future female schizophrenic increased opportunity to marry and start a family before she becomes ill. The net effect of such social forces of selection results in twice as many children being born to schizophrenic mothers as to schizophrenic fathers, thus feeding the myth of schizophrenogenic mothering. In the three studies that provide data on the matter, the *risk* of developing schizophrenia in the offspring of schizophrenic mothers is the same as that observed in the offspring of schizophrenic fathers. The phrase "schizophrenic mother" can now be expunged from the scientific literature.

Genetic, Reactive, and Adaptive

Conventional wisdom says that although only 13 percent of the children of schizophrenics are themselves schizophrenic, many more, perhaps another 50 percent or so, are conspicuously abnormal psychiatrically. If this were true, we would be forced to revise our genetic theory to say that schizophrenia is inherited via a dominant gene, a gene that does not transmit schizophrenia itself, but a schizophrenia-related illness, or to adopt a more psychogenic [originating in the mind] theory of cultural transmission. Three early German studies on the children of schizophrenics, including the Kallmann one, are the sources of this belief in high rates for combined deviance. We find the data untenable in light of newer studies.

Manfred Bleuler, carrying on his father's work in Switzerland (1978), found a surprisingly high percentage of normal children among the offspring of the schizophrenics he and his father had studied. The younger Bleuler followed the patients for more than two decades and knew them well; he knew their own histories, the histories of their spouses, and the histories of their marriages. He considered fully 74 percent of the children over age 20 to be completely normal. His own explanation is informative.

> If the hitherto prevailing dogma . . . is to be retained, to the effect that over half the children of schizophrenics are in some way abnormal (and therefore basically "undesirable"), it is in serious need of more exacting definitions. These children can only fit that classification if "abnormal," "pathological," or "undesirable" are terms to be applied even to those whose behavior becomes different from and more difficult than that of their basic nature because of an added stressful situation. They will not fit that classification if the normal person is permitted to exhibit behavior traits in stressful situations that might be difficult to distinguish from abnormal or psychopathic behavior patterns.

This quotation makes clear that the kinds of psychopathology [dysfunction] observed in the relatives of schizophrenics, especially in the children, can be both genetically transmitted and reactive and even adaptive to the presence of a psychotic, obnoxious, and guilt-provoking parent in one's psychological space. . . .

At Super-High Risk: The Offspring of Two Patients

Despite the rarity of matings between schizophrenic mothers and schizophrenic fathers, there are five completed studies to learn from. The total number of adult offspring in these studies is small, with an age-corrected sample size of only 134 risk lives observed, but the results were similar enough across studies to be taken seriously. Early workers were eager to study these matings because the crosses might reveal Mendelian patterns. If schizophrenia were caused by a dominant gene, 75 percent of the children would be affected. If it were a recessive, 100 percent would be. (And . . . if it were transmitted simply by exposure to schizophrenic parents or parenting, 100 percent would be.) The results were fairly uniform. About one-third of the children of two schizophrenic parents were schizophrenic. With appropriate correction for age, this yields a lifetime maximum risk of 46 percent. The studies also showed, however, that the children of two schizophrenics were at considerably higher risk for other psychiatric abnormalities. The largest percentage were neurotic, rather than psychotic, but some of them (perhaps as many as one-fourth) were normal. This final result is amazing, considering how much instability there must be in lives of children who have two schizophrenic parents. How can upbringing in a household loaded with stress be a major factor contributing to schizophrenia if one-fourth of the children who have problem genes from both sides of their inheritance and who live in a family disrupted by two crazy parents turn out to be normal? What a tribute to the resilience of the human body and spirit—and good genetic luck! The interaction of stress *plus* specific genetic vulnerability could produce such results.

"There is simply no evidence in the most highly touted studies for a genetic factor for schizophrenia."

Schizophrenia Is Not Genetic

Peter R. Breggin

Peter R. Breggin, a psychiatrist with a private practice in Bethesda, Maryland, believes that what is commonly called "schizophrenia" is not a medical disease, but a psychological and spiritual crisis ("schizophrenic overwhelm"). In the following viewpoint, which is excerpted from his book *Toxic Psychiatry*, Breggin argues that the popular belief that schizophrenia is a genetic disease is based on fallacious scientific evidence. Rather than revealing the genetic basis of a disease, says Breggin, studies indicate that schizophrenia has an environmental origin.

As you read, consider the following questions:

1. According to Breggin, why did the Danish study by Seymour Kety and his colleagues disprove the genetic origin of schizophrenia?
2. What two factors in Pekka Tienari's 1987 study support the theory that environmental factors play a role in the development of schizophrenia, according to the author?
3. According to Breggin, what was the "logical fallacy" in the 1988 study by Robin Sherrington?

What the [psychiatric] profession communicates to the public through the media is summed up in a newspaper headline: GE-NETIC BASIS OF SCHIZOPHRENIA SAID TO BE FOUND.

Books written for laypeople also make the claim that the hereditary basis of madness is a fact rather than a bias or a conjecture. In the 1985 mass-market book *The New Psychiatry*, psychiatrist Jerrold S. Maxmen cites adoption studies and concludes, "These findings provided overwhelming evidence that genes were the principal source of schizophrenia." Assertions of this kind are so frequent that even sophisticated scientists in other fields assume that schizophrenia must have a proven genetic link. . . .

What the Experts Tell the Profession About Genetics

Within the confines of professional books and reviews, the claims are considerably more muted, if still badly exaggerated. In *Biological Psychiatry* (1986), in a chapter entitled "The Genetics of Psychiatric Disorders," Steven Matthysse and Seymour Kety acknowledge "the absence of a consistent and generally accepted mode of genetic transmission of schizophrenia." They repeat a constant theme in the professional literature: "The task is a daunting one, but it must eventually be carried out. . . ." Notice the use of "eventually." Kety himself jointly authored the key study cited by Maxmen in *The New Psychiatry*, and even Kety doesn't think it proves the case for a genetic origin.

In Armand Nicholi, Jr.'s *The New Harvard Guide to Psychiatry* (1988) the chapter on "Genetic and Biochemical Aspects of Schizophrenia" is again written by Kety and Matthysse. Their opening statement is hardly the stuff to run to newspapers with: "Psychiatric genetics, in its relatively short history, has encountered unusual difficulties in understanding and interpretation." One problem is that schizophrenia is still difficult to define, so much that "there is little reason to insist that it represents a single disease." Needless to say, that makes it difficult to discover schizophrenia's presumed genetic origin.

Schizophrenia does tend to run in families. About one in ten families with a schizophrenic parent will have a schizophrenic offspring. To their credit, Kety and Matthysse concede the fact that this "does not necessarily constitute strong evidence for the operation of genetic factors." Families share both a genetic and an environmental influence. "Pellagra, which also shows a strong familial tendency, was at one time erroneously regarded by some on that basis as a simple genetic disease," these researchers point out. It turned out to be due to niacin deficiency. Similarly, families share political outlooks, national feelings, cultural values and prejudices, and language; but nowadays scientists do not consider these traits to be genetic in origin.

Identical twins have shown a tendency toward concordance

for schizophrenia; that is, if one of the identical twins displays symptoms of schizophrenia, so does the other, but usually much less than half the time.

Can we think of any good reasons, other than genetics, why madness might sometimes afflict both members of a pair of identical twins? Indeed, wouldn't we *expect* it to happen sometimes as a result of the similarity of their environments as children? Especially in the decades in which these studies were done, parents typically tried to rear twins with a rigorous sameness, right down to their clothing. Compounding this trend, twins themselves often go through periods where they try to look and act alike, and where they feel themselves drawn together and dependent on each other as a unit.

Since their sex is always the same, identical twins are especially likely to face more nearly identical environmental stresses than do fraternal twins or other siblings. Any sexual or physical abuse probably would be aimed at both of them at the same time.

Sexy Stories

Genetic theories are widely accepted simply because we've heard so much about them. The popular press seems particularly inclined to publicize research with a biological bent, perhaps because reporters share the general public's biases or because hard science claims make for sexier stories. Millions of readers open their newspapers and magazines to find articles based on the unproven assumption that our emotions can be explained by our brain chemistry.

Alfie Kohn, *American Health*, April 1993.

While twin studies may seem straightforward, in fact they are not. In the best book about genetics and psychiatry, *Not in Our Genes* (1984), R. C. Lewontin, Steven Rose, and Leon Kamin question the methodology of the twin studies, including whether the twins were really identical and whether their diagnoses were reliable. The authors confirm that in most instances, when one identical twin becomes schizophrenic, the other does not. They conclude that the twin data is more compatible with an environmental influence than a genetic one.

In "Biological Theories, Drug Treatments, and Schizophrenia: A Critical Assessment," in the Winter 1986 *Journal of Mind and Behavior*, David and Henri Cohen similarly conclude that "the only unquestionable result of twin genetic studies is that they demonstrate the extensive contribution of 'environmental' factors to the etiology of the disorder." This is so seemingly out of step with what the public is told, it bears repeating: identical twin studies support an environmental theory of schizophrenia rather than a genetic one.

What about the more definitive study of identical twins raised apart from their families? When laypersons think of twin studies proving the genetic basis of schizophrenia, they naturally assume that the studies are of twins raised apart. But no such studies of psychiatric disorders exist. The numbers of identical twins raised apart are simply too small to study a problem that affects a tiny fraction of the population. It's a case of the public filling in the blanks with information that isn't there.

The Most Relied-On Genetic Study

When the twin studies failed to produce the hoped-for data, genetic researchers turned to studies of children raised more or less apart from their parents. In an NIMH [National Institute of Mental Health]-sponsored Danish-American study, adopted children in Denmark who developed schizophrenia were located. Then their biological families were located and evaluated to see if they, too, had schizophrenic members. If so, it was reasoned, then a genetic factor might be at work, since the adopted children presumably had been raised in a "normal" environment separate from their parents.

These studies are by far the most often cited in support of the genetic theory of schizophrenia, and the investigators came with the highest possible credentials. Seymour Kety was a psychiatry professor at Harvard, and psychologist David Rosenthal and psychiatrist Paul Wender were at the National Institute of Mental Health. Fini Schulsinger was the chief psychiatrist in Copenhagen.

When I located the original 1975 summary report on the Danish study by Kety and his colleagues in the book *Genetic Research in Psychiatry*, I was shocked by what I found. There was no increase in so-called schizophrenia among the close biological relatives, including the mothers, fathers, full brothers, and full sisters. Thus the studies actually tended to *disprove* the genetic origin of the presumed illness.

So what data were they using to prove a genetic tendency? They had made a most strange finding: *the half-brothers and half-sisters on the father's side did have an increased rate of "schizophrenia."* In other words, we have a miracle gene that skips the biological mothers, fathers, brothers, and sisters—and even the biological half-brothers and sisters on the mother's side—and strikes only the half-siblings on the father's side.

Obviously this finding is so ridiculous, so clearly an error or a chance finding, that Kety, Rosenthal, Wender, and the other investigators are reluctant to describe their full data to their colleagues. Therefore, the actual nature of the alleged genetic tendency goes unmentioned in their reviews and requires deep digging into the original data itself.

Furthermore, the NIMH study involved so few families that this peculiar finding of increased diagnoses of schizophrenia among the half-siblings on the father's side depended on one large family with six offspring who supposedly were suffering from schizophreniclike disorders. One must wonder if there was incest or some other abusive practice occurring on the paternal side of this family.

House of Cards

In April 1990 I had the opportunity to debate one of the authors of the study, Fini Schulsinger, in a public forum at the University of Copenhagen. I repeated the point about the unaccountable loading of his study with a group of distant relatives made up of half-brothers and -sisters on the father's side. Did he produce some statistics to prove me wrong? To the contrary, he conceded the point. Yet the whole genetics of schizophrenia rests on this house of cards. What hocus-pocus!

This is only the beginning of the flaws in this study, but I think it is sufficient to make the point.

As the authors of *Not in Our Genes* observed, the weaknesses of the Danish study are so obvious that it's hard to understand how "distinguished scientists" could have promoted them as valid. In the March 16, 1990, *Psychiatric News*, Yale psychiatrist Theodore Lidz reminded readers of his own earlier criticisms. "Our published reexamination of the Danish-American adoption studies show that the researchers' interpretations of their data are untenable, distorted to support their hypothesis."

Environmental Origin Confirmed

There is simply no evidence in the most highly touted studies for a genetic factor for schizophrenia. Instead, their failure to detect *any* genetic influence tends to confirm an environmental origin for schizophrenic overwhelm [the psychological and spiritual crisis that is labeled "schizophrenia"]. It discredits psychiatry that these studies have been used to prove the opposite of what they really show and that the public has been consciously propagandized with misleading information.

A more recent study by the Finnish psychiatrist Pekka Tienari and several other investigators, including the American Lyman Wynne, was published in 1987 in *Schizophrenia Bulletin* (vol. 13, no. 3). Like the Danish study, it studied children who became schizophrenic after being adopted away from their original families. Tienari finds some evidence for a genetic influence, but hidden in the fine print is the fact that the children had lived with their original parents until up to the age of four years and eleven months. Whatever apparent genetic influence Tienari found could easily be due to early environmental exposure to the biological parents.

A much more striking finding was generated by Tienari's careful psychological examination of the adoptive parents. In every case that a child became diagnosed as schizophrenic there was serious diagnosed mental disorder in one of the adoptive parents. Tienari states flatly, "There were no borderline or psychotic offspring who were reared in healthy or mildly disturbed families." He concludes that *environment must play a role in the development of schizophrenia.*

If there is any pattern here, it is that the genetic hypothesis remains unproven, while the environmental hypothesis has been confirmed repeatedly by the very studies aimed at proving a genetic component.

The Diminishing Evidence

Because of psychiatry's influence in the media, most people think that there is a growing body of studies supporting the genetic origin of psychiatric disorders, such as so-called schizophrenia.

In reality, literature supporting a genetic cause for "schizophrenia" has grown sparser over the years. We have fewer and fewer studies claiming a genetic basis. Old ones have become discredited by the hundreds, while new ones are rare indeed. If anything, the evidence seemed much more convincing in the 1930s and 1940s, when genetic researchers inspired Hitler's eugenic legislation and the enforced sterilization of tens of thousands of people in the United States and then in Germany. At that time, dozens of progenetic studies typically were cited in reviews. If there has since been a scientific revolution in genetic psychiatry, it has been in the opposite direction—toward discrediting the old studies and casting skepticism on the few new ones. But that's not what the public is told.

The public has been encountering another kind of genetic study—those claiming to have located specific genes for specific psychiatric problems, such as schizophrenia, depression, and alcoholism.

In the British journal *Nature,* in November 1988, a team headed by Robin Sherrington of the Molecular Psychiatry Laboratory of the University of London reports locating a gene for schizophrenia on "the long arm of human chromosome 5" in seven families from England and Iceland. The exact gene could not be identified, but it was thought to be dominant. Those carrying it would supposedly become schizophrenic or have a related disorder. "This report," they claim, "provides the first strong evidence for the involvement of a single gene in the causation of schizophrenia."

An editorial in the same issue of *Nature* proclaimed a breakthrough in psychiatry: "New research has shown some schizophrenia to be, in part, genetically determined." The president-elect of the American Psychiatric Association, Herb Pardes, leaped on the promotional opportunity and proclaimed the study to be a "tremendous advance." Newspapers all over the world carried the story without a hint of skepticism.

Absurdities Revealed

Apart from the hazard of making too much of a single study, there was a logical fallacy in this one that rendered it highly suspect from the start. When scientists succeed in locating a single dominant gene for a physical disease, such as Huntington's chorea, their finding makes sense because the disease is already known to be transmitted by a dominant gene as a result of studying the medical family tree of the patients. If one parent has Huntington's, for example, the odds are exactly fifty-fifty that each of the offspring also will have it. But this is not the case with so-called schizophrenia. Every family study—including the ones we have looked at—shows that a single dominant gene does not exist for people diagnosed as schizophrenic. This has been known for decades. So anyone familiar with the field could have dismissed the discovery of a dominant gene even before looking at the study. Yet the study was heralded by psychiatry as a powerful confirmation of its genetic bias.

An actual examination of the study brought out more absurdities. Drawing on seven families, it contained 104 individuals. From the family tree reproduced in the study we find the following examples of extraordinary prevalence for schizophrenia and other disorders among these families: one set of parents had five of seven children with psychiatric disorders, including three who were said to be schizophrenic or otherwise psychotic; another had four out of seven with diagnosed schizophrenia or other psychoses; another had seven out of ten with psychiatric disorders. The typical rate for children diagnosed as schizophrenic in families with a schizophrenic parent usually is estimated to be less than 10 percent. These families could vie to be in the *Guinness Book of World Records* for being the most crazy family.

What can be learned from such a group of families in terms of schizophrenia? Probably nothing. It would be far more interesting to check out the patterns of child abuse and neglect required to produce such rampant misery.

Curiously, the same issue of *Nature* contains a study in which James Kennedy and his colleagues find, as the title states, "Evidence Against Linkage of Schizophrenia to Markers on Chromosome 5 in a Northern Swedish Pedigree." The Swedish study specifically and precisely refutes the English study.

Now, the English study has gone the way of all such studies, lost in the shifting sands of science; yet the public has never heard the refutations.

Despite the single-minded promotion of genetic explanations in both the psychiatric and the popular press, occasionally a more realistic appraisal crops up. The March 1987 issue of *Psychiatric Times* carried an article headlined CONFIDENCE WANES IN SEARCH FOR GENETIC ORIGINS OF MENTAL ILLNESS. It declares, "The reason: Researchers are finding it difficult or impossible to replicate earlier reports claiming to trace various psychiatric illness to particular chromosomal locations." Genetic advocate Elliot Gershon of NIMH is quoted as admitting, "The major problem is all the nonreplications." It concludes, "But so far the evidence is so equivocal that some competent observers deny that there is any convincing evidence for the genetic basis of any major psychiatric illness.". . .

A Journey of Renewal and Growth

In summary, we do not fully understand the human experience that gets labeled schizophrenia, but we have some good ideas about its environmental origin and psychospiritual meaning. . . . We also know a lot about helping people get through the experience in a creative, valuable manner when they ask for and desire our help. What begins as disintegration or breakdown, a psychospiritual overwhelm, can become a journey of renewal and growth. It often involves facing meaningful conflicts about the nature of life, love, relationships, and responsibility. It gains its particular flavor, which has been called madness, from its often flamboyant psychospirituality, combined with its typically overwhelming feelings of fragmented identity, humiliation, and helplessness.

Instead of offering human understanding to these overwhelmed people, psychiatry has fabricated biological and genetic explanations. It has used these explanations to justify a massive drug assault that has taken a profound toll in terms of damaged brains and shattered lives.

*"Exposure to the A2 influenza virus during the
second trimester [of fetal development] increases
the risk of later schizophrenia."*

Influenza During Gestation Causes Schizophrenia

Eadbhard O'Callaghan et al.

The authors of the following viewpoint review the incidence of
schizophrenia among individuals who were born during and
close to an influenza epidemic in England and Wales in 1957.
They conclude that exposure to the virus during the second
trimester of fetal development increases the risk of schizophrenia later in life. The authors are Eadbhard O'Callaghan, who is
a consultant psychiatrist at Cluain Mhuire Family Centre in
Dublin, Ireland; Pak Sham, Nori Takei, and Robin M. Murray
who are with the Institute of Psychiatry in London, England,
where Murray is the head of the department of psychological
medicine, Sham is a lecturer, and Takei is a research psychiatrist; and Giles Glover, who is senior medical officer at
Wellington House in London, England.

As you read, consider the following questions:

1. Why are their results unlikely to have been caused by
   seasonal fluctuations in the general population birthrate,
   according to the authors?
2. Do the authors have evidence that the mothers of the
   schizophrenics studied were infected with the influenza
   virus?
3. According to the authors, who seems to be at greater risk of
   developing schizophrenia as a result of exposure to influenza,
   men or women?

Individuals born in late winter and early spring are more likely to develop schizophrenia than those born at other times of the year, a reproducible and widely observed seasonal effect that is most striking among those without a family history of the disorder. Is there some season-dependent environmental factor which causes neuro-developmental damage in the prenatal or perinatal period that in turn increases the risk of later schizophrenia? Maternal influenza is one of many possible candidates. Influenza epidemics occur frequently in autumn and winter months, and psychotic states were reported after the 1919 pandemic. S.A. Mednick et al have reported an increased risk of schizophrenia among those who were in their second trimester of fetal life when Helsinki, Finland, was subject to the 1957 pandemic of A2 influenza [caused by the type A2 virus], but studies in Scotland and the USA did not show a relation between prenatal exposure to influenza and risk of schizophrenia. We set out to investigate whether the 1957 pandemic of A2 influenza in England and Wales was followed by an increase in the births of individuals who have subsequently been diagnosed as schizophrenic.

Data Gathered

A2 influenza arrived in the United Kingdom in the summer of 1957; from serological data gathered during the epidemic, the peak incidence of new infections occurred from mid-September to mid-October. Reported claims for sickness benefit are consistent with this interpretation, because they refer to claims for illness during the week before the claim was made; although there was some geographical variation, the total number of claims nationwide increased rapidly from about Sept 15, reached a peak during the first week of October, and fell considerably by the end of that month.

Data were analysed for 12 consecutive months; to follow the sampling methods of two earlier studies, and to allow estimation of the time in pregnancy when exposure most probably occurred, these periods ran from the fifteenth day of one month to the fourteenth day of the next. The first period therefore included all those born on Aug 15, 1957, to Sept 14, 1957, and so on to period 12 (July 15, 1958, to Aug 14, 1958). If the epidemic was indeed at its peak from Sept 15 to Oct 14, 1957, people born in the first period were most likely to have been exposed to influenza in the second month after birth, those born in period 7 would most probably have been exposed to the infection in the fifth month in utero, and those born in period 12 would not have been exposed at all.

Data from the Mental Health Enquiry for first discharges from hospital between 1976 and 1986 were sought for all individuals born in the United Kingdom between Aug 15, 1957, and Aug 14, 1958, who had a primary discharge diagnosis of schizophrenia. . . . Similarly diagnosed schizophrenic patients born in the corresponding periods (1-12) of the previous two and the next two years (from Aug 15, 1955, 1956, 1958, and 1959) were taken for comparison and to control for the known season-of-birth effect for schizophrenia. Data were obtained from the following regional health authorities in England and Wales: North-west Thames (1976-1984), Oxford (1979-1986), Wales (1976-1980), South West (1978-1987), North West (1976-1986), Mersey (1976-1981), Trent (1979-1986), and Yorkshire (1976, 1978, and 1980-1984).

An Improbable Event

339 schizophrenic patients in these health regions were born during the index year and 1331 in the 4 control years. The number of index and control patients were compared for each of the 12 periods (see table).

Table 1: **Distribution of Affected Births Aug 15, 1957-Aug 14, 1958, Compared with Average for Control Years (Aug 15, 1955-Aug 14, 1957, and Aug 15, 1958-Aug 14, 1960)**

	All		Men		Women	
Period*	Control[†]	1957/58	Control[†]	1957/58	Control[†]	1957/58
1	24	24	15.25	13	8.75	11
2	34	31	22.75	23	11.25	8
3 (9)	23.75	29	17	17	6.75	12
4 (8)	25.5	35	15	25	10.5	10
5 (7)	27.25	24	17	16	10.25	8
6 (6)	27	23	19.75	17	7.25	6
7 (5)	25.5	48	16.25	26	9.25	22
8 (4)	30.75	32	20.75	22	10	10
9 (3)	26.75	17	17.75	8	9	9
10 (2)	28.75	29	19	21	9.75	8
11 (1)	30.5	26	17.5	20	13	6
12	29	21	17.25	17	11.75	4

*Numbers in parentheses indicate month of gestation (for index year) during peak of 1957 A2 influenza epidemic.
†Multiply by 4 for total births in the 4 control years studied.

Eadbhard O'Callaghan et al., *Lancet*, May 25, 1991.

There is a significant difference in the distributions of schizophrenic births in 1957/58 compared with the control years. The most striking difference was seen in period 7 (February/March, 1958) of the index year: individuals born in this period were in their fifth month of fetal development when the influenza epidemic was at its peak. Fig 1 shows the ratio of affected births in the index year compared with average numbers over the 4 control years: there is an 88% excess of such births in period 7. . . . The observed number . . . represents a highly improbable event. This result is unlikely to be caused by fluctuations in the general population birth rate, because the number of births in England and Wales in February and March, 1958 (126, 959), is very similar to the average for the same months in the control years (126, 327). When the results were considered separately for men and women, the difference between the index and control years was significant for women but not for men (see table 1).

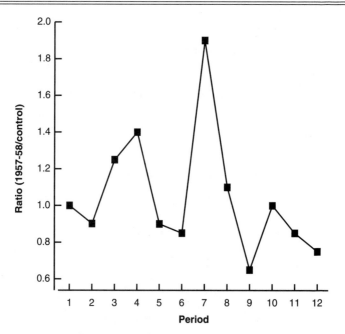

Fig 1: Ratio of affected births (study period/average for previous 2 and next 2 years).

Eadbhard O'Callaghan et al., *Lancet*, May 25, 1991.

Our findings support Mednick et al's report that exposure to the A2 influenza virus during the second trimester increases the risk of later schizophrenia. Our data do not cover the whole of England and Wales, and several years of discharge records are missing from several regional health authorities, but we think it unlikely that a sampling artifact beyond our control might have biased the results towards an excess of future schizophrenia in those exposed to influenza at the time predicted in the original report. We also have no direct evidence that the mothers of the individuals who developed schizophrenia were infected with the virus, and it is not certain whether the virus crosses the placenta. Nevertheless, maternal influenza during pregnancy is associated with an increase in congenital abnormalities of the central nervous system, particularly anencephaly [absence of all or a large segment of the brain], and mothers infected with influenza in the autumn of 1957 had twice as many children with congenital malformations as did uninfected controls. Female fetuses appear to have a greater risk of abnormalities in the central nervous system as a result of such infections, but it is unclear whether this is due to greater susceptibility, or because affected male fetuses have a greater risk of spontaneous abortion. Although a test for interaction by sex on our data did not reach significance, both our data and those of R.E. Kendell and I.W. Kemp show a more obvious schizophrenogenic effect on female than on male fetuses. Schizophrenia usually presents earlier in men than in women, and in a young sample such as ours one might expect many more affected men than women—despite an overall male:female ratio of 1.97:1 in the index year, the ratio fell to 1.18:1 for period 7.

"Prenatal exposure to influenza and schizophrenia are unrelated."

Influenza During Gestation Does Not Cause Schizophrenia

Timothy J. Crow and D. John Done

In the following viewpoint, Timothy J. Crow and D. John Done reject the contention that prenatal exposure to influenza causes the development of schizophrenia later in life. The authors document the rates of schizophrenia among the children of women who suffered from influenza while pregnant during an influenza epidemic in 1957 and conclude that no correlation exists. Crow is head of the psychiatry division of the Clinical Research Centre at Northwick Park Hospital in Harrow, England. Done is senior lecturer in the psychology department of the University of Hertford in Hatfield, England.

As you read, consider the following questions:

1. What do the authors believe is the probable origin of schizophrenia?
2. On what point do the authors dispute the study by O'Callaghan and colleagues?
3. How many of the 945 mothers who suffered from influenza in the second trimester of pregnancy gave birth to children who later became schizophrenic, according to Crow and Done?

From Timothy J. Crow and D. John Done, "Prenatal Exposure to Influenza Does Not Cause Schizophrenia," *The British Journal of Psychiatry* 161 (September 1992):390-93, with permission of the Royal College of Psychiatrists.

The hypothesis that schizophrenia is caused by a virus was originally proposed in relation to psychoses observed following the 1919 influenza epidemic. Karl Menninger considered that approximately a third of the illnesses that he had observed in influenza sufferers were like dementia praecox [schizophrenia]. He suggested that dementia praecox might be caused by the virus, although he subsequently retracted in 1928—"I think I said seven years ago that influenza caused psychosis. I have grown older since and I hope, wiser. I have certainly changed my mind."

Others have formulated versions of the viral theory. The attraction of such theories is that they provide an environmental explanation (and a putative cause therefore apparently more accessible to remedy) of a disease that otherwise appears to be of an inscrutable but probably intrinsic and genetic origin. The flaw of viral theories is that they provide no explanation for the ubiquitous and approximately constant occurrence of the illness; in spite of claims to the contrary the evidence for horizontal transmission (i.e. contagion) is not compelling.

The hypothesis that schizophrenia is caused by the influenza virus has been resuscitated in the proposal that the pathogenic infection occurs not at the time of onset of psychosis in adult life but *in utero*. Any theory of an origin of schizophrenia in early life (including the genetic one) has the capability of accounting for the observation that some sufferers are noted to have been unusual, for example by their relatives, many years before the first psychotic symptoms appeared. However, to explain onset in adult life on the basis of influenza infection *in utero* requires an additional postulate, for example an interaction between a static lesion and a programme of development, since there is no evidence that the influenza virus (unlike herpes viruses) is re-expressed as viral particles after a long latent period.

Is There a Relationship?

The evidence to date relates (mainly) to the 1957 epidemic. S.A. Mednick *et al* (1988) and E. O'Callaghan *et al* (1991) have claimed that there was an excess of births of people who later developed schizophrenia during this epidemic. This claim has not been supported in two other studies. [R.E. Kendell and I.W. Kemp found a correlation in Edinburgh but not in the rest of Scotland. E. Fuller Torrey, studying a population much larger than the other studies, found no correlation in the United States.] The largest studies have failed to demonstrate an effect.

It is implausible to suggest that if the schizophrenogenic effect of the 1957 influenza epidemic was genuine, that it was present in Finland and England & Wales and Edinburgh, Scotland, but absent in the rest of Scotland and the US. The virus that caused this pandemic cannot have changed. If the effect was real it should have been more apparent in the Scottish sample and most securely have been demonstrated in the US sample. Yet there is no increase in the rate for Scotland, and Torrey *et al* conclude that "there was no significant elevation of the schizophrenic birth rate immediately preceding, during, or after the 1957 influenza epidemic". If Mednick *et al*'s finding is extrapolated to the US study [by Torrey], an excess of 981 cases of schizophrenia born to mothers who were exposed to influenza in the second trimester would be expected. If O'Callaghan *et al*'s interpretation of their findings was correct, 321 extra cases in a single month in the US sample would be expected. Even if such cases had been distributed over a longer time interval than they were in Europe, they would have been readily detectable. But there is no sign of any such increase in the figures of Torrey *et al*. An effect that disappears as sample size increases cannot be regarded as a reliable finding.

A curious feature unremarked upon by O'Callaghan *et al* is the form of the curve in the monthly laboratory reports of influenza and its relation to the apparent excess of births of those later to suffer from schizophrenia. Whereas the former shows, as one would expect from an infection that travels around the country, a curve that extends to affect at least three months (a rise in August with a peak spread through September and October, and a fall in November—the data are described as monthly but the graph shows some observations were made more frequently than this), the plot of schizophrenic births shows a spike that is limited to one month (period 7—corresponding to exposure in the 5th month of pregnancy) with no excess in either the preceding or succeeding months (periods 6 and 8 corresponding to the 4th and 6th months of pregnancy). It is surprising (if the relationship is not a chance finding) that the dependent variable (schizophrenic births) shows a temporal distribution that is more restricted than the change (incidence of influenza) to which it is suggested it is causally related. O'Callaghan *et al* draw attention to the spike in period 7 as a "highly improbable event", but have not presented an analysis that includes the adjacent months.

A More Direct Test

A more direct test of the hypothesis is to examine whether mothers who actually suffered from influenza in their pregnancies gave birth to more children who became schizophrenic. We [along with E.C. Johnson] studied admissions to psychiatric hospitals of patients included in the British Perinatal Mortality Survey and the National Child Development Study (NCDS), whose ante- and perinatal histories, including infections, were documented at the time of birth. All children born in England, Scotland and Wales in the week 3-9 March 1958 were included.

The sample consisted of those whom O'Callaghan *et al* suggest are at greatest risk of subsequent psychotic illness as a result of their mother's exposure to influenza in the supposedly critical fifth month of pregnancy, and Mednick *et al* regard as at risk as a result of exposure in the second trimester.

Cases were identified (with the help of statisticians in each of the regional health authorities) by a search in the Mental Health Enquiry records (that were continued until 1985, when persons in the survey were 27 years old [onset of schizophrenia usually occurs by the patient's early 20s]) for individuals born that week. Psychiatric diagnoses were established by retrieving the case notes and applying the criteria of the Present State Examination [a standardized diagnostic method]. Influenza during pregnancy was documented by an interview with the mother conducted by the midwife who was also required to consult medical records relating to the pregnancy.

Table 1: **Infection with Influenza in Pregnancy in Relation to Subsequent Psychiatric Illness in the Child**

	Number of subjects	Maternal influenza in trimester[1]		
		1	2	3
Total Psychoses	16,268	231	945	675
total	89 exp[2]	1.3	5.2	3.7
	obs	0	8	5
broad schizophrenia	57 exp	0.8	3.3	2.4
	obs	0	3	4
narrow schizophrenia	34 exp	0.5	2.0	1.4
	obs	0	1	3
affective illness	32 exp	0.5	1.9	1.3
	obs	1	5	1

1. Trimester 1 = June to August 1957; trimester 2 = September to November 1957; trimester 3 = December 1957 to March 1958.
2. exp = expected, obs = observed.

Timothy J. Crow and D. John Done, *British Journal of Psychiatry*, September 1992.

Table 1 shows rates of influenza in 16,268 mothers in the NCDS, together with information on whether their children had by 1985 been admitted to a psychiatric unit and acquired a diagnosis—either of schizophrenia, by a broad or a narrow definition, or of affective [mood] disorder. . . .

Even though the influenza epidemic reached a peak and 945 mothers were affected in the trimester that Mednick *et al* and O'Callaghan *et al* regard as especially risky, only one child had later schizophrenia as defined by narrow diagnostic criteria, and three children by a broader definition, figures closely comparable with the rates in children of non-infected mothers and with population expectation. . . .

An Erroneous Assumption

The significance of the findings for the influenza hypothesis are best seen if one extrapolates the interpretations of Mednick *et al* and O'Callaghan *et al* to this study. Mednick *et al*'s interpretation is that 1.87 times the usual rate of schizophrenic births occurred in the general population for births between 15 February and 14 May 1958, and O'Callaghan *et al*'s interpretation is that 1.88 times the usual schizophrenic birth rate occurred between 15 February and 14 March 1958. Both authors attribute the excess to the exposure of mothers to the 1957 epidemic.

Since the week in which the NCDS sample was collected (3-9 March 1958) is included in both time periods, Mednick *et al* and O'Callaghan *et al* would predict an 87% to 88% increase in schizophrenic births in this week. Calculations based upon various population-based estimates of schizophrenia suggest that the observed number of schizophrenic births in this week corresponds quite closely to expectation. Nonetheless, one could make the assumption that the observed rates are indeed inflated by 87% to 88% as a result of mothers being infected with influenza during pregnancy. In other words, 0.87/1.87 of the total will be attributable to influenza. According to this assumption, the excess number of births due to influenza by broad criteria will be 26.5, and 15.8 by narrow criteria. But if this excess of births is, as Mednick *et al* and O'Callaghan *et al* suppose, due to maternal exposure to influenza, these numbers should appear in the column relating to the second trimester in Table 1. Thus where the figure of 3 appears in the category of broad schizophrenia there should be a further 26.5 cases, and where the figure of 1 appears in the category of narrow schizophrenia there should be a further 15.8 cases. Even if one assumes that twice as many cases of influenza went undetected as were actually reported in the NCDS sample, the expectations of Mednick *et al* and O'Callaghan *et al* would be of a further 8.8 cases of broad schizophrenia, and of 5.3 cases of narrow schizophrenia. The fact that no single extra case of schizophrenia is observed in these cells indicates that the interpretations of Mednick *et al* and O'Callaghan *et al* of their own data are in error.

We concluded that prenatal exposure to influenza and schizophrenia are unrelated. Those who believe otherwise must answer two questions:

(a) Why is the supposed relationship not seen in the US sample?

(b) Why do 945 mothers with influenza in the second trimester not have more than the expected three children (by age 27 years) with schizophrenia?

The proponents of the hypothesis may be tempted to argue that the causation of schizophrenia is multifactorial, and that prenatal infection with influenza could still account for a small but unidentified fraction of cases. We believe this temptation should be resisted. No aetiological factor other than a genetic one has been established, although the nature of the genetic contribution (mode of transmission, persistence of the gene in spite of a fertility disadvantage) is obscure. It contributes little to assert that any particular environmental factor has not been excluded as a cause of a small but undefined group of cases. Scientific progress depends upon replicable findings. The putative effects of prenatal exposure to influenza on the incidence of schizophrenia are not of this nature.

"Birth complications, neonatal complications, and pregnancy complications are all relevant to the development of schizophrenia."

Obstetrical Complications Contribute to Schizophrenia

Suzanne N. Brixey et al.

The following viewpoint is the result of a research project at Villanova University in Pennsylvania, where Bernard J. Gallagher III is a professor of psychiatric sociology, Joseph A. McFalls Jr. is a professor of sociology, and Lisa Ferraro Parmelee is a professor of history. Suzanne N. Brixey is a medical student at the University of Virginia in Charlottesville. These authors present evidence that complications during gestation, birth, and early infancy contribute to the risk of developing schizophrenia later in life. According to the authors, risk factors include fetal hypoxia (an oxygen deficiency), low birth weight, developmental problems, and exposure to viruses and stress.

As you read, consider the following questions:

1. How are obstetrical complications (OCs) defined by the authors?
2. Do the authors believe that a single virus is the sole cause of schizophrenia?
3. Why is the timing of fetal exposure to a virus important, according to the authors?

From Suzanne N. Brixey et al., "Gestational and Neonatal Factors in the Etiology of Schizophrenia," *Journal of Clinical Psychology* 49, no. 3 (May 1993):447-54. Copyright 1993 by the Clinical Psychology Publishing Company, Inc., Brandon, VT 05733.

Schizophrenia is a debilitating and mysterious psychosis. Although the causes of schizophrenia continue to elude researchers, there has been much progress in ascertaining concrete etiologies [causes]. Until the 1970s, schizophrenia was widely perceived by mental health experts to be the result of environmental stressors. Although life experiences may exacerbate schizophrenia, research over recent decades has identified biological abnormalities as likely causes. This viewpoint is a review of a specific group of biogenic factors—those that are imposed during pregnancy and around the time of birth. Events during the embryonic development of a fetus can have debilitating effects on fetal brain formation. Noxious experiences that affect intrauterine development, such as infections, toxins, maternal stress, hypoxia [a deficient amount of oxygen reaching the body tissue], or a variety of other factors, may result in an increased predisposition to schizophrenia.

The gestational period is defined here as the period of pregnancy (approximately 280 days). The neonatal period pertains to the newborn infant. Prenatal complications, that is, complications during the period before birth, and perinatal complications, that is, complications during the period that traditionally is defined as shortly before and after birth (from the 28th week of gestation to 1-4 weeks after birth), are all classified under the heading of obstetrical complications because more current research does not distinguish among pregnancy, birth, and neonatal complications.

Obstetrical Complications

Obstetrical complications (OCs) can be defined as physical deviations from the expected course of fetal development during pregnancy, labor or delivery, or the early newborn period. Studies have shown that birth complications (BCs), neonatal complications (NCs), and pregnancy complications (PCs) are all relevant to the development of schizophrenia.

Schizophrenia has been linked with OCs in a number of different populations, including adult schizophrenics; schizophrenics adopted while very young; schizophrenic children of low-income schizophrenic mothers; high-risk offspring who became schizophrenic; and schizophrenics within a pair of discordant, monozygotic twins [a pair of identical twins in which one becomes schizophrenic and the other does not]. In one study, J. Parnas et al. uncovered pregnancy and birth complications in 67% of 166 schizophrenic patients, a radically higher percentage than in the nonschizophrenic population. Although no specific complication was identified, a trend of increased stress before or at the time of birth appeared to be especially relevant. . . .

The majority of OCs appear to be linked with fetal hypoxia, a deficient amount of oxygen reaching the body tissue. Brain structure and function associated with schizophrenia may be sensitive to even moderate levels of hypoxia, especially in the presence of a genetic predisposition. Numerous studies report that hypoxia is common in prolonged labor and that hypoxia is significantly more prevalent among birth mothers of schizophrenics than among those of nonschizophrenics. Animal studies also indicate a significant change in brain metabolism, overall brain growth, and cellular differentiation as a result of fetal hypoxia. According to T.F. McNeil, "the specific OCs most characteristic of childhood psychotics across different studies were toxemia [the presence of toxic substances in the blood], bleeding during pregnancy/threatened spontaneous abortion, and asphyxia, all of which imply [risk for] schizophrenia.". . .

Low birth weight also has been correlated positively with increased incidence of schizophrenia. According to T. McNeil and L. Kaij, schizophrenics differ from controls in overall combined gestational age, length, and birth weight. Some more specific studies report that schizophrenics weigh an average 6 ounces less than their siblings at birth. In birth weight analyses of monozygotic twins discordant for schizophrenia, a majority of the twins with schizophrenia have had a significantly lower birth weight than their respective twins. . . . Other analyses identified low birth weight as a risk factor for schizophrenia along with such factors as OCs and a family history of schizophrenia. . . .

Viral Infection

Infectious agents may induce schizophrenia by directly infecting the brain as in the case of Creutzfeldt-Jakob disease, where a congenital infection directly attacks the brain. Causal infection in this disease occurs in infancy and results in late life dementia as well as a decrease in brain mass. Similarly, schizophrenia involves a reduction in brain mass that may result from an infectious agent. Opinion is divided, however, on the specific pathways by which an infectious agent may induce the psychosis. . . .

The risks of birth complications, abnormal prenatal developments, and chronic viral acquisition in the fetus are increased greatly by a viral infection in the mother. A virus during pregnancy may disrupt maternal physiology and directly infect the fetus or may cause direct brain damage to the offspring later in life as a result of its presence in the central nervous system (CNS) (as in the case of an enterovirus). A viral etiology for schizophrenia makes sound theoretical sense, but researchers have yet to document a link between schizophrenia and any *specific* viral agent. While a number of studies report elevated antibody production to numerous familiar viruses, these findings have not been replicated thoroughly. Even though a virus cannot be isolated, however, this does not discount a viral etiology. . . .

Many researchers predict that no specific virus will be identified as the sole cause of schizophrenia; rather, a family of viruses will be implicated. Perhaps a family of viruses may account for the heterogeneity seen among schizophrenic patients. Additionally, a viral etiology may be especially relevant to issues of seasonality of birth [a disproportionate number of schizophrenics are born in winter] and geographical prevalence [large numbers of schizophrenics are concentrated in cities and in certain geographical areas], as well as unusual immunological responses seen in schizophrenic patients. A pregnant woman is presumed to have a compromised immune system and, thus, to be more susceptible to viral infections during the winter months. A viral hypothesis is not only consistent with the winter-born phenomenon; it also is correlated directly with infection rates in the general population in given birth years. One study of 3,246 schizophrenics discovered that "The winter birth-seasonality effect was greater in the years directly following those marked by high levels of infectious disorders than in years directly following those with low incidences of . . . diphtheria, pneumonia and influenza" [according to C.G. Watson, T. Kucala, C. Tilleskjor, and L. Jacobs]. E. Fuller Torrey reports an increase in schizophrenic births as a result of a corresponding increase in measles, polio, varicella-zoster [chicken pox], and influenza during the prenatal period in two different states. And L.E. Barr, S.A. Mednick, and P. Munk-Jorgensen confirmed Mednick's conclusion that a positive association exists between the risk of viral infection during the second trimester of pregnancy and the probability of being hospitalized as an adult schizophrenic.

An American Study

Studies have been carried out on the occurrence of pregnancy and birth complications (PBCs) in persons who later develop schizophrenia. An American study utilized retrospective histories from the mothers plus birth records and compared the patients with schizophrenia with normal sibling controls; the study found significantly more complications with pregnancy and birth among the patients with schizophrenia.

E. Fuller Torrey and Charles A. Kaufmann, *Handbook of Schizophrenia, Vol. 1: The Neurology of Schizophrenia*, H.A. Nasrallah and D.R. Weinberger eds., 1986.

Place of birth adds another element to the application of a viral etiology. A fetus with a genetic vulnerability, born in winter in an urban environment, is more likely to suffer CNS damage as the result of infection. Therefore, it is not surprising that the incidence of schizophrenia in high-risk urban winter-born adults is 23.3%, dramatically more than that of the general population (1%) or even the overall high-risk population (8.9%). . . .

E. O'Callaghan, P. Sham, N. Takei, G. Glover, and R.M. Murray report an 88% difference between the usual hospital admission rate for schizophrenics and the number admitted 20 to 30 years after the fall 1957 influenza epidemic in England and Wales. They hypothesize that this was the result of cerebral cortex damage caused by exposure to influenza during the mother's pregnancy.

Most researchers believe more emphasis should be placed on the *timing* of the fetal exposure to infection rather than on the *type* of infection, particularly because of the importance of fetal neural development in the second trimester. While exposure to A2 influenza, for instance, during the first trimester leads to observable central nervous system abnormalities, exposure in the second trimester actually may play a greater role in increasing the risk of adult schizophrenia. Mothers in Helsinki, Finland, whose fetuses were exposed to the 1957 type A2 influenza epidemic during the second trimester of development had an increased risk of their children's being diagnosed schizophrenic as adults. In fact, the expected number of schizophrenic patients among that birth cohort was doubled.

Fetal exposure to a virus is not a sufficient cause of schizophrenia because not all fetuses exposed to the influenza virus develop adult schizophrenia. Logic dictates that an infection only increases the risk for the psychosis in persons who already are genetically predisposed. . . .

Developmental Deficits and Stress

Children of schizophrenic parents typically have lower birth weight than normal controls, although they have about average length, head circumference, and shoulder circumference. High-risk children tend toward unusual growth patterns and uncharacteristic development of their musculoskeletal systems during infancy. Intrauterine growth retardation usually is attributed to a low ponderal index (weight to length ratio).

Some [including J. Marcus et al.] propose a "genetically determined neurointegrative deficit" in conjunction with external variables that result in schizophrenia. These deficits include poor perinatal performance in motor and sensorimotor skills in the first year, low birth weight, and an increased vulnerability to external insults. . . . Others hold that a vulnerable infant is less able to maintain its own homeostasis in its nervous system. Consequently, high-risk infants have a lower threshold for disequilibrium within the CNS. According to J.D. Guy, L.V. Majorski, C.J. Wallace, and M.P. Guy, schizophrenics have an increased rate of minor physical anomalies (MPA), which result from a malformation in the first trimester. Such a deformation may be the result of genetic factors in addition to teratogenic agents [which cause developmental malformations] such as infection, anoxia [severe hypoxia], and nutritional deficiencies. N. Andreason et al. determined that schizophrenics (especially males) have smaller frontal lobes, cerebrums, and craniums. Head size determination occurs early in life, which supports early developmental dystrophy rather than atrophy in later years. Developmental deviations and neuromotor deficits also have been linked to OCs in high-risk infants. . . .

Consistently, schizophrenic mothers report unwanted pregnancies accompanied by fear, anxiety, and depression. E. Walker and E. Emory reported that mothers with any psychiatric disturbance have an increased stress level during pregnancy. Gestational and neonatal stress may factor in with other variables, such as genetic predisposition, in producing schizophrenia in the offspring.

Hypoxia, Viruses, and Genetics

Evidence to date indicates a high correlation between schizophrenia and natality factors. Although OCs do not automatically induce schizophrenia, they clearly appear to increase the likelihood of adult schizophrenia. This connection must be analyzed more extensively in carefully designed studies. Perinatal hypoxia surfaces repeatedly in a number of studies designed to assess the causal role of OCs, thyroid abnormalities, stress, and other insults. Hypoxia is known to cause minor physical anomalies and may be the causal factor in neurointegrative deficits, both of which frequently are associated with schizophrenia. The role of hypoxia in disrupting normal brain development must be explored during all embryological stages.

It is interesting to note that viral infections also can increase the likelihood of OCs, which, again, may result in hypoxia. A virus can exist undetected in the brain and still cause profound psychological change. Viral particles inhibit the functioning of neurotransmitters and damage brain structures. Viral antibodies also can mimic or block brain cell function. Respiratory viruses deserve particular attention, especially in light of the dramatic increase in hospital admissions for schizophrenia two or three decades after major influenza epidemics. Again, it is the timing of the insult on the fetal brain that appears to be especially critical. The second trimester has been targeted regularly in research on the effect of viral exposure and autoantibodies on the fetus.

The etiological influences of hypoxia and viral infections do not discount the role of genetic factors. In fact, it is logically consistent to assume that there may be a combined influence, as in the case of a child who is more genetically susceptible to certain families of viruses or the effects of hypoxia. Another scenario is a stressful gestation of a genetically vulnerable fetus exposed to a viral infection. The viral infection could cause an OC, resulting in hypoxia and an ultimate brain development deficit. Clearly, there is no singular cause of schizophrenia with the possible exception of excessive genetic loading. But even genetic testing may be altered by gestational and neonatal factors. This was dramatically clear in the case of the famous Genain quadruplets [described in *The Genain Quadruplets*, a book edited by David Rosenthal], all of whom became schizophrenic to varying degrees. At one time, the explanation for the variation in their symptoms rested on concepts such as child-rearing. But today it appears as though the real explanation is that two of the quads had OCs that the others were fortunate to avoid. As stated earlier, much of today's thinking about the etiology of schizophrenia is biogenic. What is needed now is more finely tuned research on the impact of adverse experiences between conception and the time of birth.

6 $\mathring{}$ VIEWPOINT

---

*"The generic category of [pregnancy and delivery
complications] is not associated with an elevated
risk for psychiatric diagnosis."*

Obstetrical Complications
Do Not Cause Psychiatric
Disorders

Stephen L. Buka, Ming T. Tsuang, and Lewis P. Lipsitt

Stephen L. Buka is an assistant professor of maternal and child
health at the Harvard School of Public Health in Boston,
Massachusetts. Ming T. Tsuang is a professor of psychiatry and
head of the Harvard Department of Psychiatry at the Massachusetts Mental Health Center and the Brockton/West Roxbury
Veterans Administration Medical Center. Lewis P. Lipsitt is a professor of psychology and medical science at Brown University in
Providence, Rhode Island. In the following viewpoint, these authors describe a study they conducted from which they conclude
that pregnancy and delivery complications (PDCs) do not increase the risk of adulthood psychiatric problems.

As you read, consider the following questions:

1. What are the three subcategories of PDCs identified by the
   authors?
2. According to the authors, what six variables were used to
   select the normal comparison subjects?
3. How do the authors account for the finding that PDCs are
   associated with a reduced risk of some psychiatric conditions?

From Stephen L. Buka, Ming T. Tsuang, and Lewis P. Lipsitt, "Pregnancy/Delivery
Complications and Psychiatric Diagnosis," *Archives of General Psychiatry* 50 (February
1993):151-56, ©1993, American Medical Association. Reprinted with permission.

This viewpoint addresses the long-term psychiatric sequelae [aftereffects] of pregnancy and delivery complications (PDCs). This area of research has received considerable attention since the historic work of B. Pasamanick et al, who suggested that complications of pregnancy and delivery might produce ". . . a continuum of reproductive casualty extending from death [which] might descend in severity through cerebral palsy, epilepsy, mental deficiency, and perhaps even to behavior disorder." Although the neurologic consequences of adverse events during the prenatal and perinatal periods are known, the behavioral and emotional impacts of such events are still largely undetermined.

Early attempts to address this issue employed case-control designs of treated samples with psychiatric disorders and hospital, sibling, or population controls. In a previous report, we reviewed the methodologic limitations of these studies. Briefly, these include inappropriate control groups, nonstandardized diagnostic procedures resulting in overly broad and indefinite psychiatric groupings, inclusion of a large and heterogeneous set of maternal, obstetric, and infant-based events under the general heading of "PDCs," and noncomparable obstetric records for the case and control subjects.

Key Questions

Despite the serious design problems that may potentially arise from the case-control method, these studies as a group continued to show elevated rates of PDCs for a variety of psychiatric disorders ranging from childhood behavioral problems to adult schizophrenia. The mounting volume of some 100 studies of this type seemed to indicate that PDCs might indeed be a global risk factor for the development of many forms of psychiatric conditions. Key questions that remain unresolved from these studies include the following:

1. Would the association between PDCs and psychiatric outcomes remain, in studies of improved design?

2. Is the association causal or the result of confounding by some third factor such as socioeconomic status of the family, access to prenatal care, or genetic predisposition to psychiatric disorder?

3. Which psychiatric diagnoses are and are not associated with conditions of pregnancy and delivery?

4. What are the critical PDCs that act as risk factors for various psychiatric outcomes? . . .

The current study was conducted to contribute to the research base on the psychiatric consequences of PDCs through a long-term prospective investigation that addressed the major methodologic limitations of prior studies. Our objectives were to quantify the relative risk of developing various psychiatric diagnoses for complicated vs normal pregnancies/deliveries and to assess the relative risks associated with certain specific categories of PDCs, including chronic fetal hypoxia [a deficient amount of oxygen reaching the body tissue], other complications, and preterm birth. We hypothesize that the generic category of PDCs is not associated with an elevated risk for psychiatric diagnosis, but that the subcategory of chronic fetal hypoxia, particularly in combination with preterm birth, does constitute a risk factor for various diagnoses, particularly psychotic disorders and cognitive impairment. . . .

Table 1: **Lifetime Prevalence of Diagnoses Based on Diagnostic Interview Schedule/*DSM-III* Criteria Among Normal Pregnancies/Deliveries and Pregnancies and Deliveries with Complications (PDCs)**

	Lifetime Prevalence, %	
Diagnosis	Normal *(n = 320)	PDCs (n = 373)
Alcohol abuse/dependence	23.4	22.5
Drug abuse/dependence	24.1	20.9
Antisocial personality disorder	8.1	8.8
Affective disorders	15.0	15.6
Anxiety disorders	19.4	20.6
Psychotic disorders	1.2	1.1
Cognitive impairment	1.9	3.2

*n = sample size

Stephen L. Buka, Ming T. Tsuang, and Lewis P. Lipsitt, *Archives of General Psychiatry*, February 1993.

The study sample was drawn from 4140 pregnancies enrolled at the Providence, Rhode Island, Center of the National Collaborative Perinatal Project (NCPP) between 1960 and 1966. Extensive obstetric, neurologic, psychologic, and sociodemographic information from the prenatal period through age 7 years was collected prospectively for these subjects. Approximately one half of the 7000 data items collected for these subjects pertained to pregnancy and delivery events. Follow-up assessments were conducted at 4 and 8 months and 1, 3, 4, and 7 years. On average, 75% of the sample participated in any given assessment; 82% of the original birth cohort were seen at the final 7-year assessment.

Although routinely used in the clinical and research literature, the conditions of PDCs, chronic fetal hypoxia, and prematurity have been defined in many different ways. Based on reviews of the literature, clinical consultations, and prior analyses of the NCPP data set, we derived the following conceptual and operational criteria. The general category of PDCs included any deviations from a normal course of pregnancy and delivery. Three subcategories were defined: (1) chronic fetal hypoxia (severe and prolonged eclampsia [toxemia: the presence of toxic substances in the blood]; maternal hypertension, hypotension, anemia, and/or diabetes); (2) prematurity (gestational age of 36 weeks or less); and (3) other complications (placental problems [abruptio, infarct, previa]; cord problems [around-neck, knot, prolapsed]; prolonged labor; breech delivery; maternal shock, neonatal asphyxia, respiratory distress syndrome and/or apnea [transient cessation of breathing]). Any subject who did not meet these criteria was classified as a normal pregnancy and delivery.

All 4140 members of the study cohort were classified according to these criteria, and a sample of 1068 subjects was selected for follow-up. The goal of the sampling design was to select equal groups of subjects with and without PDCs that were comparable with respect to known correlates of both PDCs and psychiatric disorder. All cases of relatively rare PDCs (eclampsia, placenta problems, breech delivery) were selected. The remainder of the PDC sample was selected by random stratified sampling to generate approximately equal numbers of subjects from each of the PDC subgroups. Finally, normal comparison subjects were selected, category-matched on six variables (race, sex, parity [number of children previously borne], date of birth, maternal age, and maternal education) to be comparable with the PDC sample.

Follow-Up and Assessment

The last contact with these subjects had been at their 7-year assessment, some 11 to 21 years before the current investigation. Subjects were located at ages 18 to 27 years through a variety of sources that included information recorded at the 7-year assessment, telephone and town directories, motor vehicle and voter registration lists, and contact with state and local agencies. Initial contact and requests for consent were made by telephone and/or letter. Subjects were informed that they were among a large group of participants in the original NCPP study who were being recontacted for interviews on their physical, mental, and social development since childhood. The 3-hour interviews were scheduled at the subjects' convenience at their home, the study center, or by telephone. In total, 15% of the interviews were conducted by telephone. Informed consent forms were read to the subject who either signed the form or gave oral consent (for telephone interviews) prior to any questioning. All interviews were conducted "blind" with respect to perinatal status and the study hypotheses.

Adult psychiatric status was assessed with a battery of instruments designed to measure psychiatric diagnosis, cognitive and psychosocial functioning, and family history of mental disorders. This analysis will focus solely on lifetime psychiatric diagnoses, which were assessed through the administration of version III of the Diagnostic Interview Schedule (DIS) of the National Institute of Mental Health, Bethesda, Maryland. The DIS is a completely structured interview form constructed to gather information about current and lifetime psychiatric symptoms. This information is organized for computer diagnostic assessment using *DSM-III* [the third edition of the American Psychiatric Association's *Diagnostic and Statistical Manual of Mental Disorders*]. . . . The DIS has satisfactory measurement and administrative properties for the ascertainment of psychiatric diagnoses within large community samples. This analysis will focus on lifetime diagnoses, that is, whether a person has ever met criteria for a particular psychiatric diagnosis. Thus, information from the DIS is used to determine the lifetime prevalence (or cumulative incidence) of specific symptoms and diagnoses in the study sample, according to *DSM-III* criteria.

Table 2: **Lifetime Prevalence Diagnoses Based on Diagnostic Interview Schedule/*DSM-III* Criteria Among Pregnancy and Delivery Complication Subgroups**

| | Lifetime Prevalence, % | | | |
Diagnosis	Normal *[n = 320]*	Chronic Hypoxia *[n = 192]*	Other Complications *[n = 196]*	Preterm Births *[n = 118]*
Alcohol abuse/dependence	23.4	20.3	24.0	25.4
Drug abuse/dependence	24.1	18.8	23.0	22.0
Antisocial personality disorder	8.1	7.8	10.2	11.0
Affective disorders	15.0	15.6	13.8	19.5
Anxiety disorders	19.4	21.4	22.4	13.6
Psychotic disorders	1.2	2.1	0.5	0.0
Cognitive impairment	1.9	3.6	1.0	5.1

*n = sample size

Stephen L. Buka, Ming T. Tsuang, and Lewis P. Lipsitt, *Archives of General Psychiatry*, February 1993.

A number of procedures were implemented to enhance the reliability of the DIS lay interviews. First, interviewers were trained for 4 weeks by clinicians and mental health researchers using the instructional materials and procedures recommended by the developers of the DIS. Interrater agreement was satisfactory, as assessed by independent ratings of video tapes and volunteer subjects. Initial field interviews were monitored by senior research staff who were experienced with the interview. Interrater agreement was reassessed near the completion of the study and again found to be satisfactory. Finally, a variety of data management efforts were implemented to ensure the quality and consistency of the computer-coded interview data prior to running the diagnostic algorithms.

The primary hypothesis for investigation was that subjects with histories of PDC—chronic fetal hypoxia, prematurity, and/or other complications—have a greater cumulative incidence or lifetime prevalence of major psychiatric diagnoses than the normal pregnancy/delivery subjects. To examine this hypothesis, data analyses compared the lifetime rates of several major *DSM-III* diagnostic categories for each perinatal group. . . .

Perinatal Classification and Psychiatric Illness

Results of the analyses conducted to test the primary study hypothesis are presented in Tables 1 and 2. Table 1 compares the lifetime prevalence of six major diagnostic categories between the normal pregnancy/delivery and PDC subjects. . . . There were no statistically significant differences between the lifetime prevalence of psychiatric diagnoses of these two groups. Mild or severe cognitive impairment was more common among the PDC group. This indicates that, controlling for differences in gender, age, socioeconomic level, race, and family history of mental illness between the two groups, the odds of a lifetime diagnosis of cognitive impairment in the PDC group was 1.4 times that of the normal group. Drug abuse/dependence was slightly less common among the PDC group, but neither of these differences was significant.

Of the 373 subjects with PDCs, 192 had experienced chronic fetal hypoxia, 118 were preterm births, and 196 had experienced other complications (listed above). These classifications are not mutually exclusive; many subjects had experienced multiple PDCs. Table 2 displays the lifetime prevalence of the six diagnostic categories for each of these PDC subgroups. The lifetime prevalence rates for each perinatal group were compared with those of the normal pregnancy/delivery group . . . , again controlling for gender, age, socioeconomic level, race, and family history of mental illness. With the exception of cognitive impairment, there was little evidence of increased lifetime prevalence of psychiatric diagnosis in association with these specific PDC subgroups. The prevalence of mild or severe cognitive impairment was statistically greater among the preterm birth group and marginally greater among the chronic fetal hypoxia group. On the contrary, the subjects classified as having been exposed to chronic fetal hypoxia were less likely to report drug abuse/dependence than were the normal subjects. Similarly, the preterm subjects were at diminished risk for anxiety disorders. The prevalence of psychotic diagnoses (schizophrenia, schizophreniform disorder) was somewhat higher among the chronic hypoxia sample; however, this difference was not significant.

As noted earlier, 15% of the assessments were conducted by telephone, for which the validity of structured psychiatric interviews has not been established. Accordingly, all of the above analyses were repeated for only those subjects who had participated in face-to-face assessments. The results of the analyses were essentially unchanged. . . .

Control of Measurement Error

Systematic and random errors in the assessment of both pregnancy/delivery conditions and psychiatric disorders have plagued earlier research efforts in this area and must be considered before a final interpretation of the present study results. The pregnancy and delivery data in this investigation were of the highest quality. All data were collected prospectively according to standardized research protocols and monitored with a variety of quality assurance methods. Of greater concern were the procedures used to diagnose psychiatric disorders in a large-scale field study of this type. The measurement properties of the DIS have been assessed and are satisfactory. In the current study, training efforts, monitoring of interviews in the field, interrater agreement checks, and data management procedures support the reliability and validity of our administration of the DIS. . . .

With the exception of cognitive impairment among the preterm subjects and the chronic fetal hypoxia group, and psychotic disorders also among the chronic fetal hypoxia group, this study failed to confirm prior reports of a positive association between PDCs and adult psychiatric disorder. At least for the particular PDCs examined in this study, the "continuum of reproductive casualty" does not appear to extend to adult psychiatric diagnoses. On the contrary, the results indicate a reduced risk of certain diagnoses in association with PDCs. Two possible explanations could account for this "protective" effect of PDCs. First, since several of the PDCs under investigation have been shown to correlate with lower IQ scores, the lower rates could result if subjects with low IQs, in general, tended to report fewer symptoms and diagnoses on the DIS than those with higher IQs (with presumably greater verbal abilities). We investigated and rejected this hypothesis and found no relationship between premorbid IQ scores (at age 7 years) and the number of symptoms reported on the DIS. In contrast, there was preliminary evidence to suggest that the health and functional consequences of PDCs in certain instances contributed to the development of overly protected and less-outgoing children, who, in turn, are less likely to engage in antisocial and substance-using activities.

Although not statistically significant, the observation that subjects exposed to chronic fetal hypoxia were twice as likely to develop a psychotic disorder as the normal control subjects offers some further support for the potential etiologic role of PDCs in the development of psychoses. However, with a mean age of 23.0 years, the subjects in this study had not yet passed the period of risk for the development of psychotic illness. Further follow-up efforts with this cohort are needed to increase the sample size and include subsequent cases of psychotic disorder with later ages of onset. In addition, further studies are warranted of longitudinal samples that include detailed pregnancy and delivery data and will yield sufficient numbers of cases of psychotic disorder, either large perinatal cohorts or high-risk samples.

Our failure to confirm earlier reports of an association between PDCs and psychiatric diagnoses may result from the methodologic efforts instituted to reduce random and systematic biases in the study procedures. Unlike most earlier investigations, the present study includes detailed, accurate, and unbiased measures of both pregnancy and delivery events (due to the existence of the prospective and standardized research protocols used in the NCPP project) and psychiatric diagnoses. Our sampling procedures, subject location procedures, and statistical analyses have largely eliminated the potential sources of confounding due to sociodemographic variables and family history of mental illness that were typically unaddressed in earlier studies. We conclude that many of the previously reported positive findings in this area of research result from incomplete control of these potentially confounding factors. However, it is possible that our vigorous control of these factors at the design and analysis stages may have obfuscated potentially informative mechanisms of the development of psychiatric illness that accounted for associations detected in earlier reports. Further analyses will consider the interactive relationships of gender, socioeconomic level, and family history of disorder in the etiology of specific diagnoses. In addition, this report has considered only psychiatric diagnoses based on *DSM-III* criteria. Adverse effects of PDCs may result in less extreme functional impairments.

Periodical Bibliography

The following articles have been selected to supplement the diverse views presented in this chapter.

Paul Bebbington et al.   "Life Events and Psychosis: Initial Results from the Camberwell Collaborative Psychosis Study," *British Journal of Psychiatry*, January 1993. Available from Mercury Airfreight International Ltd. Inc., 2323 Randolph Ave., Avenel, NJ 07001.

Tony Dajer   "Divided Selves," *Discover*, September 1992.

Bruce P. Dohrenwend et al.   "Socioeconomic Status and Psychiatric Disorders: The Causation-Selection Issue," *Science*, February 21, 1992.

Alfie Kohn   "Back to Nurture," *American Health*, April 1993.

Graham Lucas   "Stress and Mental Health," *The Practitioner*, May 1992. Available from Royal Sovereign House, 40 Beresford St., London SE18 6BQ, UK.

Robin M. Murray et al.   "Genes, Viruses and Neurodevelopmental Schizophrenia," *Journal of Psychiatric Research*, vol. 26, no. 4, 1992. Available from Pergamon Press Inc., 660 White Plains Rd., Tarrytown, NY 10591-5153.

Eadbhard O'Callaghan et al.   "Season of Birth in Schizophrenia: Evidence for Confinement of an Excess of Winter Births to Patients Without a Family History of Mental Disorder," *British Journal of Psychiatry*, June 1991.

David Reiss et al.   "Genetics and Psychiatry: An Unheralded Window on the Environment," *American Journal of Psychiatry*, March 1991. Available from the American Psychiatric Association, 1400 K St. NW, Washington, DC 20005.

Pak C. Sham et al.   "Schizophrenia Following Pre-natal Exposure to Influenza Epidemics Between 1939 and 1969," *British Journal of Psychiatry*, April 1992.

E. Fuller Torrey   "Are We Overestimating the Genetic Contribution to Schizophrenia?" *Schizophrenia Bulletin*, vol. 18, no. 2, 1992. Available from the Government Printing Office, Washington, DC 20402.

E. Fuller Torrey and Ann Bowler   "Geographical Distribution of Insanity in America: Evidence for an Urban Factor," *Schizophrenia Bulletin*, vol. 16, no. 4, 1990.

Are Mental Health Treatments Beneficial?

Mental Illness

Chapter Preface

Since its introduction in 1988, the drug Prozac (fluoxetine) has been increasingly accepted as a safe and effective treatment for severe depression. It has also been widely prescribed for milder disorders, such as dysthymia—a less-than-major form of depression. For patients with a range of symptoms, according to psychiatrist Peter D. Kramer, the drug has done more than cure depression; it has displayed "the power to transform the whole person." In his best-selling book *Listening to Prozac*, Kramer describes how Prozac alters the personalities of his patients, making them more relaxed, confident, and successful both socially and professionally.

Some people fear that Prozac and other drugs that can shape personality have the potential to induce mass conformity. For example, they contend that the personality traits enhanced by Prozac are those favored by American society; so by taking the drug, patients are forcing themselves into conformity with their social and professional environments. David J. Rothman, a professor of social medicine and history at Columbia University, notes that in Kramer's patients, most of whom are women, Prozac effects changes consistent with the values of male-dominated, American capitalism: "Prozac emerges not only as a male-gendered drug, but also as a quintessentially American drug . . . [that] promotes adroit competitiveness. It is . . . an office drug that enhances the social skills necessary in a postindustrial, service-oriented economy."

Others are less concerned that drugs like Prozac will enforce social conformity. Kramer acknowledges Prozac's potential to force women into accord with American capitalism, but he also notes its power to liberate women from traditional female roles. He writes that Prozac "allows women with the traits we now call 'overly feminine,' in the sense of passivity and a tendency to histrionics, to opt . . . for a spunkier persona." Moreover, while Kramer concedes that drugs could eventually become tools in the service of mass conformity, he believes that such an outcome is unlikely because of America's "pharmacological Calvinism"—the belief that it is morally wrong to take drugs merely to feel good.

Whether Prozac portends a future of drug-induced conformity or the freedom to create one's own personality, the dispute over Prozac reveals that mental health treatments can be the subject of careful scrutiny and divisive argument. In the following chapter, the safety, efficacy, and legitimacy of several types of treatment are debated.

"Psychotherapy will continue to occupy a prominent place in the future of psychological treatments."

Psychotherapy Is Effective

Masahisa Nishizono, John P. Docherty, and Stephen F. Butler

In the following viewpoint, Masahisa Nishizono, John P. Docherty, and Stephen F. Butler discuss conflicting studies on the effectiveness of psychotherapy and conclude that both long-term and short-term psychotherapy are valuable for understanding and treating personality disorders, although short-term therapy is increasingly predominant. Nishizono is with the department of psychiatry at the Fukuoka University School of Medicine in Fukuoka, Japan. Docherty is with the division of psychiatry at National Medical Enterprises in Santa Monica, California. Butler is with Northeast Psychiatric Associates at Brookside Hospital in Nashua, New Hampshire.

As you read, consider the following questions:

1. What is "transference," according to the authors?
2. According to the authors, why was "time-limited psychotherapy" developed?
3. On what basis do the authors question the validity of the study by Svartberg and Stiles?

From "Evaluation of Psychodynamic Psychotherapy" by Masahisa Nishizono, John P. Docherty, and Stephen F. Butler, pp. 131-38, 142-44, of *Treatment of Mental Disorders: A Review of Effectiveness*, edited by Norman Sartorius, Giovanni de Girolamo, Gavin Andrews, G. Allen German, and Leon Eisenberg. Geneva, Switzerland: World Health Organization and Washington, DC: American Psychiatric Press, Inc., 1993, ©1993, World Health Organization. All rights reserved. Reprinted with permission.

The birth of modern psychotherapy is commonly traced to Josef Breuer's famous patient Anna O. who gained relief from her hysterical difficulties by means of the *talking cure*. Sigmund Freud, Breuer's young colleague, built on Breuer's early insights. His subsequent discoveries of psychological dynamics ushered in a revolution that continues to have profound effects on contemporary clinical thinking and practice. The method and theory of therapy pioneered by Freud and Breuer, and then later developed by Freud into psychoanalysis, branched into a variety of approaches, subsumed under the rubric of psychodynamic or psychoanalytic psychotherapy.

Earlier in this century, most mental health professionals underwent extensive training in psychodynamic theory and therapy. Over the last 20 to 30 years, however, many nonpsychodynamic treatments have emerged. For example, pharmacotherapy, other somatic therapies, social skills training, recreation therapy, and occupational therapy and rehabilitation have all been demonstrated to be important, effective remedial procedures for various mental disorders. In addition, other psychotherapy approaches, such as cognitive therapy, have been developed as alternatives to psychodynamic psychotherapy.

These treatment developments and the current climate of concern about the cost-effectiveness of mental health treatments have raised the question of the role of psychodynamic theory and treatment in modern psychiatry. . . .

Definition of Psychodynamic Psychotherapy

Psychodynamic psychotherapy, as discussed here, refers to psychological treatment based on methods that were developed and refined by Freud, including those approaches that have evolved from Freud's seminal ideas. In general, psychodynamic theory assumes that symptoms and maladaptive patterns of relating reflect underlying conflicts that have their origin in conflicted relationships with significant others in the past, usually the parents. By ascertaining the nature of these conflicts, the meaning of heretofore inexplicable behaviors and symptoms can be understood. This understanding, when imparted to the patient in a deep, experiential manner, usually involving a corrective experience in the relationship with the therapist, promotes growth and maturation of personality in the individual. The individual becomes more capable of controlling anxiety, anger, and depression and achieves a deepening sense of personal capability in managing problematic interpersonal relationships. The resulting improvement in life satisfaction and more rewarding relationships presumably lessens the debilitating symptoms associated with the mental disorders.

To facilitate the therapist's understanding, the various schools of psychodynamic psychotherapy provide perspectives on personality development that essentially are maps for guiding the therapist's formulation of a patient's diagnosis (i.e., a conception of what is "wrong") and for guiding interventions. All dynamic therapies follow the same basic outline for conceptualizing the therapeutic endeavor. As Freud observed, despite the patient's conscious endorsement of the therapeutic aim of release from symptoms, the therapist meets with "a violent and tenacious resistance, which persists throughout the whole length of treatment." These resistances reflect the maladaptive patterns of behaving that sustain the symptoms and prevent change. Transference occurs when these maladaptive patterns incongruently become manifested in the relationship with the therapist. Analysis of this reaction to the therapist—that is, analysis of the transference—is the sine qua non of dynamic therapy. All dynamic therapies assume that, in some manner or another, the patient repeats attitudes and emotional reactions from earlier relationships with the therapist. It is thought that this repetition within the therapeutic relationship of earlier relationship problems permits the therapist to facilitate changes in emotional problems that originated in the past.

Essentials of the Psychotherapeutic Process

The most important elements in the process of therapy may be summarized as follows:

1. The first and foremost therapeutic element involves the formation of a therapeutic relationship (often referred to as the therapeutic alliance, working alliance, or helping alliance). Achievement of such an alliance requires empathy and empathetic listening by the therapist and the development in the patient of trust in the therapist and the feeling of being cared for and understood.

2. As the therapist works to develop the alliance, he or she encourages free expression by the patient. The therapist listens carefully to the statements of the patient, attempting to understand what the patient is communicating. During this process it is necessary to clarify ambiguous comments and cryptic explanations and to help the patient confront accounts of significant events that are contradictory.

3. Eventually the patient's conflicts are brought to light in the therapist-patient relationship (i.e., the transference). Conflictual themes common to the patient's relationship-experience in earlier life, the present therapeutic relationship, and extratherapeutic relationships in daily life point to the patient's core areas of conflict.

4. As these conflicts emerge in the therapeutic relationship, the therapist draws the patient's attention to them through

the use of interpretations. These interpretations usually link patterns of relating to significant others across the various relationship domains (past, present, and the therapeutic relationship).

5. During the therapeutic process, the therapist strives to minimize responding to the patient's transference in a countertherapeutic manner (that is, acting out the countertransference) and, thus, reinforcing the conflictual mode of interaction.

6. Thus therapeutic change is hypothesized to occur via two primary mechanisms. One is as a result of the therapist's pointing out (interpreting), rather than acting out (countertransference), the patient's conflicts. This fosters the patient's awareness of hitherto unconscious or automatic maladaptive modes of relating. The second is the therapist's affording the patient the experience of new, more mature and satisfying modes of relating within the therapeutic relationship itself. This fosters the development and expression of such modes of relating in daily life.

The first analyses of patients by Breuer and Freud were only a few months long; a few were as short as a single session of several hours duration (i.e., the cases of Katharina [Breuer and Freud 1895] and Gustav Mahler [D. Jones 1955]). Rapidly, however, psychoanalysis became virtually defined by its frequency (four or five times per week), its duration (5 to 7 years), and use of the couch. Efforts to extend psychotherapy to more patients and more disturbed patients led to variations in the standard, psychoanalytic technique. Currently, psychodynamic psychotherapy typically involves one or two meetings per week with the therapist and patient facing each other. These weekly sessions may continue for several years.

Time-limited psychotherapy was developed as a further attempt to make psychotherapy more accessible. In contrast to 300 to 500 hours typical of a course of psychoanalysis, time-limited dynamic psychotherapy generally means about 12 to 40 weekly sessions. This type of brief psychotherapy is also termed *focal psychotherapy*, because the effort is to shorten the work by limiting the content of the therapy to a single, central dynamic focus. More recent versions of brief dynamic therapy outline specific procedures for developing a dynamic focus, typically in interpersonal rather than intrapsychic terms. The therapist avoids digression away from the defined focus and relates the focal pattern to the state of the patient-therapist relationship and the presenting symptoms. Given the dramatically shrinking funding resources for mental health care in general, it seems likely that the future of psychodynamic psychotherapy will increasingly take the form of these brief, dynamic psychotherapies.

In 1952, Hans Eysenck challenged the psychiatric field, which at that time was dominated by psychoanalysis, when he purported to show that response rates to psychotherapy were no greater than would be expected with the passage of time (i.e., the *spontaneous remission* concept). Nearly 35 years later, Michael Lambert et al., in their comprehensive and rigorous review of the psychotherapy research literature, were able to draw the following conclusion:

> Psychotherapy outcome research shows that some control patients improve with the passage of time, that a variety of placebo control procedures produce gains that exceed those in no-treatment controls, and that psychotherapies produce gains that exceed those obtained through the use of placebo controls. Psychotherapists are more than "placebologists."

Lasting Gains

Fifty years ago, any proof that psychotherapy worked rested largely upon personal testimonials. People who had been in therapy said it helped, and therapists saw clients get better, but hard numbers were scarce. And there was no shortage of scoffers, among them British psychologist Hans Eysenck, who in a famous 1952 critique asserted that two thirds of neurotic individuals got better—with or without therapy.

Today, researchers have enough data to refute Eysenck's charge with conviction. In a review of psychotherapy studies, psychologists Michael Lambert and Allen Bergin write: "There is now little doubt that psychological treatments are, overall and in general, beneficial, although it remains equally true that not everyone benefits to a satisfactory degree." Investigators have repeatedly shown that clients with diverse problems who receive a broad range of therapies improve more than they would with no treatment, with "placebo" treatment or through spontaneous recovery, and that the gains are lasting.

Erica E. Goode with Betsy Wagner, *U.S. News & World Report*, May 24, 1993.

In addition, these authors also documented that the gains made in psychotherapy tend to be lasting. However, despite these optimistic conclusions, psychotherapy research has failed to identify any theory or set of techniques as clearly superior, in general, to any other. L. Luborsky et al. evoked the *Alice in Wonderland* quality of this predicament by quoting the dodo bird's ruling, "Everybody has won and all must have prizes." Recent work with highly selected patients presenting with specific diagnoses, such as obsessive-compulsive disorder or panic disorder, appears to establish some superiority of one treatment over others. Such highly specialized treatments notwithstanding, the general finding with psychiatric patients remains "no difference" between treatments.

Long-Term Versus Short-Term Therapy

Investigations of the effectiveness of long-term psychotherapy and its relative effectiveness vis-à-vis short-term or less intensive dynamic psychotherapy have yielded equally equivocal findings. On the other hand, K.I. Howard et al. plotted improvement rates for a large number of studies as a function of time and concluded that 50% of patients show significant improvement by the eighth session and 75% by the 26th session (consistent with the 25-session limit of many brief dynamic therapies).

Evaluation of such findings must consider the inherent limitations . . . of research with long-term psychotherapies. For pragmatic reasons, research on long-term therapies usually involves observation of therapies in naturalistic studies, resulting in loss of experimental control possible in studies of shorter duration. Because more severely disturbed patients often end up in longer term or more intensive treatment, naturalistic studies may be biased and random assignment to long- or short-term treatment can be hard to implement. Furthermore, patients continuing in longer term therapy are presumably working on issues not directly reflected in symptom checklists, so the effects of such treatment are not detected by standard measures. While the position that these are additional benefits of long-term treatment needs to be supported by research, it is certainly premature to accept the alternative conclusion, namely that long-term treatment is without value.

Research on Short-Term Therapy

Because of the practical difficulties of research on long-term treatment, the main body of dynamic research to date involves the brief dynamic therapies. Two reviews of the literature on the effectiveness of brief dynamic psychotherapy demonstrated the difficulties of achieving a clear consensus from these data. The first is a meta-analysis by M. Svartberg and T.C. Stiles, which reported "a small but significant superiority" of brief dynamic psychotherapy to waiting list patients at posttreatment, a small-sized inferiority to other treatments at posttreatment, and a large-sized inferiority to other treatments at 1-year follow-up. These authors continued by noting that brief dynamic psychotherapy performed as well as other therapies with mixed neurotic patients "unless the patients were young or therapists are clinically experienced."

P. Crits-Christoph, on the other hand, conducted a meta-analysis and arrived at quite different conclusions. He included only state-of-the-art psychotherapy studies that used a treatment manual, involved bona fide patient groups, and used therapists trained in brief treatment. He found that brief dynamic psychotherapy demonstrated large effects relative to waiting list controls, slight superiority to nonpsychiatric treatments (e.g., placebo, clinical management, self-help groups, low contact control), and equal effects to other psychotherapies and medications.

As with any single study, the conclusions of meta-analyses may be limited by such factors as sample size, quality of the studies included, and so forth. Both meta-analyses discussed here examined very small numbers of studies (19 in the Svartberg and Stiles study, 11 in the Crits-Christoph study). Of additional concern are the unexpected conclusions reached by Svartberg and Stiles. Whereas Crits-Christoph's conclusions are consistent with the general understanding of outcome data, Svartberg and Stiles' conclusions appear to contradict generally accepted views. Clearly, counterintuitive conclusions, such as Svartberg and Stiles' finding that experienced or trained therapists are a detrimental factor in the effectiveness of brief therapy, require close examination of a study's assumptions and methodological sophistication. Nine of the 11 studies reviewed by Crits-Christoph were published since 1987 (one 1989 study was unpublished), while 16 of the 19 studies reviewed by Svartberg and Stiles were published before 1987. The use of older studies raises the possibility, for example, that the "experienced" therapists in the studies examined by Svartberg and Stiles may not have had specific training in brief therapy and may have been resistant to the brief format. As previously noted, Crits-Christoph included only studies using therapists specifically trained in brief therapy. Finally, the use of older, more poorly designed studies obliged Svartberg and Stiles to use various statistical transformations to make assumptions that may have affected the analyses in unknown ways. . . .

Specific Therapies and Combined Treatments

Because it appears that no form of psychotherapy, including psychodynamic, shows special benefits for certain types of patients, the next step will be to devote efforts to developing specific therapies for specific types of patients. While other therapies (e.g., cognitive and behavioral therapies) have well-developed treatments designed specifically for particular disorders, such as depression and panic disorders, dynamic therapies tend to be conceptualized as applicable to psychiatric patients in general. Greater efficacy, however, may be obtained by tailoring dynamic approaches to the conflicts and interpersonal problems commonly encountered in particular patient groups. Recent attempts to develop specialized dynamic treatment approaches to specific populations are J.F. Clarkin and O.F. Kernberg's treatment for borderline personality disorder and D. Mark et al.'s supportive-expressive therapy for cocaine addiction. The efficacy of these specific approaches is currently being tested.

Psychotherapy outcome research has largely been concerned with contrasting the various approaches against each other to determine the single "treatment of choice." However, a case can be made for combining different approaches. To date, investigations of combined treatments typically involved psychotherapies combined with medication treatments. For some disorders these combined treatments tend to produce more benefits than single treatments. For example, combining psychotherapy and antidepressant medication for depressed patients has been shown to produce the best outcome at 1-year follow-up when compared to either treatment alone. These conclusions were supported by a later review of combined treatments for depression. Although much work remains to be done in this area, T.B. Karasu proposed that, for depression, optimal treatment appears to be combination treatment. As he stated, "Drugs have their major effects on symptom formation and affective distress, whereas psychotherapy more directly influences interpersonal relations and social adjustment."

Psychodynamic Psychotherapy Will Endure

This is a time of change in the way mental health services are provided; the changes will affect how psychotherapists think about and use psychodynamic psychotherapy. . . . What is the role of psychodynamic theory and treatment in modern psychiatry? In essence, it will retain its traditional role, albeit in a new form. It still represents the major effort to understand or modify maladaptive patterns of interpersonal relatedness. Clearly there will be increased use of the briefer versions of dynamic treatment, increased efforts to target dynamic approaches to specific kinds of patients, and increased use of combined treatments (dynamic therapy with medication and possibly with cognitive and behavioral interventions as well). Thus, although the longer term, unfocused, intrapsychic psychoanalysis may become less frequently practiced, in this new form the utility of a dynamic, interpersonal understanding of psychopathology and the rich body of clinical observation it embodies will endure.

The clinical challenge is to understand and improve treatments for those patients who do not easily respond to the available treatments. This includes not only those who fail to respond to the treatments, but also those plagued by repeated relapses. The chronic and intractable nature of the problems endured by these individuals is not well understood. It is likely, however, that many of these people are unable to make use of standard treatments due to pervasive mistrust, immaturity, and hostility. In other words, these are patients usually described as having personality disorders. Personality disorders, in turn, are typically conceptualized as involving chronic interpersonal maladaptations. Dynamic psychotherapy directly addresses such interpersonal problems and any approach to these kinds of problems will, of necessity, make use of the understanding that dynamic theory and therapy provide of chronic interpersonal problems. The greatest strides in the science and art of psychotherapy are yet to come, and we expect that dynamic psychotherapy will continue to occupy a prominent place in the future of psychological treatments.

"Psychotherapy can't do its job anymore."

Psychotherapy Is Counterproductive

James Hillman and Michael Ventura

James Hillman is a psychoanalyst, author, and lecturer. Michael Ventura is a newspaper columnist, novelist, and screenwriter. The following viewpoint, excerpted from the book *We've Had a Hundred Years of Psychotherapy—And the World's Getting Worse*, is a dialog between Hillman and Ventura in which they agree that psychotherapy is harmful because it causes people to focus on their internal selves and to neglect the worsening social and political conditions that surround them. Furthermore, they contend, psychotherapy's emphasis on growth misconceives the nature of personality, which they see as largely changeless and possibly predetermined.

As you read, consider the following questions:

1. Why does Hillman criticize psychotherapy's emphasis on the "inner child"?
2. How does the "fantasy of growth" set people up to fail, according to the authors?
3. According to Hillman, why did the bullfighter Manolete hang onto his mother when he was a child?

James Hillman: We've had a hundred years of analysis, and people are getting more and more sensitive, and the world is getting worse and worse. Maybe it's time to look at that. We still locate the psyche inside the skin. You go *inside* to locate the psyche, you examine *your* feelings and *your* dreams, they belong to you. Or it's interrelations, interpsyche, between your psyche and mine. That's been extended a little bit into family systems and office groups—but the psyche, the soul, is still only *within* and *between* people. We're working on our relationships constantly, and our feelings and reflections, but look what's left out of that. . . .

What's left out is a deteriorating world.

So why hasn't therapy noticed that? Because psychotherapy is only working on that "inside" soul. By removing the soul from the world and not recognizing that the soul is also *in* the world, psychotherapy can't do its job anymore. The buildings are sick, the institutions are sick, the banking system's sick, the schools, the streets—the sickness is out *there*. . . .

There is a decline in political sense. No sensitivity to the real issues. Why are the intelligent people—at least among the white middle class—so passive now? Why? Because the sensitive, intelligent people are in therapy! They've been in therapy in the United States for thirty, forty years, and during that time there's been a tremendous political decline in this country.

Michael Ventura: How do you think that works?

Hillman: Every time we try to deal with our outrage over the freeway, our misery over the office and the lighting and the crappy furniture, the crime on the streets, whatever—every time we try to deal with that by going to therapy with our rage and fear, we're depriving the political world of something. And therapy, in its crazy way, by emphasizing the inner soul and ignoring the outer soul, supports the decline of the actual world. Yet therapy goes on blindly believing that it's curing the outer world by making better people. We've had that for years and years and years: "If everybody went into therapy we'd have better buildings, we'd have better people, we'd have more consciousness." It's not the case.

Ventura: I'm not sure it's causal, but it's definitely a pattern. Our inner knowledge has gotten more subtle while our ability to deal with the world around us has, well, *deteriorated* is almost not a strong enough word. *Disintegrated* is more like it.

Therapy as Child Cult Worship

Hillman: The vogue today, in psychotherapy, is the "inner child." That's the therapy thing—you go back to your childhood. But if you're looking backward, you're not looking around. This trip backward constellates what Carl Jung called the "child archetype." Now, the child archetype is by nature apolitical and disempowered—it has no connection with the political world. And so the adult says, "Well, what can I do about the world? This thing's bigger than me." That's the child archetype talking. "All I can do is go into myself, work on my growth, my development, find good parenting, support groups." This is a disaster for our political world, for our democracy. Democracy depends on intensely active citizens, not children.

By emphasizing the child archetype, by making our therapeutic hours rituals of evoking childhood and reconstructing childhood, we're blocking ourselves from political life. Twenty or thirty years of therapy have removed the most sensitive and the most intelligent, and some of the most affluent people in our society into child cult worship. It's going on insidiously, all through therapy, all through the country. So *of course* our politics are in disarray and nobody's voting—we're disempowering ourselves through therapy.

Ventura: The assumption people are working out of is that inner growth translates into worldly power, and many don't realize that they go to therapy with that assumption.

Hillman: If personal growth did lead into the world, wouldn't our political situation be different today, considering all the especially intelligent people who have been in therapy? What you learn in therapy is mainly feeling skills, how to really remember, how to let fantasy come, how to find words for invisible things, how to go deep and face things—

Ventura: Good stuff to know—

Hillman: Yes, but you don't learn political skills or find out anything about the way the world works. Personal growth doesn't automatically lead to political results. Look at Eastern Europe and the Soviet Union. Psychoanalysis was banned for decades, and look at the political changes that have come up and startled everybody. Not the result of therapy, their revolutions.

Ventura: So you're making a kind of opposition between power, political power or political intelligence, and therapeutic intelligence. Many who are therapeutically sensitive are also dumb and fucked up politically; and if you look at the people who wield the most power in almost any sphere of life, they are often people whose inner growth has been severely stunted.

To Grow or Shrink?

Hillman: You think people undertake therapy to grow?

Ventura: Isn't growth a huge part of the project of therapy? Everybody uses the word, therapists and clients alike.

Hillman: But the very word *grow* is a word appropriate to children. After a certain age you do not grow. You don't grow teeth, you don't grow muscles. If you start growing after that age, it's cancer.

Ventura: Aw, Jim, can't I grow *inside* all my life?

Hillman: Grow what? Corn? Tomatoes? New archetypes? What am I growing, what do you grow? The standard therapeutic answer is: you're growing yourself.

Ventura: But the philosopher Soren Kierkegaard would come back and say, "The deeper natures don't change, they become more and more themselves."

Hillman: Jung says individuation is becoming more and more oneself.

Ventura: And becoming more and more oneself involves a lot of unpleasantness. As Jung also says, the most terrifying thing is to know yourself.

Hillman: And becoming more and more oneself—the actual experience of it is a shrinking, in that very often it's a dehydration, a loss of inflations, a loss of illusions.

Ventura: That doesn't sound like a good time. Why would anybody want to do it?

Hillman: Because shedding is a beautiful thing. It's of course not what consumerism tells you, but shedding feels good. It's a lightening up.

Ventura: Shedding what?

Hillman: Shedding pseudoskins, crusted stuff that you've accumulated. Shedding dead wood. That's one of the big sheddings. Things that don't work anymore, things that don't keep you—keep you alive. Sets of ideas that you've had too long. People that you don't *really* like to be with, habits of thought, habits of sexuality. That's a very big one, 'cause if you keep on making love at forty the way you did at eighteen you're missing something, and if you make love at sixty the way you did at forty you're missing something. All that changes. The imagination changes.

Or put it another way: *Growth is always loss.*

Anytime you're gonna grow, you're gonna lose something. You're losing what you're hanging onto to keep safe. You're losing habits that you're comfortable with, you're losing familiarity. That's a big one, when you begin to move into the unfamiliar.

You know, in the organic world when anything begins to grow it's moving constantly into unfamiliar movements and unfamiliar things. Watch birds grow—they fall down, they can't quite do it. Their growing is all awkwardness. Watch a fourteen-year-old kid tripping over his own feet.

The Fantasy of Growth

Ventura: The fantasy of growth that you find in therapy, and also in New Age thought, doesn't include this awkwardness, which *can* be terrible and can go on for years. And when we look at people going through that, we usually don't say they're growing, we usually consider them out of it. And during such a time one certainly doesn't feel more powerful in the world.

Hillman: The fantasy of growth is a romantic, harmonious fantasy of an ever-expanding, ever-developing, ever-creating, ever-larger person—and ever integrating, getting it all together.

NON SEQUITUR *by WILEY MILLER*

SPIN THE WHEEL AND LET'S SEE WHO'S TO BLAME FOR YOUR INABILITY TO ACCEPT PERSONAL RESPONSIBILITY...

WHY PSYCHOTHERAPY DOESN'T TAKE AS LONG AS IT USED TO

©1994, Washington Post Writers Group. Reprinted with permission.

Ventura: And if you don't fulfill that fantasy you see yourself as failing.

Hillman: Absolutely.

Ventura: So this idea of growth can put you into a constant state of failure!

Hillman: "I ought to be over that by now, I'm not together, I can't get it together, and if I were really growing I would have grown out of my mess long ago."

Ventura: It sets you up to fail. That's really cute.

Hillman: It's an idealization that sets you up to fail.

Ventura: Because you're constantly comparing yourself to the fantasy of where you *should* be on some ideal growth scale.

Some Things Don't Change

Hillman: It sets up something worse. It sets up not just failure but anomaly: "I'm peculiar." And it does this by showing no respect for sameness, for consistency, in a person. Sameness is a very important part of life—to be consistently the same in certain areas that don't change, don't grow.

You've been in therapy six years and you go back home on Thanksgiving and you open the front door and you see your family *and you are right back where you were.* You feel the same as you always did! Or you've been divorced for years, haven't seen the wife though there's been some communication on the phone, but you walk into the same room and *within four minutes* there's a flare-up, the same flare-up that was there long ago.

Some things stay the same. They're like rocks. There's rocks in the psyche. There are crystals, there's iron ore, there's a metallic level where *some* things don't change.

Ventura: And if those elements did change, could change, you would be so fluid that you would not, could not, be you. You would be dangerously fluid. Where would that thing that is you reside, if the psyche didn't depend on some things' not changing? And this dependence on the changeless is far below the level of the ego's control or consent.

Hillman: This changeless aspect, if you go all the way back in philosophy even before Aristotle, was called Being. "Real Being doesn't change." That was one fantasy. Other people would say, "Real Being is always changing." I'm not arguing which one is right, I'm arguing that both are fundamental categories of life, of being. You can look at your life with the eye of sameness and say, "My god, nothing's really changed." Then you can look at it with the other eye: "My god, what a difference. Two years ago, nine years ago, I was thus and so, but now all that's gone, it's changed completely!"

This is one of the great riddles that Lao Tse talked about, the changing and the changeless. The job in therapy is, not to try and make the changeless change, but how to separate the two. If you try to work on what's called a character neurosis, if you try to take someone who is very deeply emotionally whatever-it-is, and try to change that person into something else, what are you doing? Because there are parts of the psyche that are changeless. . . .

Ventura: The fantasy of growth, the fantasy of the ever-expanding, ever-developing person—which is a very strong fantasy out there right now, especially among the educated, and among all those buyers of self-help books—doesn't take changelessness into account at all, doesn't set up a dialectic between change and changelessness. So (bringing this all back to the relation of therapy to politics) this fantasy, fed by many sorts of therapies, can't help but make people feel more like failures in the long run. Which, in turn, can't help but increase the general feeling of powerlessness.

That's a pretty vicious circle.

Therapy Internalizes Emotions

Hillman: There's another thing therapy does that I think is vicious. It internalizes emotions. . . .

I'm outraged after having driven to my analyst on the freeway. The fucking trucks almost ran me off the road. I'm terrified, I'm in my little car, and I get to my therapist's and I'm shaking. My therapist says, "We've gotta talk about this."

So we begin to talk about it. And we discover that my father was a son-of-a-bitch brute and this whole truck thing reminds me of him. Or we discover that I've always felt frail and vulnerable, there've always been bigger guys with bigger dicks, so this car that I'm in is a typical example of my thin skin and my frailty and vulnerability. Or we talk about my power drive, that I really wish to be a truck driver. We convert my fear into anxiety—an inner state. We convert the present into the past, into a discussion of my father and my childhood. And we convert my outrage—at the pollution or the chaos or whatever my outrage is about—into rage and hostility. Again, an internal condition, whereas it starts in *outrage*, an emotion. Emotions are mainly social. The word comes from the Latin *ex movere*, to move out. Emotions connect to the world. Therapy introverts the emotions, calls fear "anxiety." You take it back, and you work on it inside yourself. You don't work psychologically on what that outrage is telling you about potholes, about trucks, about Florida strawberries in Vermont in March, about burning up oil, about energy policies, nuclear waste, that homeless woman over there with the sores on her feet—the whole thing. . . .

Relationship, Work, and Community

Hillman: The thing that therapy pushes is relationship, yet work may matter just as much as relationship. You think you're going to die if you're not in a good relationship. You feel that not being in a significant, long-lasting, deep relationship is going to cripple you or that you're crazy or neurotic or something. You feel intense bouts of longing and loneliness. But those feelings are not only due to poor relationship; they come also because you're not in any kind of political community that makes sense, that matters. Therapy pushes the relationship issues, but what intensifies those issues is that we don't have (a) satisfactory work or (b), even more important perhaps, we don't have a satisfactory political community.

You just can't make up for the loss of passion and purpose in your daily work by intensifying your personal relationships. I think we talk so much about inner growth and development because we are so boxed in to petty, private concerns on our jobs.

Ventura: In a world where most people do work that is not only unsatisfying but also, with its pressures, deeply unsettling; and in a world where there's nothing more rare than a place that feels like a community, we load all our needs onto a relationship or expect them to be met by our family. And then we wonder why our relationships and family crack under the load. . . .

History as Cause?

Hillman: The principal content of American psychology is developmental psychology: what happened to you earlier is the cause of what happened to you later. That's the basic theory:

107

our history is our causality. We don't even separate history as a story from history as cause. So you have to go back to childhood to get at why you are the way you are. And so when people are out of their minds or disturbed or fucked up or whatever, in our culture, in our psychotherapeutic world, we go back to our mothers and our fathers and our childhoods.

No other culture would do that. If you're out of your mind in another culture or quite disturbed or impotent or anorexic, you look at what you've been eating, who's been casting spells on you, what taboo you've crossed, what you haven't done right, when you last missed reverence to the Gods or didn't take part in the dance, broke some tribal custom. Whatever. It could be thousands of other things—the plants, the water, the curses, the demons, the Gods, being out of touch with the Great Spirit. It would never, *never* be what happened to you with your mother and your father forty years ago. Only our culture uses that model, that myth. . . .

Reading Life Backwards

But let's say somebody looked at it differently. Let's say that what matters is that you have an acorn in you, you are a certain person, and that person begins to appear early in your life, but it's there all the way through your life. Winston Churchill, for example, when he was a schoolboy, had a lot of trouble with language and didn't speak well. He was put in what we would call the remedial reading class. He had problems about writing, speaking, and spelling. Of course he did! This little boy was a Nobel Prize winner in literature and had to save the Western world through his speech. Of course he had a speech defect, of course he couldn't speak easily when he was eleven or fourteen—it was too much to carry.

Or take Manolete who, when he was nine years old, was supposedly a very frightened little skinny boy who hung around his mother in the kitchen. So he becomes the greatest bullfighter of our age. Psychology will say, "Yes, he became a great bullfighter because he was such a puny little kid that he compensated by being a macho hero." That would be Adlerian psychology—you take your deficiency, your inferiority, and you convert it to superiority.

Ventura: That notion has seeped in everywhere—feminism and the men's movement both depend on it more than they know.

Hillman: But suppose you take it the other way and read a person's life backwards. Then you say, Manolete was the greatest bullfighter, and he *knew* that. Inside, his psyche sensed at the age of nine that his fate was to meet thousand-pound black bulls with great horns. Of course he fucking well held onto his mother! Because he couldn't hold that capacity—at nine years old your fate is all there and you can't handle it. It's too big. It's not that he was inferior; he had a great destiny.

Now, suppose we look at all our patients that way. Suppose we look at the kids who are odd or stuttering or afraid, and instead of seeing these as developmental problems we see them as having some great thing inside them, some destiny that they're not yet able to handle. It's bigger than they are and their psyche knows that. So that's a way of reading your own life differently. Instead of reading your life today as the result of fuck-ups as a child, you read your childhood as a miniature example of your life, as a cameo of your life—and recognize that you don't really know your whole life until you're about eighty—and then you're too old to get it in focus, or even care to!

"That traumas experienced as a child can be totally forgotten for decades is the great mental-health myth of our time."

Suppressed Memory Therapy Is Not Legitimate

Martin Gardner

Therapists often use hypnosis and other techniques to probe their patients' minds and uncover repressed memories of traumatic events from their pasts. In the following viewpoint, writer Martin Gardner argues that this form of therapy is based on a false premise—that people are able to block unpleasant occurrences from consciousness. Rather than uncovering memories, says Gardner, suppressed memory therapists, or "traumatists," are inducing in their patients a false memory syndrome (FMS) in which they "remember" traumatic events, usually childhood sexual abuses, that never actually happened.

As you read, consider the following questions:

1. According to Gardner, why do patients' symptoms usually get worse after "suppressed memories" are "brought to light"?
2. In what way have many states revised their statute of limitations laws, according to the author?
3. What point does Gardner attempt to make by recounting the story of Jean Piaget's fictional kidnapping?

Martin Gardner, "The False Memory Syndrome," *Skeptical Inquirer*, Summer 1993.
Reprinted with permission of the Committee for the Scientific Investigation of Claims of the Paranormal, Buffalo, NY.

In March 1992, a group of distinguished psychologists and psychiatrists, including CSICOP's [Committee for the Scientific Investigation of Claims of the Paranormal] Ray Hyman, banded together to form the False Memory Syndrome (FMS) Foundation. The organization is headquartered in Philadelphia under the direction of educator Pamela Freyd. Its purpose: to combat a fast-growing epidemic of dubious therapy that is ripping thousands of families apart, scarring patients for life, and breaking the hearts of innocent parents and other relatives. It is, in fact, the mental-health crisis of the 1990s.

The tragic story begins with Sigmund Freud. Early in his career, when he made extensive use of hypnotism, Freud was amazed by the number of mesmerized women who dredged up childhood memories of being raped by their fathers. It was years before he became convinced that most of these women were fantasizing. Other analysts and psychiatrists agreed. For more than half a century the extent of incestuous child abuse was minimized. Not until about 1980 did the pendulum start to swing the other way as more solid evidence of child sexual abuse began to surface. There is now no longer any doubt that such incest is much more prevalent than the older Freud or the general public realized.

Then in the latter 1980s a bizarre therapeutic fad began to emerge in the United States. Hundreds of poorly trained therapists, calling themselves "traumatists," began to practice the very techniques Freud had discarded. All over the land they are putting patients under hypnosis and subtly prodding them into recalling childhood sexual traumas, memories of which presumably have been totally obliterated for decades. Decades Delayed Disclosure, or DDD, it has been called. Eighty percent of the patients who are claimed to experience DDD are women from 25 to 45 years old. Sixty percent of their parents are college graduates, 25 percent with advanced degrees. More than 80 percent of their parents are married to their first spouse.

A Typical Scenario

Here is a typical scenario. A woman in her thirties seeks therapy for symptoms ranging from mild depression, anxiety, headaches, or the inability to lose weight, to more severe symptoms like anorexia. Her therapist, having succumbed to the latest mental-health fad, decides almost at once that the symptoms are caused by repressed memories of childhood abuse. Profoundly shocked by this suggestion, the woman vigorously denies that such a thing could be possible. The stronger her denial, the more the therapist believes she is repressing painful memories.

The patient may be hypnotized, or given sodium amytal, or placed into a relaxed, trancelike state. Convinced that a child-

111

hood trauma is at the root of the patient's ills, the therapist repeatedly urges the woman to try to remember the trauma. If she is highly suggestible and eager to please the therapist, she begins to respond to leading questions and to less obvious signs of the therapist's expectations.

Signe Wilkinson/Cartoonists & Writers Syndicate. Reprinted with permission.

After months, or even years, images begin to form in the patient's mind. Shadowy figures threaten her sexually. Under continual urging, these memories grow more vivid. She begins to recognize the molester as her father, or grandfather, or uncle. The more detailed the visions, the more convinced both she and the therapist become that the terrible truth is finally being brought to consciousness. To better-trained psychiatrists, these details indicate just the opposite. Childhood memories are notoriously vague. Recalling minute details is a strong sign of fantasizing.

As the false memories become more convincing, the patient's anger toward a once-loved relative grows. The therapist urges her to vent this rage, to confront the perpetrator, even to sue for psychic damage. Stunned by their daughter's accusations, the parents vigorously deny everything. Of course they will deny it, says the therapist, perhaps even suppress their own memories of what happened. The family is devastated. A loving daughter has inexplicably been transformed into a bitter enemy. She may join an "incest survivor" group, where her beliefs are reinforced by hearing similar tales. She may wear a sweatshirt saying, "I survived."

No one doubts that childhood sexual assaults occur, but in almost every case the event is never forgotten. Indeed, it festers as a lifelong source of shame and anger. Studies show that among children who witnessed the murder of a parent, not a single one repressed the terrible memory. Not only do victims of child incest not repress such painful memories (to repress a memory means to completely forget the experience without any conscious effort to do so); they try unsuccessfully to forget them. That traumas experienced as a child can be totally forgotten for decades is the great mental-health myth of our time—a myth that is not only devastating innocent families but doing enormous damage to psychiatry.

In the past, when juries found a parent guilty of child incest, there has been corroborating evidence: photos, diaries, letters, testimony by others, a history of sexual misconduct, or even open admission of guilt. Juries today are increasingly judging a parent guilty without any confirming evidence other than the therapy-induced memories of the "victim."

Patients as well as their families can be scarred for life. They are led to believe that bringing suppressed memories to light will banish their symptoms. On the contrary, the symptoms usually get worse because of traumatic breaks with loved ones. Moreover, this treatment can also cause a patient to refuse needed therapy from psychiatrists who have not fallen prey to the FMS epidemic. Pamela Freyd has likened the traumatists to surgeons doing brain surgery with a knife and fork. Others see the epidemic as similar in many ways to the great witch-hunts of the past, when disturbed women were made to believe they were in Satan's grip. The Devil has been replaced by the evil parent.

Satanic Cults and Abductions by Aliens

FMS takes many forms other than parental sexual abuse. Thousands of victims are being induced by traumatists to recall childhood participation in satanic cults that murder babies, eat their flesh, and practice even more revolting rituals. Although there is widespread fascination with the occult, and an amusing upsurge in the number of persons who fancy themselves benevolent witches or warlocks, police have yet to uncover any compelling evidence that satanic cults exist. Yet under hypnosis and soporific drugs, memories of witnessing such rituals can become as vivid as memories of sexual abuse.

Thousands of other patients, highly suggestible while half asleep, are now "remembering" how they were abducted, and sometimes sexually abused, by aliens in spaceships from faraway planets. Every year or so victims of this form of FMS (assuming they are not charlatans) will write persuasive books about their adventures with extraterrestrials. The books will be heavily advertised and promoted on talk shows, and millions of dollars will flow into the pockets of the authors and the books' uncaring publishers. Still another popular form of FMS, sparked by the New Age obsession with reincarnation, is the recovering of memories of past lives.

Pop-psychology books touting the myth that memories of childhood molestations can be suppressed for decades are becoming as plentiful as books about reincarnation, satanic cults, and flying saucers. Far and away the worst offender is a best-seller titled *Courage to Heal*, by Ellen Bass and Laura Davis. Although neither author has had any training in psychiatry, the book has become a bible for women convinced they are incest survivors. Davis thinks she herself is a survivor, having recalled under therapy being attacked by her grandfather. A survey of several hundred accused parents revealed that in almost every case their daughters had been strongly influenced by *Courage to Heal*. . . .

Worthless Evidence

The fact that a memory has been recovered after a period of alleged repression is sufficient to show that the so-called memory is worthless as evidence of any actual occurrence outside that person's mind or brain. A tale supported only by a recovered memory merits exactly the same credence as we would accord to a story whispered in someone's ear by Wotan or Jupiter.

David Ramsay Steele, *Liberty*, March 1994.

From the growing literature of FMS cases I cite a few typical horrors. A 28-year-old woman accuses her father of molesting her when she was six months old. "I recall my father put his penis near my face and rubbed it on my face and mouth." There is not the slightest evidence that a child of six months can acquire lasting memories of *any* event.

Betsy Petersen, in *Dancing with Daddy*, tells of being convinced by her therapist that she had been raped by her father when she was 3. "I don't know if I made it up or not," she told the therapist. "It feels like a story," he replied, "because when something like that happens, everyone acts like it didn't."

In 1986 Patti Barton sued her father for sexually abusing her when she was seven to fifteen months old. She did not remember this until her thirty-second therapy session. She recalls trying to tell her mother what happened by saying, "Ma, ma, ma, ma!" and "Da, da, da, da!"

Geraldo Rivera, in 1991, had three trauma survivors on his

Geraldo television show. One woman insisted she had murdered 40 children while she was in a satanic cult but had totally forgotten about it until her memories were aroused in therapy. Well-known entertainers have boosted the FMS epidemic by openly discussing their traumas on similar sensational talk shows. Roseanne Barr learned for the first time, while in therapy, that she had been repeatedly molested by her parents, starting when she was three months old! Her story made the cover of *People* magazine. Barr's parents and sisters deny it and have threatened legal action. A former Miss America, Marilyn Van Derbur, has been in the news proclaiming her decades-delayed recollection of abuse by her father, now deceased.

An Alarming Trend

It is an alarming trend that a dozen states have revised their statute-of-limitations laws and now permit legal action against parents within 3 years of the time the abuse was *remembered!* In 1990 the first conviction based on "repressed memory" occurred. George Franklin was given a life sentence for murdering an 8-year-old in 1969 almost entirely on the basis of his daughter's memory, allegedly repressed for 20 years, of having witnessed his murdering her friend. A year later a Pennsylvania man was convicted of murder on the basis of a man's detailed account of what he had seen when he was 5, but had totally forgotten for 16 years.

Although therapists usually deny asking leading questions, tapes of their sessions often prove otherwise. If no memories surface they will prod a patient to make up a story. After many repetitions and elaborations of the invented scenario, the patient starts to believe the story is true. One therapist, who claims to have treated 1,500 incest victims, explained her approach. She would say to a patient: "You know, in my experience, a lot of people who are struggling with many of the same problems you are have often had some kind of really painful things happen to them as kids—maybe they were beaten or molested. And I wonder if anything like that ever happened to you?" Another traumatist says: "You sound to me like the sort of person who must have been sexually abused. Tell me what that bastard did to you."

The FMS epidemic would not be so bad if such therapists were frauds interested only in money, but the sad truth is that they are sincere. So were the doctors who once tried to cure patients by bleeding, and the churchmen who "cured" witches by torture, hanging, and burning.

Better-trained, older psychiatrists do not believe that childhood memories of traumas can be repressed for any length of time, except in rare cases of actual brain damage. Nor is there any evidence that hypnosis improves memory. It may increase certitude, but not accuracy. And there is abundant evidence that totally false memories are easily aroused in the mind of a suggestible patient.

A two-part article by Lawrence Wright, "Remembering Satan" (*New Yorker*, May 17 and 24,1993), tells the tragic story of Paul Ingram, a respected police officer in Olympia, Washington, who was accused by his two adult daughters of sexually abusing them as children. Ingram's family are devout Pentecostals who believe that Satan can wipe out all memories of such crimes. Ingram remembered nothing, but after five months of intensive questioning, he came to believe himself guilty. Psychologist Richard Ofshe, writing on "Inadvertent Hypnosis During Interrogation" (*International Journal of Clinical and Experimental Hypnosis*, 11:125-155, 1992), tells how he fabricated an imaginary incident of Ingram's sexual abuse of a son and daughter. After repeated suggestions that he try to "see" this happening, Ingram produced a written confession!

Jean Piaget, the Swiss psychologist, tells of his vivid memory of an attempted kidnapping when he was two. The thief had been foiled by Piaget's nurse, who bravely fought off the man. When Piaget was in his teens the nurse confessed that she made up the story to win admiration, even scratching herself to prove there had been a struggle. Piaget had heard the story so often that it seeped into his consciousness as a detailed memory.

Paul McHugh, a psychiatrist at Johns Hopkins University, in"Psychiatric Misadventures" (*American Scholar*, Fall 1992), writes about a woman who under therapy came to believe she had been sexually assaulted by an uncle. She recalled the exact date. Her disbelieving mother discovered that at that time her brother was in military service in Korea. Did this alter the woman's belief? Not much. "I see, Mother," she said. "Yes. Well let me think. If your dates are right, I suppose it must have been Dad."

Some Hopeful Signs

Although the incest-recall industry is likely to grow in coming years, as it spreads around the world, there are some hopeful signs. Here and there women are beginning to discover how cruelly they have been deceived and are suing therapists for inducing false memories that caused them and their parents great suffering. They are known as "recanters" or "retractors."

Another welcome trend is that distinguished psychologists and psychiatrists are now writing papers about the FMS epidemic. I particularly recommend the book *Confabulations* by Eleanor Goldstein, and the following three articles: "Beware the Incest-Survivor Machine," by psychologist Carol Tavris, in the *New York*

Times Book Review (January 3, 1993); "The Reality of Repressed Memories," by Elizabeth Loftus (psychologist, University of Washington), . . . and "Making Monsters," by Richard Ofshe and Ethan Watters, in *Society* (March 1993). Most of this [viewpoint] is based on material in those articles. . . .

The FMS Foundation is a nonprofit organization whose purpose is to seek reasons for the FMS epidemic, to work for the prevention of new cases, and to aid victims. By the end of 1992, only ten months after its founding, more than two thousand distressed parents had contacted the Foundation for advice on how to cope with sudden attacks by angry daughters who had accused them of horrible crimes.

I trust that no one reading this [viewpoint] will get the impression that either I or members of the FMS Foundation are not fully aware that many women are indeed sexually abused as children and that their abusers should be punished. In its newsletter of January 8, 1993, the Foundation responded to criticism that somehow its efforts are a backlash against feminism. Their reply: Is it not "harmful to feminism to portray women as having minds closed to scientific information and as being satisfied with sloppy, inaccurate statistics? Could it be viewed as a profound insult to women to give them slogans rather than accurate information about how memory works?"

The point is not to deny that hideous sexual abuse of children occurs, but that, when it does, it is not forgotten and only "remembered" decades later under hypnosis. Something is radically amiss when therapist E. Sue Blume, in her book *Secret Survivors*, can maintain: "Incest is easily the greatest underlying reason why women seek therapy. . . . It is my experience that fewer than half of the women who experience this trauma later remember or identify it as abuse. Therefore it is not unreasonable that *more than half of all women* are survivors of childhood sexual trauma."

As Carol Tavris, author of *Mismeasure of Women*, comments in her article cited above: "Not one of these assertions is supported by empirical evidence."

"The false-memory critique treats extreme examples of bad therapy as if they were mainstream practice."

Suppressed Memory Therapy Is Legitimate

David Calof

Therapists often use hypnosis and other techniques to probe their patients' minds and uncover repressed memories of past traumatic events. In the following viewpoint, David Calof defends such practices against charges that they often induce a false memory syndrome (FMS) in which patients "remember" traumatic occurrences, often childhood sexual abuses, that never actually happened. Calof is a therapist with a private practice in Seattle, Washington; the editor of *Treating Abuse Today*, a newsletter for clinicians working with sexual abuse survivors; and the author of *Multiple Personality and Dissociation: Understanding Incest, Abuse, and MPD*.

As you read, consider the following questions:
1. Why did Tom need to "pay attention to his memories," according to Calof?
2. What reasons does the author give for discouraging his clients from suing their abusers?
3. How should hypnosis be used, according to Calof?

Excerpted from David Calof, "Facing the Truth About False Memory," *Family Therapy Networker*, September/October 1993. Reprinted with permission.

Tom, a 35-year-old mortgage broker, came to see me soon after his divorce. He had never been able to sustain a loving sexual relationship for more than a couple of months, and he felt like a failure because his career was stalled. We had hardly begun the first session when he said, "I suppose you're going to tell me that I was sexually abused as a child." Tom told me that in one of their first sessions, his previous therapist had jumped to this conclusion and he had quit treatment after a couple of weeks.

Later in the session, when I routinely asked about familial alcoholism, drug addiction and sexual or physical abuse, Tom told me that while growing up, an older cousin had often beaten him, but neither the cousin nor anybody else had ever sexually abused him. And so our therapy began.

Over the months, as his trust in me grew, Tom confided that he occasionally had memory lapses and could not recall his whereabouts for hours. Sometimes, he heard voices, and he found personal checks written on his account—in his handwriting—that he could not remember writing. He found a marijuana pipe in his bedroom, even though he was a conservative man who condemned drug use, and he even found women's clothing in his closet, although he had no idea how these items had gotten there.

Five or six months into therapy, he began to have nightmares and disturbing daydreams of forced, mutual masturbation with an older man. He could not see the man's face. When I asked him about these images, he put them down to an "overactive imagination."

The images stopped for several months and then returned more clearly and insistently. Sometimes, they were accompanied by a terrible pain or a feeling of fullness in his bowels. One day, he came into my office looking pale and drawn. He was afraid to sleep at night, and he told me he had been bleeding anally off and on since our last session.

Ammunition for Critics

Up until this point, Tom's case would seem to offer plenty of ammunition for critics of the way therapists handle cases in which the possibility of childhood abuse is raised. After all, even though Tom had no memories of sexual abuse, one therapist had suggested it to him early in therapy. Disturbing images involving sexual activity appeared only after he began seeing me. Perhaps they were an iatrogenic [therapist-caused] artifact of therapy. Clearly, Tom had a fragmented sense of self and his bleeding was the kind of symptom that Freud once described as "hysterical." Many therapists would have considered Tom a "borderline" client whose tenuous sense of self made him highly suggestible, often inconsistent and occasionally dishonest. Perhaps, despite

119

my best intentions, Tom had tried to please me by cooking up "memories" of sexual abuse, and perhaps he was looking for a single, simple explanation for his present difficulties.

Fearing his bleeding was caused by cancer, Tom went to his doctor. After an examination, he was told that he had a kind of severe anal scarring that often results from forced sex. The doctor's diagnosis crystallized something for Tom that had existed only in memory fragments at the edge of his consciousness before then. He began to remember being repeatedly sexually abused by his older cousin throughout his childhood.

Such cases are not rare. During the past 20 years, I have worked as a therapist and consultant with more than 400 people who were cruelly and repeatedly beaten or sexually abused as children. While some came into therapy with memories of relatively minor abuse, very few could recall severe abuse. Many of these clients did not begin therapy concerned with memories of abuse. They wanted to lose weight, or have better relationships; they were suicidal or insomniac, or were compulsively cutting themselves. They were prostitutes, business executives, paramedics and therapists. Some had dangerous hobbies, such as mountain climbing, or they frequently had sex with strangers without using condoms. Others had eating disorders or failed marriages. They were all suspicious and self-deprecating.

Symptoms of Trauma

But what stood out in many of these cases, apart from the initial presenting complaints, were symptoms common to other trauma victims, including survivors of such public horrors as the bombing of Dresden, the camps at Auschwitz, the massacred villages of Vietnam, Guatemala and Bosnia, the killing fields of Cambodia and the torture chambers of Brazil. Like survivors of these public traumas, my clients had dissociative symptoms, such as sleepwalking and memory disturbances, as well as signs of post-traumatic stress, such as flashbacks, sleep disturbances and nightmares. They wanted to be anonymous, or were socially withdrawn. They were depressed or had other mood disturbances. They often tended to minimize or rationalize painful present realities, and they suffered from feelings of numbness, emptiness and unreality.

Unlike the survivors of publicly acknowledged disasters, however, they did not know *why* they felt that way. Their memories of the traumas were often fragmented into bewildering mosaics or missing altogether. Often, they were veterans of intensely private wars that had taken place in barns, attics and suburban houses with the blinds drawn. Their wounds were never reported in newspapers or discussed with family members. There were rarely any witnesses other than the people who hurt them.

120

Like most traumas, their childhood rapes and beatings were encoded into memory in fragments, in a state of terror, when their hearts and minds were flooded with adrenaline. They didn't remember them the way one remembers a walk in the park, and they doubted the fragments they did recall.

Misunderstanding Therapy

Since 1991—in response to an outpouring of uncertainty and horror generated by the stories some abuse survivors tell—believers in what has come to be called "false memory syndrome" have advanced the idea that patients who claim to recover repressed memories are the hapless victims of irresponsible therapists. According to this scenario, such therapists use hypnosis to implant memories where there are none, encourage so-called "borderlines" to believe their fantasies and urge adult survivors to confront and sue their parents.

In the past 20 years, I have supervised and consulted with many hundreds of therapists. In all that time, I've worked with perhaps a dozen who were doing the kind of bad therapy that has recently received so much media attention: therapists who hadn't resolved their rage about their own abuse and were sending their clients out as proxies to seek justice; others who had lost their boundaries and entered into a romantic relationship with a client, taken clients into their homes, given them money or hidden them from authorities and other family members. I have encountered far more therapists who do another kind of bad therapy by denying and minimizing their clients' experiences.

The false-memory critique treats extreme examples of bad therapy as if they were mainstream practice. It seems to arise from basic misunderstandings of what therapy is and what therapists do. It assumes there is some economic and emotional payoff for therapists in implanting memories of abuse when nothing of the sort has actually taken place. It ignores the fact that people who have been repeatedly abused tell their stories reluctantly and disbelieve themselves. Taking on the identity of a trauma survivor brings far more stigma than specialness. . . .

Memory Suppression Is Real

Let's take a look at some of the major misconceptions that underlie the current debate about false memory:

It is preposterous to think that someone could entirely forget repeated rape that occurred over years. Such "uncoverings" must be the mutual delusion of therapist and client.

Memory disturbance after shocking and horrifying events is so well-documented among survivors of other types of verified trauma that it is listed in the DSM-III-R [the American Psychiatric Association's *Diagnostic and Statistical Manual of*

Mental Disorders, 3rd ed., rev.]. Bruno Bettelheim, for example, wrote eloquently of repressing his memories of Dachau and Buchenwald:

> A split was soon forced upon me, the split between the inner self that might be able to retain its integrity, and the rest of the personality that would have to submit and adjust for survival.

> Anything that had to do with the present hardships was so distressing that one wished to repress it, to forget it. Only what was unrelated to present suffering was emotionally neutral and could hence be remembered.

A study conducted in postwar Britain found that in times of public emergency, 15 percent of all hospital psychiatric admissions were for psychogenic amnesia. Winnie Smith, a former army nurse and author of *American Daughter Gone to War*, writes that she forgot, for 16 years, whole segments of her traumatic experiences as a critical care nurse in Vietnam. Why, then, are we so suspicious about the years of self-protective forgetting by those who were sexually abused?

Avoiding the Truth

The issue of child sexual abuse and memory is incredibly complex. It is not enough to simply ask, "Did the abuse happen or not?" The truth is not so easily uncovered. The question has been answered over and over, by thousands of women, "Yes, it did happen," and still they are doubted and not believed. To acknowledge these memories would demand a commitment to dealing with the structural changes necessary to end the sanctioning of child sexual abuse in this country. Few people are willing to take that on. Instead, groups of people desperately search for other possibilities—anything to avoid the truth that lots of children get raped by adults. Wishing for and constructing other "explanations" won't ever change that.

Off Our Backs, February 1994.

If such memories were induced only by pesky therapists, survivors of childhood abuse would not spontaneously recover them outside therapy. But they do. According to Jack Kornfield, a well-known California psychologist and teacher of Buddhist meditation, women on month-long silent meditation retreats have spontaneously remembered long-forgotten incest. "I've known of many cases in which these women have gone back to their families and received confirmation," says Kornfield. After hearing a radio report about a pedophile priest arrested for molesting children, John Robitaille, a Providence, Rhode Island, public-relations man, suddenly recalled having been sexually abused at the age of 11 by the same priest. And in a *New York Times* article, Los Angeles attorney Shari Karney, who had never been in therapy, described recalling her incest experience in an overwhelming flashback while cross-examining a man accused of molesting his daughter.

The Importance of Memory

Therapists believe that recovering traumatic memories will magically "cure" their patients.

The point is not to force memories of horrible things to the surface but to live free of the aftereffects of traumatic experiences. Tom, for example, needed to pay attention to his memories, not to persecute or blame his cousin but because he had a lifetime of practice at ignoring his own experience. He needed to learn to listen to intuitions and physical sensations in order to navigate effectively in his present world.

Like many adult survivors of unresolved childhood trauma, Tom minimized the damaging effects of ill treatment by others. Some women who were sexually abused as children, for instance, become so practiced at ignoring danger signals that they put themselves in harm's way and are raped again as adults. It is important for them to piece together their childhood experiences and to trust their present responses; otherwise, they may endlessly recreate the preconditions of trauma. Tom didn't trust his perceptions. When he disagreed with his boss over an important business decision, he found himself unable to make his point. Later, when the deal turned sour, his boss was furious that he had failed to alert him.

Providing a Forum

Therapists pressure clients to jump to the conclusion that they've been abused.

When I do my best work, I mirror back to my clients the things they put into the room and then disown—their dreams, body sensations, horrific drawings, writing, memories. At the same time, I try always to stay half a step behind them as they wrestle with the conflict between believing and not believing their memories. My job is not to advocate for any version of reality. It is to provide a forum where they may sit with all sides of their inner conflicts. I often ask, "What do these images or sensations mean to you?" I do not encourage clients to seek external validation, from me or anyone else; it's much more important that they stew in their ambivalence and uncertainty and decide for themselves what their memories mean. . . .

Because of the ramifications in the world outside the therapy room, therapists should get external verification before assuming that childhood sexual abuse took place.

I have no interest in such a task. I am a therapist, not a detective. When clients come to me and genuinely risk disclosing and exploring their life's issues, the therapeutic relationship must be, as it always has been, a sanctuary—confidential, private and safe.

I work in the aftermath of shattering experiences. I am less interested in the pinpoint accuracy of every detail of clients' memories than I am in the chronic, debilitating aftereffects. I am not piecing together legal evidence. It is well beyond the usual clinical covenant for therapists to enter into their clients' lives as researchers, detectives, solicitors or professional chroniclers.

I usually discourage abused clients from suing their perpetrators, and over the years, only a handful have gone to court. Lawsuits usually take more from the client than they are worth even if they prevail. Clients who are at a deep therapeutic impasse sometimes prematurely try to staunch their feelings of loss and try to validate their perceptions and their suffering by involving the legal system.

The Role of Hypnosis

Therapists using hypnosis often unwittingly suggest traumatic memories.

False-memory advocates set up a straw man, suggesting that hypnotists don't know how undependable hypnotically refreshed memory can be. But, in fact, we know that hypnosis can distort memories by conflating them with present beliefs and feelings. I use hypnosis all the time, but rarely to discover "what really happened.". . .

Hypnosis is not truth serum. The essence of its therapeutic value is that it can alter someone's attitude toward his or her traumatic memories and blend past impressions with present-day realities and beliefs. In this way, adult insights may be brought to bear on childhood perceptions. This complex interplay between memory and hypnosis can create memory distortion, and there is no way to distinguish this from true recall without corroboration. We do need to be careful. Clients under hypnosis are highly suggestible, and their "memories" can be altered by unwitting suggestions or leading questions. Clinicians must be cautious about suggesting content and use open-ended ways of providing empathy, support and validation. If hypnosis is used for searching out memories at all, it is best to wait until the client has been able to accept some of his or her memories already, and is willing and committed to exploring for further traumatic content.

However, I frequently use hypnosis in other ways with trauma survivors. It has been recognized since at least World War I as a valuable adjunct treatment for trauma. With Tom, for example, hypnosis made the painful process of therapy easier on him. At the beginning of therapy, I used hypnosis to create positive expectations—saying, for example, "You'll find it easier to talk about things . . . this will be a place you experience some sense of discovery and expectancy, a place where you will learn to feel safe."

Later, when he was nearly overcome by memories and was having trouble sleeping and working, I used hypnosis to help him contain his pain by suggesting, "When you need to go to work, you can put these matters in the back of your mind and not be plagued by them as you work. When we work together, you can take them out again." While Tom was in trance, he put his memories in a time-lock vault and buried them under a tree between sessions.

Later, hypnosis was valuable in cognitive restructuring. Tom was able to correct his post-traumatic distortions, including the idea that he was a wimp who had failed to stop his cousin from abusing him, and would therefore fail at everything else. Otherwise, therapy might have simply condemned him to reliving his abusive memories endlessly.

That is how I usually use hypnosis—not to search out recalcitrant memories. My practice is to wait for traumatic content to bubble up, rather than go looking aggressively for it. I believe that clients want to remember and tell their stories. If I provide a supportive, consistent, caring and empathic context, the client's story will eventually come into the room. If it doesn't, I look first at problems in our relationship and not to hypnosis.

The Sanctuary of Therapy

As in other areas of clinical practice, there are few definitive research findings about the treatment of adult survivors. Like all therapists, clinicians who work with survivors must carefully look to their practices to test the validity of their methods and assumptions. The tough-minded questions we must ask ourselves are, "What are the effects of our assumptions and methods on our clients? Do they get better when we treat them as trauma survivors?"

Tom felt he had permission to explore his nightmares and body sensations only after a doctor told him he had been physically scarred. In therapy with me, he had found a place where he would be believed, supported and not abandoned, no matter what memories or sensations he reported. I believe his memories emerged partly because I had helped him create a safe place for them. . . .

When the time was right, Tom pieced together his traumatic memories and his life changed. Within a year, his nightmares, night terrors and strange physical symptoms ended. For years, he had been impotent except during one-night stands with strangers.

After therapy, that changed. He remarried, went back to school for an advanced degree and moved up in his profession.

Tom was able to get corroboration for his memories, but many adult survivors do not. In most cases, this is simply not possible. What is important is not for clients to find external validations of these memories, but for them to learn to trust their perceptions and pay attention to the truth of their lives. The sanctuary of therapy is one place where many clients find they can confront their past instead of endlessly and numbly reenacting it. After two decades of working with abuse survivors, I know that listening to their stories and helping them explore the truth of their experiences has enabled many to turn their lives around. For now, that is the best—and the most satisfying—proof I can advance that the stories told me were true.

"A person grows by taking in something human
from another person, a process that I find more
appealing than taking a pill."

Drug Therapy
May Harm Society

Richard S. Schwartz

In the following viewpoint, Richard S. Schwartz discusses a hypothetical drug—a "mood brightener" that would make nondepressed people feel good all the time—in order to illustrate the
ethical problems posed by drug therapy (psychopharmacology).
Schwartz argues that while drugs are beneficial in the treatment
of serious depression, such a mood brightener (inspired by the
real drug Prozac) would prove harmful by disconnecting individuals from reality and encouraging uncritical conformity to cultural norms. Schwartz is director of the adult outpatient clinic at
McLean Hospital in Belmont, Massachusetts, and an assistant
clinical professor of psychiatry at Harvard Medical School.

As you read, consider the following questions:

1. According to the author, who are more realistic, depressive
   people or non-depressive people?
2. What is "affect tolerance," according to Schwartz?
3. According to the author, which is more powerful, culture
   or psychiatry?

Richard S. Schwartz, "Mood Brighteners, Affect Tolerance, and the Blues," *Psychiatry* 51
(Nov. 1991):397-402. (References and notes in the original article have been deleted here.)
Reprinted by permission of the Guilford Press, New York.

Recently, a colleague [Robert Aranow] challenged me to think seriously about a hypothetical medication—a "mood brightener . . . [that would] brighten the episodically 'down' moods of those who are not clinically depressed, without causing euphoria or the side effects that have accompanied the mood elevators of abuse." Fluoxetine [Prozac] is a significant step in that direction, he argued, and we would inevitably possess drugs that "reduce the common experiences of drudgery such as going to work on Monday mornings for those who, at present, are not seen as suffering from a mood disorder, without obvious side effects or 'impairment' in judgment." He suggested that we had best begin now to consider the implications of such medicines.

I intended to put off my colleague in favor of more immediate concerns, but his challenge stayed with me. That night, I found myself thinking of a song by Mississippi John Hurt called "Got the Blues Can't Be Satisfied." The singer tells a story of infidelity and murder. He has killed his girlfriend and her lover, but he turns quickly from the tragic events themselves to the problem of bearing their emotional impact. He searches for an anodyne, a drug to relieve the pain "or lessen the sense of misfortune" (*Oxford English Dictionary*). He sings:

> Whiskey straight will drive the blues away.
> That be the case, I want some for today.

I am certain that he finds his whiskey. Yet the song concludes:

> Still got the blues and still ain't satisfied.

Now why, I wondered, is the singer still not satisfied? Is it simply because whiskey straight is not, of course, the ideal mood brightener that my colleague postulates? Or is it also because aspects of reality can and should transcend the attempts at mood adjustment to which all of us are understandably drawn at one time or another in our lives? Mr. Hurt's song grants reality its emotional power. Who would not in the face of tragedy? I trust that none of us, on hearing a similar story from a patient, would see distracting him from his grief as our primary task. When tragic events recede into the past, however, or when patients come to us with everyday misfortunes, we encounter a wider range of professional responses.

Responsiveness to Reality

I nonetheless believe that the aspects of reality to which we must remain emotionally responsive include not only the extremes of trauma, but the mundane details of ordinary life—details such as a monotonous and devaluing job, a more subtly unsatisfying romance, in fact, the aspects of life that form the subjects of many other blues songs. Of course, I enter a dangerous realm here. When I write that we *must* remain emotionally responsive, I really mean that we *ought to*—the telltale sign of a moral statement. The concept of mood brighteners provokes questions not only about psychiatric effectiveness but about what we wish to be and the nature of the good life, the central concerns of moral philosophy. Since I am far from qualified to review centuries of philosophical effort in this area, I will rest content to touch on some aspects of it that are visible from clinical psychiatry.

The importance I place on responsiveness to "reality" as an essential aspect of our humanity does not lead me to argue against antidepressant medication. The treatment of a severe depressive illness is an attempt to restore a state of normal human responsiveness to an individual unnaturally cut off from that state. Our language reflects this fact. The concept of "endogenous" depression emerged from efforts to explain the apparent unresponsiveness of many depressed patients to the world around them. The phrase *restricted range of affect* is an attempt to describe one aspect of the depressed patient's absence of expectable human reactivity. Recovery from a depressive illness therefore involves an act of connection, an act of integration. Following successful treatment, the individual is more connected with both his humanity and his world.

An Act of Disconnection

When instead you create a chemical change of mood in the absence of a pathological state (for the moment I will assume that at least severe depression can be distinguished clearly from health), you inevitably do just the opposite. It is an act of disconnection. You bring about a break, however small, between the individual and either his external reality or his humanity, by which I mean his tendency to react "humanly" to external circumstance. Either you have reduced his awareness of what is going on around him or you have reduced his capacity to care about it in the ways that human beings have historically cared as far back as myths and legends take us. I oppose making that break.

But here my argument begins to spiral. We have much more of a muddle than I have admitted so far. Problems arise in three areas. First, an individual's responsiveness to the world around him is shaped and distorted by many forces other than psychopharmacology. Second, the question of what constitutes an accurate perception of and responsiveness to reality (essentially the definition of reality) is by no means a simple one. Third, there is the possibility of conflict between a philosopher's allegiance to truth and a doctor's responsibility to alleviate pain. I will attempt to address briefly each of these points.

Chemicals are not the only forces that mediate between external circumstance and individual response. Music certainly does,

129

whether singing the blues or listening to Bach. Psychotherapy also operates at the same boundary. At the level of the individual, psychological defenses mediate between experience and response. Psychotherapy changes an individual's response to his experience by transforming his psychological defenses. And, like our universal mood brightener, psychotherapy does not limit its scope to persons with an illness. In its early years, psychoanalysis faced some of the same accusations that we hear today against mood brighteners—it would strip people of creativity and foster complacency by eliminating internal conflict. The problem cannot be reduced to a psychotherapy/psychopharmacology boxing match. Instead, I would like to look more closely at their similarities.

"...IS IT MY IMAGINATION OR DOES IT SEEM LIKE EVERYONE IS TAKING PROZAC ?..."

Bill Schorr reprinted by permission of UFS, Inc.

Leon Grinberg defines the goal of psychoanalysis as "the search for truth about oneself." It is a noble goal and I sincerely hope that some individuals will continue to seek psychoanalysis with that aim in mind. But surely psychotherapy has a different goal, a "therapeutic" goal, consistent with a doctor's dual responsibilities to cure or to relieve suffering. The difference is clearest in the psychotherapy of depression precisely because depressive thinking raises fundamental questions about the validity of experience and the nature of reality.

Cognitive therapy, and I believe that elements of all effective psychotherapy can most clearly be described in cognitive terms, prescribes for patients more "rational" ways to think about the world. The explicit theoretical assumption of cognitive therapy is that depressive thinking is distorted and that the cured patient ends up with a more realistic view of the world. Unfortunately, the assumption may simply be wrong. In a review paper entitled "Painful truths about depressives' cognitions," C. Layne writes:

> Empirical research indicates that depressives are cognitively realistic, while nondepressives are cognitively distorted.... Normals appear to be less in touch with reality than are depressives. Normals are even less in touch than are depressed outpatients and even hospitalized inpatients! . . . The major implication of the empirical literature is that depressives' thoughts are painfully truthful, whereas nondepressives' thoughts are unrealistically positive.

This summary statement oversimplifies a complex body of literature, but it underlines an ongoing controversy about who among us sees the world most clearly. Particular areas in which depressives seem to have their feet more squarely on the ground than nondepressives include predicting their performance relative to others on a task, understanding the limits of their control over the outcome of games of chance, monitoring and assessing their own skilled and unskilled social behavior, and judging themselves equally responsible for previous successes and failures on a task rather than seeing themselves as more responsible for their successes than for their failures. The common theme appears to be a more realistic but maladaptive awareness of their limitations. Intriguingly, this conclusion does not depend on the severity of depression. The studies [from which this conclusion is drawn] look at groups ranging from mildly depressed nonpatients to seriously depressed inpatients. The conclusion is also specific to depression and not a characteristic of psychiatric patients in general. Experimental results are the same whether the control group consists of nondepressed psychiatric patients or "normals."

We Are All Tainted

The importance of these findings is that drug-free normal life loses its claim to the moral high ground of realistic perception. I can even add an analyst's obligatory quote from Freud to bolster that position. In *Mourning and Melancholia*, he wrote that the depressive "seems to us justified in certain other self-accusations; it is merely that he has a keener eye for the truth than other people who are not melancholic." We are all tainted. In order to function in the world, we all distort our vision, whether by psychological defenses or chemicals. Thinking back to John Hurt, if we look clear-eyed at the world, we will have the blues. Now I favor opening up our eyes as much as we can bear, but when we all shade our eyes to some degree, how can I, as a doctor, claim the right to withhold a mood brightener from someone who wishes less pain?

I think I have arrived at my future practical clinical stance, particularly since the distinction between depression and un-happiness, clear at the extremes, remains murky at the border and I suspect always will be. I learned long ago that I cannot ac-curately predict which patients with chronic dysphoria [unhap-piness] will respond to antidepressants. Recent research on the diagnoses of dysthymia [a form of depression less severe than clinical depression] and depressive personality makes the dis-tinction even harder to grasp. But the argument in my own mind goes further. It is an argument that I might even share with future patients by way of offering an informed choice.

Bearing the Truth Through Bearing Feelings

Robert Langs has written a paper titled "Truth therapy, lie therapy." Perhaps there are ways of approaching psychotherapy that help a person to face the truth rather than offer a soothing lie. I believe that central to any "truth therapy" would be some version of the concept of affect tolerance. Simply put, affect tol-erance means that you can stand to feel what you feel. It is the opposite of a mood brightener, whether of the chemical or psy-chological variety. The more affect you can bear, the more you can look reality in the eye without either comforting distortions (i.e., mood brighteners) or a collapse into a nonfunctional state of depression or disorganization. The greater your capacity to be aware of reality and to bear the feelings stirred up by that awareness, the greater the range of adaptive responses that you can consider. Affect tolerance is a psychoanalytic concept but, under different guises, it figures prominently in a wide range of theories about how psychotherapy helps. It may offer us a way to avoid the conclusion that the only way we can make people feel better is to make them either less aware or less human. Perhaps feeling better is not synonymous with feeling happy.

I will not review the various theories about how affect toler-ance develops, although the subject comes up in analytic writ-ings about anxiety, depression, trauma, and substance abuse—all subjects relevant to the question of mood brighteners. Instead I will limit myself to considering the role of identification in its development, a subject more prominent in clinical discussions than in the psychotherapy literature. This discrepancy may be due to the importance placed on the subject by influential oral teachers such as Elvin Semrad. W.W. Meissner has explored in detail the relationship between identification and learning. In clinical discussions, however, the idea of identification with the therapist's capacity to bear the patient's feeling states represents an extension of the concept of identification "with the analyst in his analytic activity" into the realm of affective experience, [according to W. Hoffer]. Many clinicians believe that affect tolerance increases during successful psychotherapy in part because the patient identifies with the therapist—that is, identifies with his ability to bear the patient's feelings, as well as his own. The process usually begins with the patient's internalizing the therapist's voice or comforting presence but one hopes that it proceeds to the point where the patient experiences his new capacity to bear feeling states not as a foreign presence within him but as an integrated part of his own identity. The model combines within one developmental sequence two of the three "nonspecific therapeutic change agents" that T.B. Karasu identifies as common to all forms of psychotherapy, affective experiencing and cognitive mastery. In this model, a person grows by taking in something human from another person, a process that I find more appealing than taking a pill. I have no illusion that it can treat the psychiatric illness effectively treated by medications, which I gladly use and will continue to use, but I would hold out for it as the "treatment" of choice in helping a well person deal with life.

The Dominance of Culture

Questions about mood brighteners, however, will not be resolved mainly by psychiatrists or philosophers. The interface between external circumstance and individual response is subject to forces much more compelling than the reasoning and interventions of either of those two puny groups. The sum of these complex forces is what we call our *culture*. Culture can be understood as an immensely powerful "psychosocial" phenomenon that not only mediates between external reality and individual response but even defines what a normal human response is. If our culture came to accept the widespread use of mood brighteners, we would simply have a shift in the definition of normal human response and that would be that. As psychiatrists, we may have some effect on our culture's definition of normal, but the influence flows much more decisively in the other direction. Psychiatry's embeddedness in its social context was the essential observation of the antipsychiatry movement [led by Thomas Szasz, R.D. Laing and D. Cooper]. While those writers underestimated the capacity of psychiatrists (including themselves) to see beyond their cultural expectations and even to provide their culture with genuinely new knowledge, their basic caution should not be ignored.

A specific example of the interaction between culture and medication in the management of feelings will illustrate some of the complexity of the problem. It will also demonstrate that we are further along with some of the technology than we may suspect. A group at Yale [S. Jacobs, J.C. Nelson, and S. Zisook] has studied the treatment of "depressions of bereavement" with antidepressant medication. They find "preliminary evidence for the use of antidepressants in treating the persistent major depressive syndromes observed late in the course of bereavement." That's good news, but what do they mean by "late in the course of bereavement"? The authors do not specify the duration of bereavement in their sample, but the introduction suggests that they are concerned with depression that persists one year after a loss.

Encouraging Conformity

A strikingly divergent view of bereavement may be found in Anthony Storr's book *Solitude:*

> Mention was made of certain psychic activities, like incubation, which require long periods of time for their completion. Mourning is another example of a process which may be very prolonged indeed. In rural Greece, bereaved women mourn for a period of five years. During this time, the bereaved woman wears black, visits the grave of the deceased daily, and begins by conducting conversations with the departed.

Storr in turn quotes from L.M. Danforth, *The Death Rituals of Rural Greece:*

> A new social reality is constructed which enables the bereaved to inhabit more fully a world in which the deceased plays no part. . . . The process is brought about through a gradual reduction in the intensity of the emotions associated with death, through the formation of new social relationships with new significant others, and through the constant confrontation with the objective facts of death, climaxing in the exhumation of the bones of the deceased. The result of this process is as complete an acceptance of the final and irreversible nature of death as is possible.

Here is a culture with impressive affect tolerance. I will sidestep the sexual politics suggested by the apparent absence of a similar extended ritual for widowers. I will even concede that, as a clinician, I was delighted to learn that I had another treatment option in unresolved grief reactions. Even so, we have an interesting situation. Our culture expects that normal grieving will be a relatively short process. Naturally, there are individuals who cannot conform to cultural expectations. We can now bring their grieving to an end "on time" with desipramine [an antidepressant]. A medication can be used (and I am sure will be used) to support our cultural expectations about normal mourning. Any pressure to reconsider those norms will be further reduced because psychopharmacology can make it possible for more of the population to conform. We have a circular interaction in which cultural norms elicit pharmacologic interventions which in turn reinforce cultural norms.

Paradoxical Potential

The anxiety that I have about a universal mood brightener is not anxiety about pharmacology. It is anxiety about the potentially overwhelming synergy between pharmacology and culture, in which culture is an equal, if not more powerful player. The power of psychiatric discoveries to change our society remains latent in the absence of that synergy. Huxley's Brave New World is not a sinister place primarily because of its science. The real danger begins where biological and psychosocial experts get together.

Lionel Trilling considered Freud's emphasis on biology (his problematic drive theory) "a liberating idea . . . [because] it suggests that there is a residue of human quality beyond the reach of cultural control." Psychopharmacology is a remarkable field because, like the developing science of genetics, it can potentially extend the reach of culture into the previously protected realm of our biological nature. Both enterprises have the paradoxical potential to liberate us by reducing the limits imposed on us by illness and to imprison us by increasing the degree of uniformity that society may demand of us. Individuals in all societies have used psychoactive substances episodically to alter their perceptions and responses. Since chronic intoxication was generally incompatible with either effective functioning or good health, they faced an inevitable return to their original mental state. As we control the side effects of mood brighteners, however, the need for that return disappears. With that change, we begin to transform not just how we are responding but who we are. I have seen too much of the suffering that depression brings to argue against traveling further down that path. But I wonder where it will take us.

"*Psychopharmacology has become, like Freud in his day, a whole climate of opinion.*"

Drug Therapy Will Not Harm Society

Peter D. Kramer

Peter D. Kramer, a psychiatrist who prescribes Prozac in his private practice, is an associate clinical professor of psychiatry at Brown University and the author of the best-selling book *Listening to Prozac*, from which the following viewpoint is excerpted. Although he concedes that Prozac and other drugs could conceivably harm society by fostering cultural conformity, Kramer argues that such a development will be prevented by America's "pharmacological Calvinism"—a belief that taking drugs for pleasure is morally wrong. He concludes that the growing prevalence of drug therapy (psychopharmacology) will alter the way people conceive of their personalities, their psychological states, and their physiologies.

As you read, consider the following questions:

1. According to Kramer, what is a thymoleptic?
2. What is an "antidepressant," according to the author?
3. What are the two historical conceptions of opium that Kramer mentions?

The debate about Prozac was catalyzed by a young Harvard psychiatrist, Robert Aranow, who challenged his colleagues to consider the ethical implications of "mood brighteners," a phrase he coined after seeing Prozac exert a dramatic effect on certain of his less ill patients. Aranow defined mood brightener as a medicine that can "brighten the episodically down moods of those who are not clinically depressed, without causing euphoria or the side effects that have accompanied the mood elevators of abuse," such as cocaine or amphetamine. Aranow stressed the lack of side effects in order to sharpen the discussion: once we set aside the argument that drugs are bad because they harm people physically, we are forced to focus on whether we really want to be able to use drugs to improve normal people's mood.

Until the advent of Prozac, most ethical questions involving psychotherapeutic drugs turned on clinical tradeoffs: For which indications may highly addictive medications be prescribed? Ought coercion to be permitted in the administration (to gravely disturbed or dangerous patients) of drugs that alleviate psychosis but can cause neurological damage? What constitutes informed consent regarding risks and benefits of medications given to the mentally ill? And so on.

Prozac made Aranow wonder about the ethical implications of a drug that demands no tradeoff. He further highlighted this issue by formulating a second concept, "conservation of mood." Amphetamine, cocaine, heroin, opium, alcohol, and other street drugs used to elevate mood all ultimately result in a "crash." Under conservation of mood, there are, Aranow notes, no shortcuts to happiness: "In effect, there has been an unspoken assumption that . . . any substance that induces an elevation of mood above an individual's long-term baseline will eventually result in an opposite equivalent or greater decline." What goes up must come down. What interested Aranow was the consequences of mood-elevating drugs that violate the principle of conservation of mood.

A Familiar Case

Aranow's inspiration was a familiar-sounding case. The patient was a forty-four-year-old woman who two days each week tended to feel apathetic and unable to complete her usual tasks. She met criteria for none of the depressive disorders, though she did appear to have a "personality disorder" characterized by dependency and passive aggression. One gets the impression that the patient may have struck her doctors as a whining complainer. She requested Prozac to give her energy on her down days. Her doctors suggested that psychotherapy would be more effective, but at the patient's insistence Prozac was prescribed. Six weeks later, she reported that she had much more energy, optimism, and self-confidence: "This is the way I have always wanted to feel." Twice she was weaned off Prozac, and each time she returned to her normal, unsatisfactory level of functioning. Back on the medication, she found her energy and optimism returned. She never became manic and never suffered a collapse in mood.

This case led Aranow to challenge his colleagues to think about the implications of a harmless drug that could "reduce the common experiences of drudgery such as going to work Monday mornings for those who, at present, are not seen as suffering from a mood disorder. . . ."

A Transforming Drug

My impression, on listening to the medical ethicists and reading their essays [written in response to Aranow's challenge], was that they had captured important concerns regarding the potential corrosive effects of mood brighteners on individuals and on society. Their arguments expressed in formal terms certain quiet worries I had felt on first working with Prozac. At the same time, I found the mood-brightener discussion unsatisfying. . . . The concept of mood brightener just will not do—it arises from the limited idea of an "antidepressant," when what we are dealing with is a thymoleptic, a drug that acts on personality. . . .

Part of what may bother us is the nature of the changes that Prozac can accomplish. Michael McGuire [a California psychiatrist with a background in animal ethology] hypothesized that low mood in dysthymic women [those who suffer from less-than-major depression] results from a mismatch between the personality with which they enter adulthood and the one their culture rewards. It follows that a mood elevator for dysthymics, at least one that works through altering temperament, will necessarily be a drug that induces "conformity." I put "conformity" in quotation marks because here it means conformity to traits that society rewards, which might well be rebelliousness, egocentricity, radical self-confidence, or other qualities that lead to behaviors we ordinarily call nonconformist. (The evolutionary model [which holds that unpleasant moods are vital for species adaptation and survival] entails certain paradoxes. It holds that in a given society an "antidepressant" is any chemical that leads to a rewarded personality—different cultures may have quite different antidepressants. In a culture that rewards caution, a compulsiveness-inducing drug might produce the temperament that leads to social rewards and thus brightened mood.) What are the implications of a drug that makes a person better loved, richer, and less constrained—because her personality conforms better to a societal ideal? These moral concerns seem at least as complex as those attending a drug that just inherently makes a person happy. In terms of its interaction with cultural norms, a transforming drug might be even more ethically troubling than a mood brightener.

NON SEQUITUR by WILEY MILLER

©1994, Washington Post Writers Group. Reprinted with permission.

Consider the Greek widow who over the course of five years is given a chance to allow her feelings to attenuate. She lives in an affect-tolerant culture, though she may be far from affect-tolerant [able to bear anxiety and depression]: the widow may be rejection-sensitive and for that reason in need of an especially long time to recover after the death of a husband. Perhaps rural Greek society is organized precisely to allow widows with low affect tolerance to recover at their own pace. In an affect-tolerant traditional culture, rejection-sensitivity might be an adaptive trait. A more assertive widow, or one quicker to heal, would find the society stifling and infuriating: she might be happier in a less affect-tolerant culture, and indeed might find that rural Greek society makes impossible demands that she is temperamentally ill-equipped to meet.

To say that our society is less affect-tolerant is to say that it favors different temperaments. The Greek society is not preferable, just more comfortable for certain people. But it may be in our society that what doctors do when they treat mourning with medication goes far beyond elevating mood: they are asking a fragile widow to adopt a new temperament—to be someone she is not.

A Spunkier Persona

Prozac highlights our culture's preference for certain personality types. Vivacious women's attractiveness to men, the contemporary scorn of fastidiousness, men's discomfort with anhedonia [an inability to experience pleasure] in women, the business advantage conferred by mental quickness—all these examples point to a consistent social prejudice. The ways in which our culture favors one style over another go far beyond impatience with grief.

A certain sort of woman, socially favored in other eras, does poorly today. Victorian culture valued women who were emotionally sensitive, socially retiring, loyally devoted to one man, languorous and melancholic, fastidious in dress and sensibility, and histrionic in response to perceived neglect. We are less likely to reward such women today, nor are they proud of their traits.

We admire and reward a quite different sort of femininity, which, though it has its representations in heroines of novelists from Jane Austen to Fay Weldon, contains attributes traditionally considered masculine: resilience, energy, assertiveness, an enjoyment of give-and-take. Prozac does not just brighten mood; it allows a woman with the traits we now consider "overly feminine," in the sense of passivity and a tendency to histrionics, to opt, if she is a good responder [to the drug], for a spunkier persona.

Fostering Conformity?

The Mexican poet and essayist Octavio Paz has put the issue of American expectations of women in the context of our form of economic organization: "Capitalism exalts the activities and behavior patterns traditionally called virile: aggressiveness, the spirit of competition and emulation, combativeness. American society made these values its own." Paz acknowledges that the position of women under American capitalism is legally and politically superior to that of women under Mexican traditionalism. But American social equality, Paz contends, comes in the context of a masculine society, in terms of values and expectations; Mexican society, though deplorable in the way it treats women, is more open to values Paz calls feminine.

Does Prozac's ability to transform temperament foster a certain sort of social conformity, one dominated in this case by "masculine" capitalist values? Thymoleptics are feminist drugs, in that they free women from the inhibiting consequences of trauma. But the argument can be made that, in "curing" women of traditional, passive feminine traits and instilling in good responders the attributes of a more robust feminine ideal, Prozac reinforces the cultural expectations of a particularly exigent form of economic organization.

Seducer or Enabler?

This issue of conformity and psychotropic medication is an old and fascinating one. Consider opium. In the romantic imagination—I am thinking of Thomas De Quincey's *Confessions of an English Opium Eater*, and Coleridge's "Kubla Khan"—opium is an instrument of nonconformity, a source of sustenance for the individual imagination. But in Marx's metaphor for religion, "the opiate of the masses," opium is an instrument of conformity, a substance that deadens mind and body to pain or injustice against which one ought properly to rebel.

On the one hand, Prozac supports social stasis by allowing people to move toward a cultural ideal—the flexible, contented, energetic, pleasure-driven consumer. In the popular imagination, Prozac can serve as a modern opiate, seducing the citizenry into political conformity. The poet James Merrill writes of "The stick / Figures on Capitol Hill. Their rhetoric, / Gladly—no rapturously (on Prozac) suffered!" On the other hand, Prozac lends, or creates, confidence. It catalyzes the vitality and sense of self that allow people to leave abusive relationships or stand up to overbearing bosses. The impact of such a medicine remains unclear: perhaps the apparent liberation it offers is merely the freedom to be hyperthymic [optimistic, energetic, and confident], that is, to embody a cultural ideal; or perhaps it allows formerly inhibited people to exercise power in social or political arenas that previously made them uncomfortable, where they may be disruptive of the status quo.

Early in this century, psychotherapy was criticized for inducing adaptation to the dominant culture; even if it contained a radical critique of that culture, psychotherapy was ultimately an agent of stasis. This argument applies well to Prozac. The counterargument is that Prozac, like psychotherapy, emboldens the inhibited and the injured. My own sense is that psychotherapy has been on balance a progressive force, and I suspect the same will prove true of Prozac.

Prozac and Social Coercion

The concern that Prozac raises regarding social coercion is that, once a transforming drug is available, people might be forced to take on new personalities. I am not thinking of drugs in the hands of a totalitarian state, though the interaction of psychotropic drugs and totalitarianism is always terrifying, but of the benign coercion that pervades all mass societies.

The ethics of drugs and social coercion have been most thoroughly addressed around the issue of steroids in competitive sports. We might say that a mentally competent adult athlete should be free to choose to take steroids even if they harm his body and mind; the drugs are not being used for mere pleasure but to increase excellence, a socially valued goal. But this choice has an impact on other athletes. Ethicists have argued against enhancing athletic performance with steroids because drugs diminish fairness in sport and because medical inventions ought not to be put to such a nonmedical use. But the strongest reason for banning steroids in competition has to do with coercion, or, more precisely, "free choice under pressure," as Thomas H.

Murray puts it in his essay "Drugs, Sports, and Ethics." Once a few athletes take steroids, others remain free not to do so, but only at the cost of forsaking goals to which they have devoted many years of painful effort. The choice not to take drugs (with their attendant risks) has been diminished.

A parallel example is cosmetic surgery for breast enhancement among female fashion models. No one coerces women to have breast implants, but, according to media reports, only women with enlarged breasts receive the desirable and lucrative assignments in television and print advertising. For aspiring models, the decision whether to undergo surgery is free choice under pressure. What once was (arguably) a social good—allowing a woman to gain the appearance that gives her a sense of well-being—becomes a clear social ill, the requirement, putting it in the severest terms, that a woman undergo mutilating surgery in order to pursue her chosen career.

A Science-Fiction Horror Story

The possibility of chemical "enhancement" of a variety of psychological traits—social ease, flexibility, mental agility, affective stability—could be similarly coercive. In the science-fiction horror-story version of the interplay of drug and culture, a boss says, "Why such a long face? Can't you take a MoodStim before work?" A family doctor warns the widow, "If you won't try AntiGrief, we'll have to consider hospitalization." And a parent urges the pediatrician to put a socially anxious child on Anti-Wallflower Compound. (Parents tend to want their children to be leaders—but how does a troop of monkeys or a classroom of children function when every member has high levels of serotonin [the brain chemical that Prozac increases]?) Only slightly less nightmarish is the prospect of free choice under pressure. There is always a Prozac-taking hyperthymic waiting to do your job, so, if you want to compete, you had better take Prozac, too. Either way, a socially desirable drug turns from boon to bane because it subjects healthy people to demands that they chemically alter their temperament.

Such an outcome would clearly be bad, but it also seems unlikely, not least because of our society's aversion to prescribed medication—our "pharmacological Calvinism." That phrase was coined over twenty years ago by the late Gerald Klerman, a pioneering researcher into the outcomes of both drug treatments and psychotherapy. Thinking about psychotropics in the late sixties and early seventies inevitably was influenced by the mushrooming use of street drugs in conjunction with a variety of forms of social ferment. Klerman characterized the contrasting reactions as psychotropic hedonism and pharmacological Calvinism. He defined the latter as "a general distrust of drugs used for nontherapeutic purposes and a conviction that if a drug 'makes you feel good, it must be morally bad.' "

Study after study has shown that, when it comes to prescribed drugs, Americans are conservative. Doctors tend to underprescribe (relative to the recommendations of academic psychiatrists) for mental conditions, and patients tend to take less medicine than doctors prescribe. This appears to have been true in the "mother's little helper" period, during which Klerman formulated his dialectic, and it is true today. Relative to the practice in other industrialized countries, prescribing in the United States is moderate.

Environment Precedes Medication

Past experience suggests that we can count on our pharmacological Calvinism to save us from coercion. On the other hand, pharmacological Calvinism may be flimsy protection against the allure of medication. Do we feel secure in counting on our irrationality—our antiscientific prejudice—to save us from the ubiquitous cultural pressures for enhancement? Perhaps the widespread use of new medication will erode our "Calvinism," and then a myriad of private decisions, each appropriate for the individual making them, will result in our becoming a tribe in which each member has a serotonin level consonant with dominance.

But the pressure to engage in hyperthymic, high-serotonin behavior precedes the availability of the relevant drugs. The business world already favors the quick over the fastidious. In the social realm, an excess of timidity can lead to isolation. Those environmental pressures leave certain people difficult options: they can suffer, or they can change. Seen from this perspective, thymoleptics offer people an additional avenue of response to social imperatives whose origins have nothing to do with progress in pharmacology. . . .

The Psychopharmacologic Era

We are, it seems to me, denizens of an island whose castaways have been receiving capsules rather than notes. What is most disturbing about those capsules is how they affect even those who never take medication. Castaway or not, in the psychopharmacologic era, when we look at our children, we will attend more to their constitution. At the same time, we will worry about losses children suffer, about our failures in empathy toward them, about the myriad of pains that can elevate stress hormones and stimulate dysfunctional neuronal sprouting.

Certain people we may tolerate better, or dismiss more readily, because their struggles are so transparently responses to functionally autonomous anxiety or depression, problems in regulation of mood that they ought really to get tended to, one way or another. Where once we might have sat with a friend, puzzling over her social dilemmas, now we will smile knowingly, wondering which subculture will best tolerate her quirks, or which medicine might enhance her appeal or her social skills.

We may become more aware of our own feelings of confidence or despondency, noting how they respond to our social circumstances—how applause is a tonic for us, how loss devastates. We will no doubt worry over our depressions as once we worried over carcinogens: are they causing covert damage? An unreliable lover enrages us—he is doing not just psychic but physical harm; we assume the two are much the same. Or we see our spouse as a sort of first neurotransmitter in a cascade of chemicals, one who keeps our serotonin levels high. We are keenly aware of our temperament, our psychic scars, our animal nature. Assessing both ourselves and others, we find ourselves attending to strange categories: reactivity, aloneness, risk and stress, spectrum traits, dysthymic and hyperthymic personality. We understand that our reliance on biological categories has run far ahead of the evidence, but we are scarcely able to help ourselves. . . .

Is Prozac a good thing? By now, asking about the virtue of Prozac—and I am referring here not to its use in severely depressed patients but, rather, to its availability to alter personality—may seem like asking whether it was a good thing for Freud to have discovered the unconscious. Once we are aware of the unconscious, once we have witnessed the effects of Prozac, it is impossible to imagine the modern world without them. Like psychoanalysis, Prozac exerts influence not only in its interaction with individual patients, but through its effect on contemporary thought. In time, I suspect we will come to discover that modern psychopharmacology has become, like Freud in his day, a whole climate of opinion under which we conduct our different lives.

"Jolting the human brain with 80 to 150 volts of electricity is an injurious treatment."

Electroconvulsive Therapy Is Harmful

Seth Farber

Electroconvulsive therapy (ECT) is a treatment for depression, schizophrenia, and other mental disorders in which an electrical current is applied to the patient's brain in order to induce a seizure. In the following viewpoint, Seth Farber argues that rather than a legitimate treatment for mental illness, ECT is a form of social control that causes brain damage and memory loss. Farber is a counselor in New York City, a member of the board of directors for the Network Against Coercive Psychiatry, and the author of *Madness, Heresy, and the Rumor of Angels: The Revolt Against the Mental Health System*.

As you read, consider the following questions:

1. According to Farber, where did Ugo Cerletti receive the inspiration for ECT?
2. How did psychiatrists of the 1940s think ECT worked, according to the author?
3. According to Farber, why is "new modified" ECT just as harmful as "old classical" ECT?

From Seth Farber, "Romancing Electroshock," *Z Magazine*, June 1991. Reprinted with permission.

As a therapist, philosopher, and human rights activist I am appealing to all individuals of conscience to step forward and oppose the resurgence of electroconvulsive treatment. Listen to the words of Leonard Frank, shock survivor, writer, and editor of *The History of Shock Treatment*, and act accordingly. "If the body is the temple of the spirit, as I believe, the brain may be seen as the body's inner sanctum, the holiest of holy places. To invade, violate and injure the brain as electroshock unfailingly does is a crime against the spirit, a desecration of the soul.". . .

On February 11, 1991, the Board of Supervisors of the city of San Francisco took an unprecedented action and voted seven to four in favor of a resolution introduced by Supervisor Angela Alioto opposing the use and public financing of electroconvulsive treatment (ECT). The resolution also urges the State Legislature of California to strengthen the state's informed consent laws related to ECT. The resolution was passed after the Board heard approximately fifteen hours of testimony over a three-day period from ECT supporters and critics including many shock survivors (such as Leonard Frank), as well as professionals critical of ECT including Dr. Peter Breggin, psychiatrist and author of *Electroshock: Its Brain-Disabling Effects*. . . .

Memory Loss and Brain Damage

Although the hearing was open to the public, out of more than 40 shock survivors who gave testimony, only one believed ECT had any value. Camille Moran, an activist who had had shock treatment, appealed to the Board of Supervisors: "My own head was used for a wall socket. It was as if I was being murdered many times, and during the last one I was conscious. ECT left me with terrible headaches, memory loss, learning disability, and seizures. A grand mal seizure is not an act of compassion. No one should be able to steal our memories. We need them to work through, to find the dignity of our humanity. No one has the right, though they have the power, to burn, batter, and blast someone's head into convulsions. . . . Please don't let our city pay any money to these Dr. Mengele doctors for shock treatment, and try to get it banned at the state level. . . . We need our right to say no to being tortured."

Margie Butler, former dance therapist at Berkeley's Herrick Hospital testified "They [the shock patients] just sat there numb and some of them stayed that way for days and weeks. One patient came to me and said she really didn't want shock treatment but the psychiatrists were trying to pressure her into it. . . . They evidently pressured her into it because three days later she came to me a zombie. . . . I love those people and after that I quit."

Jay Mahler testified, "There's nothing more horrible than to be completely without memory, to not know who you are, where you are, to not know your name." . . .

Marilyn Rice, former economist for the U.S. Department of Commerce and founder of the Committee for Truth in Psychiatry, the national organization of shock survivors, has been attempting since 1980 to get the FDA [Food and Drug Administration] to develop an informed consent statement that will tell patients that ECT causes brain damage and memory loss. She is opposed to an outright ban.

Rice's experience of disorientation and memory loss following ECT was similar to that described by the witnesses in San Francisco. But not only did Rice lose her memory, she also lost her job. The impairment to her memory made necessary an early retirement. She described her return to work following ECT: "I came home from the office after that first day feeling panicky. I didn't know where to turn. I was terrified. All my beloved knowledge, everything I had learned in my field during twenty years or more was gone. I'd lost the body of knowledge that constituted my professional skill. . . . I'd lost my experience, my knowing. But it was worse than that. I felt I'd lost myself."

Electroshock History

Electroshock was introduced in Rome in 1938 by psychiatrist Ugo Cerletti. Cerletti received the inspiration for the electroshock procedure at a slaughterhouse in Rome. In this particular slaughterhouse the hogs were first clamped by tongs on their heads and then administered an electric current of 125 volts, rendering them unconscious. During this period of unconsciousness the butchers stabbed and bled the animals without difficulty. The first human electroshock patient, identified only by his initials S.E., had been diagnosed as "schizophrenic." Surrounded by several colleagues, Cerletti applied the first shock which, because the voltage had been set too low, failed to induce a convulsion. As the psychiatrists discussed what to do next, S.E., to quote Cerletti, "who evidently had been following the conversation, said clearly and solemnly, without his usual gibberish: 'Not another one! It's deadly!'" Cerletti ordered a second and larger jolt, which caused the desired seizure.

Born in Germany in 1899, Lothar Kalinowsky went to Italy to study electroshock with Cerletti. Kalinowsky had missed the first electroshock experiment but was present at the second. In a 1988 interview, Kalinowsky was asked for his first impression of ECT. He responded, "According to my wife, because I don't remember it exactly, she claims that when I came home I was very pale and said, 'I saw something terrible today. I never want to see that again!'"

It is a sad commentary on the power of fame and fortune that

147

the man who recoiled in horror and moral outrage when first witnessing an assault on the human brain would become the champion of this kind of assault. In 1939–1940 Kalinowsky helped to introduce electroshock in France, England, the Netherlands, and the United States. The way for ECT had already been prepared by the acceptance of insulin coma therapy in the 1930s, introduced by Manfred Sakel.

Peter Breggin notes in his text on ECT, "The 1930s saw a new approach in technology. Previous assaults on the patients [in mental hospitals] had been largely directed at the whole body rather than the brain. Patients were whipped, strapped into spinning chairs, dunked into cold water, poisoned with toxic agents, bled, placed in straitjackets and thrown into solitary confinement. But with the third decade of the 20th century, psychiatrists discovered it was more efficient to attack the brain directly. . . . The widespread acceptance of insulin coma therapy in the 1930s paved the way for a variety of brain-damaging convulsive therapies, and ultimately for direct surgical destruction of the highest centers of the brain (lobotomy)."

By 1942 a national survey showed that ECT was being used in 93.8 percent of the state hospitals sampled, 79.4 percent of federal facilities, and 74 percent of private hospitals. This partially complete survey indicated that 75,000 patients had been electroshocked in a three-year period. Individuals would often be given massive numbers of treatments, frequently more than 100. The use of ECT and the other "somatic therapies" continued throughout the 1940s and 1950s.

Social Control or Cure?

Psychiatrists in those days were often quite explicit about their motives. In the nation's most popular psychiatric textbook in 1948, Arthur Noyes suggested "Experience has shown that the employment of maintenance [ECT] treatment on chronic wards has greatly simplified their management." In Lucie Jessner's and Gerard Ryan's authoritative text *Shock Treatment in Psychiatry* (1941), it was noted that ECT "quieted the noisy patients in the disturbed wards."

Institutional psychiatry wanted to have its cake and eat it too. Thus the same journals, and frequently the same individuals, who praised ECT as a means of social control in mental hospitals also averred that it was a cure for mental illness. The concept prevalent at that time was that brain damage was the therapeutic agent in electroshock as well as the other convulsive therapies then in use. Jessner and Ryan, in the same text cited above, wrote, "a certain amount of brain damage is of therapeutic value."

Lucino Bini, who collaborated with Ugo Cerletti, was encouraged by his finding that it caused "widespread and severe," "reversible and irreversible" alternations in the nervous system. In the 1940 *Journal of Neurological Psychiatry*, A. Kennedy acknowledged that convulsive therapy kills brain cells. He went on to state that the mental patient may "in the language of chess, be sacrificing a piece to win the game."

Brain Damage as Therapy

This brings us for a moment to a discussion of the brain damage produced by electroshock. Is a certain amount of brain damage not necessary in this type of treatment? Frontal lobotomy indicates that improvement takes place by a definite damage of certain parts of the brain. This position was espoused repeatedly by ECT supporters in the psychiatric journals throughout the 1940s.

Since brain damage rendered upset individuals docile, it is easy to understand why it was an effective means of ward management, but why was it therapeutic? A number of psychiatrists addressed this question. One of America's most respected psychiatrists, Abraham Myerson, wrote in 1942, "these people have for the time being at any rate more intelligence than they can handle and . . . the reduction of intelligence is an important factor in the curative process. The fact is that some of the very best cures one gets are in those individuals whom one reduces almost to amentia [a state of mental retardation]." Dr. Walter Freeman, who performed thousands of lobotomies, and whose career spanned from the 1930s to the early 1970s, and who was a professor at the George Washington University Medical School, expressed this thesis succinctly in 1941, "Maybe it will be shown that a mentally ill patient can think more clearly and constructively with less brain in actual operation."

The blunt advocacy for the "brain damage as therapy" thesis began to make a number of psychiatrists, presumably those more inclined to verbal intercourse with their clients, uneasy. Dr. Roy Grinker, a psychoanalyst, had written as early as 1940, "Interest in the uncovering of the basic psychological causes has decreased, for the busy psychiatrist hardly waits for the patient to undress in his hospital before shocking them into insensibility."

In the late 1940s and early 1950s a small group of prestigious psychiatrists, mildly critical of ECT, called for "a campaign of professional education on the limits of this technique" and even suggested that "certain measures of control might be required." By the late 1950s most promoters of ECT were denying that ECT caused any brain damage at all. As Peter Breggin, psychiatrist and critic of ECT, has noted in his book *Electroshock: Its Brain-Disabling Effects*, "The mountain of evidence indicating brain damage in human and animal studies was virtually eradicated from review articles and textbooks. The position was taken that no such evidence ever existed."

Brain Damage as Cure

To the extent that it works at all, shock [electroconvulsive therapy] has its impact by disabling the brain. It does so by causing an organic brain syndrome, with memory loss, confusion, and disorientation, and by producing lobotomy effects. For a few days or weeks the patient may be euphoric or high as a result of the brain damage, and this may be experienced as "feeling better." In the long run the patient becomes more apathetic and "makes fewer complaints.". . .

That shock works by damaging the brain and by making patients more simpleminded, less self-aware, and docile is such an obnoxious idea to most people that the theory is never presented to the public or repeated in court, even by its main proponent, Max Fink. In public Fink states that shock's mode of action is unknown and that it may correct biochemical imbalances. When interviewed for a magazine article on shock treatment in 1989 Fink declared, "I can't prove there's no brain damage. I can't prove there are no other sentient beings in the universe, either. But scientists have been trying for thirty years to find both, and so far they haven't come up with a thing."

Peter R. Breggin, *Toxic Psychiatry: Why Therapy, Empathy, and Love Must Replace the Drugs, Electroshock, and Biochemical Theories of the "New Psychiatry,"* 1991.

In the most widely disseminated texts on ECT—written respectively by Kalinowsky 1959, Kalinowsky and Paul Hoch 1961, Noyes and Lawrence Kolb 1973 and Max Fink 1977—no mention is made of the classic study by Dr. Hans Hartelius on brain cell death in cats subjected to minimal electric currents and a small number of treatments. Hartelius had concluded, "The question of whether or not irreversible damage to the nerve cells occurs must be answered in the affirmative." Nor is psychiatrist's Otto Will's study mentioned. In 1948 Will and his associates at the world-renowned St. Elizabeth Hospital issued the most detailed review of autopsy data in humans, indicating brain damage as a frequent result of ECT. D. Impastato's classic 1957 study of 254 ECT-related deaths is not mentioned. . . .

Like Wizardry

ECT's popularity faded in the mid-1950s, although it continued to be used. This situation changed in the late 1970s. (It is estimated in 1989 that 100,000 individuals received ECT.) In June 1979 the APA [American Psychiatric Association] suddenly launched an all-out media campaign to sell ECT. The initial blast was a feature article in *The New York Times Magazine* that said ECT was "like wizardry." At this point the APA seemed to face a major obstacle to its attempt to mass-market ECT as the treatment of choice for "depression" and other "mental illnesses." Almost everybody in the United States knew—in large part as a result of Ken Kesey's book and the movie based on it, *One Flew Over the Cuckoo's Nest*—that ECT was a barbaric treatment used in snake pits to subdue unruly patients.

One reflection of the public skepticism about ECT was the refusal on the part of the Food and Drug Administration to defer to the "expertise" of the American Psychiatric Association, which urged the FDA to classify the ECT device (and indirectly the treatment) as a low-risk device. The FDA elicited information on ECT and held a public hearing on the issue in May 1979. On September 4, 1979, the device was assigned to Class III by the FDA. These are devices that pose "the greatest potential health risks." This classification was made after the FDA's Neurological Device Classification Panel had identified eight risks to health caused by ECT, including brain damage and memory loss. This classification had symbolic value but little practical effect. Electroshock users did not warn potential shock recipients of the FDA's ruling. The FDA had announced in 1979 that it was going to provide information about ECT to individuals considering undergoing this treatment. This would make it more likely that ECT candidates would be informed about the dangers of electroshock since they would read a document written by the FDA. It would also mean that state informed consent laws would be something more than dead letters. Year after year passed and the FDA failed to produce informed consent forms. Consequently, the hundreds of thousands of individuals who were subjected to electroconvulsive treatment had no way of knowing *what* they were consenting to in advance.

A Brilliant Marketing Strategy

The APA continued to pressure the FDA to reclassify the ECT device as a low-risk device. (The report justifying the reclassification of ECT in the *Federal Register*, September 5, 1990, makes clear that what is in question is not the safety of the *device*, but the safety of the *procedure* itself.) Since the public was convinced that ECT was "harmful," how could the APA and its supporters manage to convince the American public that ECT was harmless? They came up with a brilliant marketing strategy. On the one hand, they omitted from their promotional material any explicit reference to the most obvious deleterious effect of ECT: brain damage. (The evidence had already been deleted from the textbooks, as stated above.) On the other hand, as if they sensed that they could not dispel the negatively charged images ECT evoked in the public mind, they attempted to link these images with the abuses of another ostensibly long gone era. They claimed that the "new modified" ECT was a completely different species than the "old classical" ECT. (It was not mentioned that many of the promoters of the new technique had had no moral qualms about using the older technique.) Anyone who opposed the new modern "humane" treatment was just not up with the times.

The fact is electroconvulsive treatment has not *essentially* changed over the years. What *has* changed is what ECT promoters say about it, what they write about in their journals and how they market it. The anesthesia and the muscle paralyzers used in the new modified ECT do not mitigate the force of the assault on the human brain. If anything, ECT users tend to use more electricity today since the drug modifications raise the subject's convulsive threshold, making it necessary to apply a larger amount of electricity to trigger the convulsion. The muscle paralyzers suppress the natural tendency of individuals to flail out in all directions when their brains are jolted. One critic has questioned whether the most salient effect of *this* modification is to reduce bone fractures (which it does in almost all cases) or to make it easier for the ECT administrator to perform the procedure while remaining oblivious to the harm that he or she is inflicting on another human being. Neurologist John Friedberg, author of *Shock Treatment Is Not Good for Your Brain*, has compared these "improvements" to "the flowers planted at Buchenwald" (the Nazi concentration camp).

Brain Damage Cover-Up

It was noted above that the shock lobby began in the 1950s to cover up the fact that electroshock caused injury to the brain. One exception was Max Fink, editor of the prestigious journal *Convulsive Therapy*. In the text he coauthored with A. C. Kahn and E. A. Weinstein in 1956, it was written "there is a relation between clinical improvement and production of brain damage." In 1958 in the *Archives of Neurology and Psychiatry*, Fink wrote, "from the data available, it is probable that the biochemical basis of convulsive therapy is similar to that of cranial-cerebral trauma." As late as 1978 Max Fink had written, "The principal complications of ECT are death, brain damage, memory impairment, and spontaneous seizure. These complications are similar to those seen after head trauma." By 1987, eight years after the APA public relations campaign for ECT began, Fink had changed his mind: "There . . . is a public image that ECT is a high risk treatment, and the public is concerned that the treatment will produce permanent brain damage. These concerns have never really been documented." Fink was finally in line with his colleagues in the APA, whose 1989 manual, *The Practice of ECT: Recommendations for Treatment, Training and Privileging*, stated that when obtaining a patient's consent for ECT, "brain damage need not be included as a potential risk."

The FDA's September 5, 1990, report (*Federal Register*) justifying its reclassification of ECT is an extraordinary document. It is clearly an effort to assist the APA in its unrelenting effort to exorcise the American public's suspicion that jolting the human brain with 80 to 150 volts of electricity is an injurious treatment. (Common sense alone would indicate this. Independent researcher Bill Cliadakis has calculated that this is an amount of electricity roughly equivalent to 100,000 times greater than the brain is used to accommodating.) The document overlooks the many animal and human autopsy studies documenting brain damage, including the studies cited above by Hartelius, Will, and Impastato. Either the authors of the FDA report failed to read the work of leading ECT critics such as Breggin or Friedberg, or they merely decided it prudent to avoid any mention of their names, or their findings. Nor is it surprising that this "hear no evil, speak no evil" document omits any reference to the argument of ECT critics that the alleged therapeutic effect of the procedure is actually a short-term personality change resulting from the brain injury and that all brain injuries produce temporary states of euphoria. The FDA contemptuously dismisses the numerous reports of memory loss that it has received from ECT patients as "anecdotal."

The heart of this document is expressed in one sentence: "*Risks associated with ECT are primarily related to the technique of administration*, which has been significantly modified over the past 40 years" (emphasis added). The claim that risks associated with ECT are primarily related to the "technique of administration" is a cheap gimmick designed to mislead the American public and cover up the truth about electroshock. The APA has been using this ploy for over a decade. Now the federal government, which the Food and Drug Administration represents, has adopted the same gimmick. The truth is electroshock was harmful in the 1940s and 1950s and it is harmful today. And it is harmful for precisely the same reason: it is an injury inflicted on the human brain.

"Hundreds of thousands of individuals—and their families—have benefited from ECT."

Electroconvulsive Therapy Is Safe

Rael Jean Isaac and Virginia C. Armat

Electroconvulsive therapy (ECT) is a psychiatric treatment method in which a seizure is induced in a patient by means of an electrical current applied to the brain. It is used to treat depression, schizophrenia, and other mental disorders. In the following viewpoint, Rael Jean Isaac and Virginia C. Armat defend the treatment against charges that it causes brain damage. Isaac received her Ph.D. in sociology from the City University of New York. Armat has written on numerous subjects for *Newsweek*, the *New York Times*, and *Reader's Digest*. Isaac and Armat coauthored *Madness in the Streets: How Psychiatry and the Law Abandoned the Mentally Ill*, from which the following viewpoint is excerpted.

As you read, consider the following questions:

1. How were fractures and frightening experiences related to ECT eliminated, according to the authors?
2. According to Isaac and Armat, what discovery allowed memory loss from ECT to be reduced?
3. Why did the movie *One Flew Over the Cuckoo's Nest* mobilize public opinion against ECT, according to the authors?

ECT [electroconvulsive therapy] has been described [by T. George Bidder] as "one of the most effective treatments in all of medicine—with a therapeutic efficacy, in properly selected cases, comparable to some of the most potent and specific treatments available, such as penicillin in pneumonococcal pneumonia."

The Origins of ECT

The history of electroconvulsive therapy is often traced by looking at early efforts to use electricity in the treatment of mental illness. As ECT expert Dr. Richard Abrams points out, this misses what is crucial to the therapy, which is the convulsive *seizure* the electricity produces; the seizure can and has been achieved in a variety of other ways. Indeed, the treatment goes back to the sixteenth century when Paracelsus administered camphor to produce convulsions in lunatics. But because others did not follow up, Hungarian psychiatrist Ladislas von Meduna was unaware of the existence of predecessors when in 1934 he injected camphor-in-oil in a schizophrenic patient who had been in a catatonic stupor for four years, not moving or eating, incontinent and tube fed. The patient fully recovered. Meduna subsequently substituted the chemical metrazol to induce the seizures.

As is often the case with major medical discoveries, the theory behind the discovery was wrong. Meduna believed incorrectly that individuals who suffered from epilepsy did not become schizophrenic. (In fact, epileptics are more liable than others to suffer from psychosis.) Wagner von Jauregg had won the Nobel Prize for introducing malaria therapy for general paresis—mental disease caused by syphilis—and Meduna reasoned that inducing epileptic fits might work a similar cure in schizophrenia.

In Italy, Ugo Cerletti, director of the University Clinic in Rome, realized that it would be much easier to induce seizures with electricity than by injection with chemicals; he was at that time using electricity to induce convulsions in animals in connection with his studies of epilepsy. The difficulty was that in his clinic's experiments, half the animals died. Lucino Bini, Cerletti's assistant, figured out the source of the problem: in their experiments one electrode was customarily put into the mouth and one into the anus, passing electricity through the heart. Bini came up with an answer: he applied the electrodes to the animal's temples, so that the current passed from one side of the brain to the other, sparing the heart.

In April 1938, the first electroshock treatment was performed on a catatonic man, around forty years old, his identity unknown, who had been found in the Milan train station without a ticket and spoke an incomprehensible gibberish. After a series of nine treatments, he improved markedly, rejoined his wife, and resumed his engineering career. . . .

In the fresh flush of therapeutic enthusiasm ECT was over-used. As [James Roy Morrison] observed: "When any new treatment comes along, it is tried on every disease from alcoholism to zoophobia, and so it was with ECT." Even when ECT was used appropriately, for schizophrenia and the affective illnesses, in the first two decades there were undeniably problems associated with its use. The experience of ECT was nothing like that of metrazol, which in the period between injection and convulsion produced sensations so terrible that it was called [by Lothar Kalinowsky and Paul Hoch] "a roller coaster to hell." But, without anesthetic, incomplete seizures from subconvulsive stimuli occurred frequently.

A Benign Experience

When ECT was administered properly, even in the treatment's first years, the experience was benign. Producer-director Joshua Logan described receiving ECT for his manic-depressive illness in the period before anesthetic and muscle relaxants:

> I could see his hand move to pull the switch, but I never saw him complete the action. In a fraction of a second, I was in total oblivion, having felt nothing. . . . I was no longer angry with the poor nun or the people who had dragged me back to the hospital. All I wanted to do was lie there and enjoy this cool peace that was flowing through me. If this was electric shock, then I wished I had it years ago.

But when there were "missed" seizures, the experience was frightening. The reaction of the catatonic man in Milan who received the first treatment would turn out to be typical. Cerletti reported that initially he used insufficient electricity to induce a convulsion; as he prepared to try a second time, the man, who had been incapable of coherent speech, suddenly said: "Not a second. Deadly." According to Kalinowsky's wife, when her husband came home after first witnessing the treatment, he told her: "I saw something terrible, I never want to see that again." Sylvia Plath, the young poet who suffered from depression and eventually took her own life, recounts her own experience of ECT, which matches clinical descriptions of incomplete seizures.

> Then something bent down, and took hold of me and shook me like the end of the world. Whee-ee-ee-ee-ee, it shrilled, through an air crackling with blue light, and with each flash a great jolt drubbed me till I thought my bones would break and the sap fly out of me like a split plant.

Nor were subjective feelings the only problem. Compression fractured vertebrae occurred in up to a third of patients, especially in young men, as a result of the force of the convulsion.

Finally, the treatment was misused. Excessive numbers of

treatments were given to some patients. While engaged in a 1960s study in England on the effects of anti-psychotic medications, Dr. Sydney Brandon discovered accidentally that there were some patients in the hospital who had been given over a thousand ECT treatments. In other cases ECT treatments were given too close together. In the late 1950s, as part of a research project, Dr. Ewen Cameron and associates performed what they called "depatterning treatment" on chronic paranoid schizophrenic patients, which involved giving them twelve electroshock treatments *per day* for a total of up to sixty treatments. Patients became profoundly disoriented, incontinent, in need of continuous nursing care. A majority reported "persisting amnesia retrograde to the depatterning . . . ranging in time from six months to ten years."

Some hospitals took up the method. The Hartford Retreat (now the Institute for Living), a private hospital in Connecticut, adopted it to buttress misguided psychoanalytic theories. The notion was that if a patient regressed to an infantile state through ECT, the psychoanalyst could then restructure his personality.

Major Problems Overcome

By the mid-1960s, however, major problems associated with ECT had been overcome. In the early 1950s, techniques were developed for using a muscle relaxant accompanied by anesthesia (with oxygen), and within a decade these were in almost universal use. Fractures and frightening experiences from missed seizures were eliminated. So major were the changes that the new procedure was called "modified ECT" to distinguish it from the original treatment. Individuals reported nothing worse than a headache and most rated the treatment less formidable than a trip to the dentist.

The only serious side effect remaining is memory loss, and for many patients this too can be minimized. In traditional "bilateral" ECT, where electrodes are placed on both sides of the head, all patients suffer temporary memory loss, and the effect is cumulative, so that the more treatments, the greater the loss. Tests of memory after ECT suggest that it is generally restored within around six months. However, a significant number of patients complain of permanent, if spotty, memory loss for autobiographical events, especially for the months directly preceding the treatment. And while few mind forgetting the period immediately preceding ECT when they were profoundly depressed, acutely psychotic, or both, a small number complain of severe, long-term memory deficits.

It was discovered in the mid-1950s that memory deficits could be sharply reduced by placing the electrodes so that electricity passed through only one, nondominant, side of the brain—so-called "unilateral" ECT. However, this did not prove to be an "answer" to the problem of memory loss in the sense that muscle relaxants are to the problem of fractures. While few clinicians are as blunt as Dr. Kalinowsky, who says, "my experience is completely negative," surveys in the 1970s found that most psychiatrists used *only* bilateral ECT because in their clinical experience it is more effective.

A Magic Wand

My biggest depressive episode took place in May 1980. . . .

Within hours of arriving at the hospital, I was very carefully treated with electric-shock therapy. ECT [electroconvulsive therapy] is horribly misunderstood. People have this ghastly image of someone standing in a tub of water and putting his finger in a socket. I knew better. I had done some shows about it. The hospital requires a release for ECT. I was so disoriented I couldn't figure out what they were asking me to sign, but I signed anyway. In my case, ECT was miraculous. My wife was dubious, but when she came into my room afterward, I sat up and said, "Look who's back among the living." It was like a magic wand.

Dick Cavett, *People*, August 3, 1992.

This is deplored by such experts on ECT as Max Fink and Richard Abrams. Conceding that from 10% to 20% of patients respond only to bilateral placement, Dr. Fink believes that because memory loss is so much reduced with unilateral placement, it should be tried first, except in special circumstances (for example, when the individual is actively suicidal). Dr. Abrams has data suggesting that unilateral can be as effective as bilateral ECT if the electrical dosage intensity is raised to approximately two and a half times threshold (the minimum electrical dosage necessary to obtain a seizure).

Ex-Patients Focus on ECT

From its inception the ex-patient movement [an alliance of a small number of ex-patients and a few disaffected psychiatrists who began an assault on psychiatric treatment in the 1970s] concentrated on ECT. *Madness Network News* [the movement's journal] provided a constant stream of articles and editorials—even whole issues—devoted to ECT. Its spinoff, the Network Against Psychiatric Assault (NAPA), described ECT as "a bogus, barbaric and destructive technological weapon," and devoted most of its energy to lobbying and demonstrating against it.

The Church of Scientology was also active, and there were activists who worked with both groups. John Friedberg and Lee Coleman, physicians close to the ex-patient movement, also served on the national advisory board of Scientology's Citizens Commission on Human Rights.

The ex-patient movement's effort to mobilize public opinion against ECT was given a major boost in 1975 when the filmed version of *One Flew Over the Cuckoo's Nest* (appearing thirteen years after the book) won the Academy Award as best picture of the year and Jack Nicholson won an Oscar for his portrayal of Patrick McMurphy. ECT is portrayed as a form of torture, administered to the hero to subdue, not treat, him. And although modified ECT had been standard for over a decade (and specifically so at Oregon State Hospital where it was filmed), *Cuckoo's Nest* shows the writhing, convulsing body of McMurphy. In real life, only his toes would have moved. For McMurphy, ECT is prelude to the dreaded (and, at the time of the film, long obsolete) lobotomy, which transforms him into a vegetable. (The American Psychiatric Association witlessly praised this film for its "timely relevance.")

Not Good for the Brain?

The ex-patients worked with a small circle of medical professionals, at the outset chiefly with then neurology resident John Friedberg. As a college student Friedberg had a brief mental hospitalization in New Haven and although he never was given ECT, felt he only narrowly escaped it. While serving as a medical resident at Pacific Medical Center, Friedberg worked closely with the Network Against Psychiatric Assault (NAPA), which he criticized for being insufficiently anti-psychiatric! The Network cooperated with a few radical psychiatrists, and Friedberg objected: "Good shrinks or bad shrinks—they all make money off human suffering. If NAPA must use them, use them like poison."

Friedberg put an advertisement in the *San Francisco Examiner*: "Electric shock therapy is not good for the brain. I would like to hear from anyone who has received these treatments." His book on ECT, which he gave the same title as the first sentence of his ad, was published by the countercultural Glide Publications late in 1975. In the same year *Psychology Today* gave Friedberg's views on ECT wide circulation by publishing his "Electroshock Therapy: Let's Stop Blasting the Brain." Even the *American Journal of Psychiatry* included one of his anti-ECT articles in a 1977 special section on ECT.

In whichever forum Friedberg wrote on ECT, his work offered little science or scholarship, but much passionate rage. The book consisted of seven of the fifteen interviews obtained in response to his anti-ECT ad, scarcely a random sample. His 1975 article in *Psychology Today* announced—without offering any evidence—that ECT was "demonstrably ineffective" and declared "ECT perpetuates a long tradition of beating up those labeled insane." The claim that modified ECT had solved problems associated with the earlier treatment? According to Friedberg: "These 'improvements' are like the flowers planted at Buchenwald."

Friedberg's article in the *American Journal of Psychiatry*, while more objective in tone, was equally distorted. For example, as proof of alleged "brain damage" caused by ECT, Friedberg cited Lucino Bini's 1938 report that mouth to rectum electrode placement in dogs produced "widespread and severe brain damage." But the brain damage had resulted from circulatory failure, and Bini's crucial contribution that made ECT possible was to realize that placing electrodes on either side of the head would avoid the often fatal passage of electricity through the heart. In a commentary accompanying Friedberg's article, Dr. Fred Frankel, head of the American Psychiatric Association's 1978 Task Force on ECT, termed it "inaccurate," "careless," and "indiscriminate," and noted that it presented "personal opinions" as if they were scholarly decisions.

A Blow on the Head?

Friedberg was soon joined in his efforts by Peter Breggin. . . . Breggin's *Electroshock: Its Brain-Disabling Effects* was published in 1979. The book's thesis was that ECT "worked" by damaging the brain in the same way as a blow on the head. The "improvements" psychiatrists claimed to see in their patients merely reflected the characteristics of a damaged brain: "the apathy, docility, suggestibility, and helplessness that so often follow brain damage, as well as the tendency to hide symptoms and complaints." In Breggin's formulation, ECT could not possibly emerge as an effective treatment. If the individual seemed to make a dramatic recovery, it was the temporary euphoria of brain damage or a pretense by the patient to make the psychiatrist stop the treatment.

ECT expert Richard Weiner of Duke University Medical School has pointed out the absurdity of Breggin's argument. Breggin claims that ECT "*always* produces serious brain damage as manifested in the acute organic brain syndrome." But *anyone* wakening from general anesthesia has such a syndrome. "Such a statement," says Dr. Weiner, "suggests that a couple of martinis or a few beers, in producing a delirious state, always leads to serious brain damage. The logical fallacy in this type of argument is apparent." Nonetheless, because the book was published by a reputable house, the Springer Publishing Co., and supposedly "proved" that ECT was a barbaric treatment, it was a powerful tool for the anti-psychiatric movement. . . .

Not until 1984 did a major review of the literature on ECT

seek to counter the distortions of Breggin and Friedberg. . . . Weiner undertook the review, which was published in the international journal *The Behavioral and Brain Sciences* (accompanied by twenty-two peer commentaries).

Weiner dismissed the animal studies from the 1940s which Breggin offered as "proof" that ECT caused massive brain damage. Actually, Weiner pointed out, those studies showed little evidence of damage, were not applicable to modern modified ECT, and in any case were so methodologically flawed as to be irrelevant to present day ECT. More recent sophisticated studies, which Weiner examined in detail, showed no evidence of damage.

Weiner also provided a lengthy evaluation of studies of memory disturbance, noting the failure of most objective tests to show long-term loss, but conceding that better tests might be needed, especially of autobiographical memory. Since there was no evidence for structural brain damage in ECT, Weiner speculated about mechanisms to explain memory loss, including a disruption of protein synthesis (it is not unlikely memory is coded in some type of protein structure), changes in neurotransmitter systems linked to memory, and the transient breakdown of the blood-brain barrier in ECT.

Weiner drew cautious conclusions: he said the evidence for brain damage was "weak," but called "for further, more definitive research." This led fellow expert on ECT Max Fink, one of the peer commentators on the article, to complain that Weiner "genuflects to avoid criticism" and that, given the body of the article, the summary should properly have read: "A reasonable scientist finds that the search has been extensive, the methods diverse, and the evidence of damage so sparse as to make the likelihood so remote as not to be a significant factor in the clinical decision to use ECT." Another peer commentator argued that it was time to stop expending so much effort on searching for damage, for which evidence was so scanty, and to investigate instead "the *changes* in the brain . . . produced by ECT that are causally associated with its therapeutic efficacy.". . .

Why Are ECT Advocates So Few?

Hundreds of thousands of individuals—and their families—have benefited from ECT. Yet only a small number have come forward publicly. If ECT is such an effective treatment, why are the vocal opponents more numerous than the vocal supporters? The major reason is the stigma associated with mental illness. (Not long ago individuals who had suffered breast cancer would not speak publicly of their experiences for the same reason.) In the case of ECT, the treatment itself is stigmatized, producing a double reluctance to come forward. Those who have benefited from ECT run the risk of both jeopardizing their careers and horrifying their friends if they come forward publicly. The same considerations do not influence those in the ex-patient movement who have chosen to make a "career" from the ex-patient role.

Family members too may be more influenced by the widespread negative view of ECT than by their own experience. We interviewed the brother of a woman who received ECT for delusional depression thirty years ago, as a sophomore at Bennington. He recounts that she went on to finish college, marry, raise three fine children, become a "crackerjack artist," a leader in her church, and do extensive volunteer work with prison inmates. (Her only further clinical depressions followed the birth of each of her children, and were controlled by medications.) Yet he remains to this day "perturbed that my parents had agreed to shock treatment which I felt was something one did as a last resort." He was convinced that "it knocked some of the spontaneity out of her"; apparently, it did not occur to him that her depression, rather than the treatment, was responsible. But Lorraine Richter of the National Depressive and Manic-Depressive Association, composed of individuals suffering from these diseases, told us: "There are many, many people who are controlled [by medications] but never really regain that zip they had. I don't think it's clearly understood but it's sort of like a chronic semi-depression."

The National Alliance for the Mentally Ill, as well as its member chapters, have largely ignored ECT, focusing almost exclusively on drug therapies. The mentally ill relatives of those who belong to the organization tend to be the most seriously ill: they suffer from schizophrenia or manic-depression. Since ECT in the last two decades has been given overwhelmingly for depression (chiefly to the elderly who are most likely to suffer serious side effects from anti-depressants), most families have had no experience with ECT.

NAMI's lack of interest is doubtless influenced by E. Fuller Torrey's otherwise excellent manual for families *Surviving Schizophrenia*, a standard reference for the family movement, which cavalierly dismisses ECT. Incredibly, it is included in the section on "Ineffective Treatments," along with psychoanalysis, group therapy, and megavitamins. Equally remarkable, in explaining the alleged "ineffectiveness" of ECT, Torrey writes that because its use "has been vigorously opposed by ex-patient groups in the United States," it is "therefore" not a realistic therapeutic alternative for schizophrenia. In other words, a vocal minority's misguided opposition becomes the reason to abandon a valuable treatment.

Periodical Bibliography

The following articles have been selected to supplement the diverse views presented in this chapter.

Keith Russell Ablow	"Psychotherapy and the Status Quo," *The Sun*, September 1993. Available from 107 N. Roberson St., Chapel Hill, NC 27516.
Geoffrey Cowley	"The Promise of Prozac," *Newsweek*, March 26, 1990.
Paul Crits-Christoph	"The Efficacy of Brief Dynamic Psychotherapy: A Meta-Analysis," *American Journal of Psychiatry*, February 1992. Available from the American Psychiatric Association, 1400 K St. NW, Washington, DC 20005.
Erica E. Goode with Betsy Wagner	"Does Psychotherapy Work?" *U.S. News & World Report*, May 24, 1993.
Leon Jaroff	"Lies of the Mind," *Time*, November 29, 1993.
Richard Leviton	"The End of Madness," *East West*, July/August 1991. Available from *Natural Health*, PO Box 57320, Boulder, CO 80322-7320.
Lotte Marcus	"Therapy Junkies," *Mother Jones*, March/April 1991.
Paul R. McHugh	"Psychotherapy Awry," *American Scholar*, Winter 1994.
Sara Rimer	"With Millions Taking Prozac, a Legal Drug Culture Arises," *The New York Times*, December 13, 1993.
Debra Rosenberg et al.	"One Pill Makes You Larger, and One Pill Makes You Small . . . ," *Newsweek*, February 7, 1994.
David J. Rothman	"Shiny Happy People," *The New Republic*, February 14, 1994.
Chi Chi Sileo	"Multiple Personalities: The Experts Are Split," *Insight*, October 25, 1993. Available from 3600 New York Ave. NE, Washington, DC 20002.
William Styron	"Prozac Days, Halcion Nights," *The Nation*, January 4-11, 1993.
Time	"Pills for the Mind," July 6, 1992.
Anastasia Toufexis	"The Personality Pill," *Time*, October 11, 1993.
Ethan Watters	"Doors of Memory," *Mother Jones*, January/February 1993.

How Should Society Respond to the Homeless Mentally Ill?

Mental Illness

Chapter Preface

Most Americans have witnessed the problems of the homeless mentally ill firsthand. As psychiatrist E. Fuller Torrey puts it, "The dimensions of the [public mental health] disaster are obvious to anyone who has been downtown in any American city [since the late 1970s]. The seriously mentally ill, who make up one-third of the total homeless population, can be seen on streetcorners chatting amiably with or responding angrily to voices in their heads."

Some commentators view homelessness among the mentally ill as a mental health problem. They argue that homelessness is often caused by the symptoms of mental illness. According to psychiatrist H. Richard Lamb, "The disabling functional deficits of major mental illness appear to be important contributing factors to homelessness among the mentally ill. These deficits include disorganized thinking and actions, poor problem-solving skills, and an inability to mobilize themselves due to depression." Consequently, Lamb and others argue that the primary need of the homeless mentally ill is assertive attention to their mental conditions—including involuntary hospitalization for those who refuse treatment.

Others, however, see homelessness among the mentally ill as primarily a social and economic problem. According to psychiatrists Carl I. Cohen and Kenneth S. Thompson, "The homeless mentally ill must first be seen as impoverished and disenfranchised, rather than diseased." They argue that homelessness among the mentally ill is caused by the same factors that lead to homelessness among the general population—a shortage of low-income housing, job losses, and inadequate welfare benefits. Therefore, according to Cohen, Thompson, and others, instead of involuntarily hospitalizing the homeless mentally ill, society should direct its attention to the overall socioeconomic problems that leave a large population of Americans, including many who are mentally ill, homeless. John Q. La Fond and Mary L. Durham, the authors of *Back to the Asylum*, contend that "by involuntarily hospitalizing the mentally ill because they are homeless, we are choosing to medicalize what is primarily a social and economic problem."

Whether their problems are primarily psychological or economic, the homeless mentally ill continue to roam the streets of America's cities. Faced with their presence, Lamb asks, "Are we a caring society or are we not?" In the following chapter, several possible societal responses to the situation of the homeless mentally ill are proposed and debated.

"*Because of their illnesses, many mentally ill individuals are unable to take advantage of living situations available to them.*"

The Homeless Mentally Ill Need Assertive Treatment

H. Richard Lamb

H. Richard Lamb argues that the problem of widespread homelessness among the mentally ill calls for a comprehensive and integrated system of mental health care that includes housing, case management, crisis intervention, and rehabilitative services. Lamb contends that because the mentally ill are often incapable of making appropriate decisions, their current legal right to refuse treatment is counterproductive. Involuntary hospitalization is sometimes necessary, he posits, so current restrictions on its practice should be eased. Lamb is a professor of psychiatry at the University of Southern California in Los Angeles.

As you read, consider the following questions:

1. According to Lamb, why are shelters inadequate to solve the problem of homelessness among the mentally ill?
2. What three factors hinder implementation of case management in large cities, according to the author?
3. According to Lamb, what professional group should be responsible for decisions about treating the homeless mentally ill?

H. Richard Lamb, "Will We Save the Homeless Mentally Ill?" *American Journal of Psychiatry* 147, no. 5 (May 1990):649-51. Copyright ©1990, American Psychiatric Association. Reprinted with permission. (References and notes in the original article have been deleted here.)

There has been much discussion about but very little definitive action on behalf of the homeless mentally ill, a problem whose very existence can only be considered incredible in a modern affluent nation. My purpose here is to advocate doing what is necessary to deal expeditiously and definitively with this problem.

What the Homeless Mentally Ill Need

The recommendations of APA's [American Psychiatric Association] Task Force on the Homeless Mentally Ill [1984], if implemented, would probably greatly reduce the prevalence of homelessness among people with major mental illness. The task force saw homelessness as but one symptom of the problems besetting the chronically mentally ill generally in the United States and called for a comprehensive and integrated system of care for the chronically mentally ill to address the underlying problems that cause homelessness. Such a system would include an adequate number and range of supervised, supportive housing settings; a well-functioning system of case management; adequate, comprehensive, and accessible crisis intervention, both in the community and in hospitals; less restrictive laws on involuntary treatment; and ongoing treatment and rehabilitative services, all provided assertively through outreach when necessary.

Little has been done, however, to implement these recommendations since they were published in 1984. Some welcome exceptions are the outreach services in New York City that include bringing patients to hospitals involuntarily, the implementation of case management strategies in some jurisdictions, and the broadening of civil commitment in some states, including outpatient commitment. Generally, when anything has been done, it has too often relied primarily on shelters. Although they are a necessary emergency resource, shelters address the symptom and do not get at the root of the problem; they are only temporary solutions from night to night.

The very fact that the homeless mentally ill are offered such facilities as shelters implies an acceptance by society of the principle that it is a basic right of the mentally ill, irrespective of their mental status and lack of competence, to refuse treatment and appropriate housing and live on the streets instead. There they live a life characterized by dysphoria and deprivation, can be victimized by any predator, and can develop life-threatening medical problems because of lack of medical intervention. Should the chronically and severely mentally ill have the right to "choose" such a life style without regard to their lack of competence to make such a decision? I think not. This is a cruel interpretation of the basic principles of civil rights that are so important to all of us in the United States.

Even a partial implementation of the recommendations of the APA task force would make a difference. Case management is an example. In a well-functioning system of case management, every chronically mentally ill person would be on the caseload of a mental health agency that would provide assertive outreach services, have sufficient staff to work intensively with these patients, take full responsibility for individualized treatment planning, link patients to needed resources, and monitor them so that they not only receive the services they need but are not lost to the system. It is reasonable to assume that such a system of case management would result in many more chronically mentally ill persons' receiving services, including housing. Moreover, much of this could be accomplished on a voluntary basis. In such a situation, the number of homeless mentally ill would undoubtedly decrease.

Can we wait still longer for this to happen? Case management has been much discussed, but in too many jurisdictions little has been done to implement it. There is every indication, especially in our larger cities, where a high proportion of the homeless mentally ill are, that not only are there insufficient funds to do this but the bureaucracies are too ponderous and inefficient to set up a comprehensive and competent case management system for the homeless mentally ill even if they had the funds.

Resistance and Functional Deficits

Moreover, a large proportion of the homeless mentally ill tend to be resistant to taking psychotropic medications, to treatment generally, and to accepting any living situation. For instance, in funding a large-scale program designed to help the homeless mentally ill, the state legislature of California stipulated that services funded by this program could only be voluntary. An independent evaluation of this program showed that, on average, about 30% of the homeless mentally ill refused housing placements offered to them as a result of voluntary outreach case management, the primary modality of the program.

Because of their illnesses, many mentally ill individuals are unable to take advantage of living situations available to them. For instance, one study found that some homeless mentally ill persons had places to live but were too paranoid to live there. The disabling functional deficits of major mental illness appear to be important contributing factors to homelessness among the mentally ill. These deficits include disorganized thinking and actions, poor problem-solving skills, and an inability to mobilize themselves due to depression. These are crucial deficits that should lead us to intervene, preferably with the patient's consent but without it if necessary. Still another major problem with a high proportion of the homeless mentally ill (probably two-thirds or more) is serious substance abuse problems over which these patients have little if any control.

What then should we do? First of all, the chronically mentally ill must be our highest priority in public mental health. A large proportion of public mental health funding, now used for other activities, should be shifted to the care and treatment of the chronically mentally ill, which would, of course, include the homeless mentally ill.

The Right to Live in Degradation

It is now nearly impossible to commit patients involuntarily, without offering the most compelling and extreme proof that they pose a danger to themselves or others. State hospitals now can hardly be persuaded even to take people who wish to be committed, unless they can prove they are dangerous to themselves or others. Mental illness is apparently the only disease requiring the sufferer to reach the worst stage before he is considered eligible for treatment. There is something wrong with this situation. . . .

It is clearly time to start reordering priorities and to begin rethinking the complex of litigated legal rights whose *primary* effect is to prevent gravely ill people from receiving treatment. It's time to start hospitalizing people who need it, and to recognize that creating a right that allows extremely disturbed people to refuse treatment amounts to the right to live in degradation.

The Wall Street Journal, September 28, 1990.

We need to take action without waiting for the ideal to happen. We want to have comprehensive and coordinated mental health systems that would engage the homeless mentally ill and help many of them voluntarily accept treatment and suitable living arrangements. But the homeless mentally ill cannot wait decades for these systems to be established. Moreover, many homeless mentally ill persons will not accept services even with assertive outreach case management. In the meantime, if homeless persons with major mental illness are incompetent to make a decision with regard to accepting treatment and/or present a danger to themselves or others or are gravely disabled, then I believe that outreach teams including psychiatrists should bring all of these patients to hospitals, involuntarily if need be. No person meeting these criteria should be left living on the streets.

A Right to Involuntary Treatment

Do these persons have a right to live on the streets? It is my belief that the question should be phrased differently—Does society have the right to deny involuntary treatment to this population? I believe the answer is no and that these persons have a right to involuntary treatment. Although being a danger to themselves or others or gravely disabled is a primary issue here and serves as legal and clinical grounds for depriving these persons of their "liberty," there are other fundamental questions. Are we physicians who care for the sick or are we not? Are we a caring society or are we not?

Although there has been hesitancy on the part of some professionals to use involuntary hospitalization, studies have shown that, after they have gone into remission, a large proportion of patients who had refused treatment state that their involuntary hospitalization was appropriate.

If after a relatively brief hospitalization (a few weeks to a few months), mentally ill individuals can be placed voluntarily in a suitable living situation with built-in ongoing treatment, then we need to have these resources available. I believe that although we should have high standards for treatment and supportive housing, we cannot in good conscience leave the homeless mentally ill on the streets while we wait for such resources to be developed. In the short run we should settle for resources that are acceptable if not ideal. Moreover, cost has to be a consideration. We have to work within the limits of what society is willing to pay.

Many chronically mentally ill people also need such mechanisms as conservatorship, outpatient commitment, and payees to assist with money management, and these should be provided as long as the patient is in need of this kind of structure in the community. By giving up a little of their liberty, many patients can remain outside of hospitals and thus retain most of their liberty.

Degrees of Structure

It is important that we recognize the needs of the homeless mentally ill. We need to recognize that the great majority need supervised housing; mainstream housing where persons live alone in their own apartments and have to manage by themselves is beyond the capability of the great majority of this population. Structure is a crucial concept; the needs of the homeless mentally ill fall on a continuum from modest amounts to moderate amounts to highly structured situations. It hardly needs to be stated that psychotropic medications are crucial, including neuroleptics, antidepressants, lithium, and others.

We are probably attempting to treat many patients in the community who cannot be managed in open community settings. These persons have a need for structure in terms of a controlled living situation where their taking of medications is supervised

170

and they are given as much freedom as they can handle but not more. For many, this will mean a locked setting. An active schedule of activities is for many patients another important way of providing structure.

Whether a patient needs a moderate or a high degree of structure should not be seen as an ideological issue but, rather, a clinical decision based on a pragmatic assessment of the needs of each individual patient. Does the patient have sufficient internal controls to organize himself or herself to cope with life's demands? To what degree do we need to add external structure to compensate for a lack of internal controls?

Some patients need more highly structured ongoing residential care in intermediate care facilities, such as California's locked skilled nursing facilities with special programs for psychiatric patients. These private sector facilities have demonstrated that good-quality care can be provided at a relatively modest cost, compared, for instance, with reopening state hospitals.

A relatively large group of patients who need highly structured 24-hour care are many of those with dual diagnoses—major mental illness and serious substance abuse problems. Probably no activity contributes more to staff burnout than trying to treat the more difficult patients with dual diagnoses in open settings.

A small but important minority of the homeless mentally ill need the highly structured setting that state hospitals provide. This should be high-quality care. But again there will be times when we cannot wait for the ideal. If funds are not available, it is more humane to place these patients in hospitals where the charts and even the staffing standards do not meet the standards of the Joint Commission on Accreditation of Healthcare Facilities than to leave these neglected human beings on the streets.

It is my belief that the time for endless (and fruitless) discussion is long past. There has been more than enough wringing of hands. The time for action is overdue. What needs to be done is abundantly clear. We need to be bold and strong of will. We must be prepared to mount a large-scale operation that will give relief to all of the homeless mentally ill. The fate of these persons with such great needs and at such great risk cannot be left in the hands of the fainthearted.

"The homeless mentally ill must first be seen as impoverished and disenfranchised, rather than diseased."

The Homeless Mentally Ill Do Not Need Assertive Treatment

Carl I. Cohen and Kenneth S. Thompson

Carl I. Cohen is a professor of psychiatry at the State University of New York Health Science Center in Brooklyn, New York. Kenneth S. Thompson is an assistant professor of psychiatry at the University of Pittsburgh in Pennsylvania. In the following viewpoint, they argue that homelessness among the mentally ill results from the same socioeconomic factors that create homelessness among the "not mentally ill." Therefore, rather than addressing the problem with assertive psychiatric regimens such as involuntary hospitalization, Cohen and Thompson favor an approach that encourages individual and collective empowerment and social integration.

As you read, consider the following questions: *

1. According to the authors, what groups were the most adversely affected by the economic policies of the 1980s?
2. Why do the mentally ill homeless refuse psychiatric and welfare services, according to Cohen and Thompson?
3. According to the authors, what percentage of single adult homeless persons is in need of acute inpatient care?

Abridged from Carl I. Cohen and Kenneth S. Thompson, "Homeless Mentally Ill or Mentally Ill Homeless?" *American Journal of Psychiatry* 149, no. 6 (June 1992):816-23. Copyright ©1992, American Psychiatric Association. Reprinted with permission. (References and notes in the original article have been deleted here.)

Within psychiatric circles, a debate has emerged between those who use "homeless" as an adjective and "mentally ill" as a noun and those who reverse the order. This is not merely a grammatical issue. Rather, . . . psychiatry faces a critical juncture in its conceptualization of the interplay of homelessness and mental illness.

The most prominent viewpoint within psychiatry has been that the fundamental problem of homeless mentally ill persons is their mental illness. From this perspective, their homelessness is important because it reflects the severity and consequences of their disease. This viewpoint rests on the notions that 1) the occurrence of homelessness among the mentally ill stems primarily from the disabling functional deficits of their disorder, and 2) the recent increase in homelessness among the mentally ill is a product of the poor implementation of deinstitutionalization. Comments by leaders of the major psychiatric organizations in this country illustrate this viewpoint. In outlining "the perspective of the American Psychiatric Association [APA]," H.R. Lamb and J.A. Talbott wrote, "How do the chronically mentally ill become homeless? . . . The chronically and severely mentally ill are not proficient at coping with the stresses of this world." Similarly, Richard Wyatt, chief of the Neuropsychiatry Branch of the National Institute of Mental Health (NIMH), declared, "America's homeless crisis began in 1963 when deinstitutionalization became law through enactment of the Mental Retardation Facilities and Community Mental Health Centers Act. . . . By law, the former residents of structured institutions became the homeless."

An Illusory Dichotomy

On the basis of these perceptions, the problems and service needs of persons who are homeless and mentally ill are conceptualized as being qualitatively different from those of "not mentally ill" homeless persons. Like the domiciled severely mentally ill population, the homeless mentally ill are viewed as requiring services from an assertive mental health care system capable of satisfying their multiple needs. Often, involuntary psychiatric hospitalization is included as a key element of such a system. The focus on these specialized needs and services leads to the view that advocacy and program planning for the homeless mentally ill population is best done separately from that for other homeless groups.

Our objective is to address this perspective by arguing that, although well-meaning, it is tenuous on empirical and strategic grounds. Underpinning our argument is the notion that the conceptual dichotomy between homeless persons with and without mental illness is largely illusory. On closer examination, "not

173

mentally ill" homeless people have many mental health problems; similarly, the "mentally ill" homeless have numerous
nonpsychiatric problems that arise from the sociopolitical elements affecting all homeless people. This alternative perspective,
although appearing to be a difference in emphasis, is a conceptual shift. Whereas the mainstream perspective acknowledges
that nonpsychiatric factors foster homelessness among the mentally ill, it is believed that mental illness is the "basic, underlying
problem" and that other forces impinge on this core deficit. Our
model views homelessness as the core element of the broader
socioeconomic and political context, which in turn becomes
intertwined with personal biography and illness. This alternative
perspective perforce spawns novel responses to homelessness
and mental illness.

Does Mental Illness Cause Homelessness?

The belief that homelessness is a problem of severe mental illness arose during the early 1980s, when the initial reports about
the new homeless appeared in the psychiatric literature. Biases
were created by methodological weaknesses in the research, particularly with respect to the settings in which observations were
made (e.g., psychiatric emergency rooms, clinical referrals), and
these biases led to inflated estimates—as high as 97%—of the
percentage of homeless who were seriously mentally ill. In recent years, however, more scientifically rigorous studies spon-
sored by NIMH have found between one-fourth and one-third of
homeless persons to be severely mentally ill. Despite the earlier
methodological flaws, it is evident that a disproportionate number of homeless persons have severe mental illness.

By dint of their training, psychiatrists have been especially
prone to concentrate on individual traits. Hence, there has been
a tendency to assume that the cognitive and behavioral styles of
the mentally ill are the primary causes of their homelessness.
Theorists who have focused on these individual characteristics
of mentally ill homeless persons point to their propensity to
"drift," to "wander," to "outrun problems," to be "disorganized,"
to have "poor problem-solving abilities," and to be unable to
"deal with even ordinary landlord-tenant situations." Nevertheless, none of these reports has been able to demonstrate how
mental illness alone causes homelessness.

A corollary of the belief that the disabilities of severe mental
illness lead to homelessness is the conviction that mental health
services should enable patients to overcome their disabilities and
thereby allow them to be domiciled in the community. From this
perspective, the increase in the occurrence of homelessness
among the mentally ill is taken as evidence of the failure of
community-based services and the policy of deinstitutionaliza-

tion. However, it is unlikely that the current practice of deinstitutionalization and community-based care is the primary reason for homelessness among the severely mentally ill. . . .

Housing and Jobs

The years since the mid-1970s have been characterized by marked social, political, and economic changes, which are much more likely to have contributed to the dramatic increase in homelessness in general, as well as among those with mental illness. For example, there has been a rapid decline in the availability of low-cost housing. J.D. Wright and J.A. Lam observed that at this stage of American history there is simply not sufficient low-income housing to accommodate the poor population; consequently, "the new homeless are largely victims of a housing market that is assuredly not of their own making." Data suggest that most homeless mentally ill persons lost their rooms in single-room-occupancy hotels or low-priced apartments not because of psychoticism but because they 1) were evicted because of renewal projects and fires, 2) were victimized by unscrupulous landlords or by other residents, or 3) could no longer afford the rent. . . .

Other major socioeconomic dislocations that have occurred since the mid-1970s include the loss of many manufacturing jobs, which have been replaced, if at all, by low-wage service positions, and the Reagan administration's targeting of social welfare programs, which led to the elimination or reduction (actual or secondary to inflation) of social welfare benefits. It is important to note that these dislocations and their effects were not randomly distributed throughout the population. Rather, during the 1980s poor and marginal populations suffered further deprivation. As a result, the nature, form, and distribution of poverty in the United States has shifted substantially in the last 20 years. The upsurge in homelessness is one example of these changes and may be best seen as the most extreme form of this new destitution. As might be expected, people of color have been differentially affected by these socioeconomic processes. For example, the percentage of poor African-Americans living in extremely poor neighborhoods increased from 25% to 40% during the 1980s. Changes of this kind account for the disproportionately high numbers of African-Americans and Latinos among the homeless, a finding that has been documented in numerous studies.

A Part of the "Underclass"

Persons with severe and persistent mental illness have been excessively burdened by these dislocations because of their symptoms, disabilities, lack of resources, dependence on others, and susceptibility to stigma, neglect, and victimization. This vulnerability has been compounded as the historical safety net for at-risk individuals provided by families and community supports has been torn asunder by the weight of poverty and its associated pathologies, such as drug use, crime, violence, and disease. Consequently, the population of severely mentally ill living in the community has been swept along with other relatively powerless and vulnerable populations, such as poor African-Americans, into increasing poverty, resourcelessness, and homelessness, to become a part of a destitute population referred to by some as the "underclass."

These processes recall longstanding historical forces in industrial society. For example, Michel Foucault noted that in seventeenth-century France such forces "seemed to assign the same homeland to the poor, to the unemployed prisoners, and to the insane." Thus, along with other homeless groups, the homeless mentally ill must first be seen as impoverished and disenfranchised, rather than diseased. From this perspective, the policy of deinstitutionalization is important because once mentally ill persons are released into the community, they are exposed to these detrimental forces. Many homeless persons with mental illness also see things this way. In a study conducted in Ohio, homeless mentally ill people identified their economic and social problems, rather than symptoms of mental illness, as the principal reasons for their homelessness. . . .

Miscommunication and Misunderstandings

Mainstream psychiatry's relatively recent recognition that homeless persons with psychiatric problems may benefit from assertive, comprehensive, and coordinated psychiatric and social welfare services is commendable. Nevertheless, it is frequently reported that the mentally ill homeless refuse these services. Before we conclude that their resistance to these services arises from their disordered thinking, we must first examine the manner in which services are offered. Although well-intentioned, psychiatry has tended to focus primarily on the psychiatric deficits of homeless people to the relative exclusion of their shared social environments, their individual and collective strengths, and their essential rights and privileges as citizens. As a result, the strategy used has been paternalistic (or maternalistic) rather than focused on context, entitlement, and empowerment. The former approach frequently engenders feelings of humiliation, although this is not fully appreciated by most service providers. As George Orwell observed in 1933, "A man receiving charity practically always hates his benefactor—it is a fixed characteristic of human nature." Because psychiatry has focused almost exclusively on pathology, there is a lack of understanding of the living conditions and life attitudes of people occupying the margins of society, leading to substantial miscommunication and misunderstandings between service providers and the served.

The problems of disempowerment and stigma are also exacerbated by psychiatry's concentration on disease and its subsequent emphasis on directing mental health services to those whose conditions meet certain criteria for chronic mental illness. This creates problems because many homeless emotionally distressed or disabled people, chronically mentally ill or not, do not view themselves as mentally ill, and some have had previous negative experiences with mental health care systems. For example, a consumer-oriented survey by P. Goering et al. indicated that part of the reason for the presumed resistance to accepting services was an incongruence between the client's priorities and the mental health services offered. Many of the homeless mentally ill persons surveyed felt disenfranchised and exhibited considerable antipathy toward any formal system. Like most people, the homeless mentally ill generally desired a safe, comfortable home and did not wish to be segregated in residences for the mentally ill, which they perceived as dangerous and stigmatizing. Hence, the form and content of disease-focused services as presently constituted often reflect insensitivity to the desires, experiences, and social world of homeless people in psychiatric distress—a point that has sometimes been missed by those (e.g., the APA Task Force on the Homeless Mentally Ill) who have viewed these individuals as primarily a subgroup of the chronic mentally ill.

Involuntary Hospitalization Is Rarely Justifiable

The failure of current approaches to engage the homeless mentally ill in services and get them off the streets has led to a mounting call by some for their involuntary hospitalization. Embedded in this demand is a belief that civil libertarians have created a situation in which the homeless mentally ill have become too entitled and are protected by stringent commitment laws that allow them to follow their own wishes and, as a result, permit them to perish in the streets with "their rights on."

Although we concur with the notion that mentally ill homeless persons who are incompetent to make decisions about accepting treatment, who are dangerous to themselves or others, or who are gravely disabled should be hospitalized against their wills, in actuality few mentally ill homeless persons meet these criteria unless the criteria are stretched beyond their intended meanings and thereby threaten the protection of human rights. In fact, an examination of data from Project Help in New York City—which is often cited as a model program for involuntary hospitalization because of its broader definitions of dangerousness to self or others—reveals that roughly two-thirds of the

An Economic Problem

What has caused the phenomenon of the still rapidly increasing new homeless? Certainly not deinstitutionalization. . . .

Most informed observers point to economic policies and issues as core causes of the new homelessness. . . . Several relate directly to housing. The first is the elimination of low-cost housing through urban renewal, removing single-room-occupancy (SRO) hotels. A second is the outcome of several small recessions during the 1980s, which resulted in fewer housing starts and placed new homes outside the reach of the middle class and led them to renovate older housing ("buying down") or to purchase condominiums converted from former apartment houses. The net effect was to put housing, including rentals, outside the purchasing power of the poor and the near poor. Third, the Reagan administration tried hard to eliminate the federal subsidy of low-cost housing, although not with complete success.

Another set of issues concerns income of the poor and near poor: regressive tax policies; reduction of welfare real income, such as Aid to Families with Dependent Children (AFDC), through inflation; and attempts to reduce welfare rolls, including attempts to reduce the number of mentally ill people receiving Supplemental Security Income (SSI).

A third set of economic variables relates to rapidly increasing costs of health care, which, combined with a large number of uninsured people, puts even routine preventive health care beyond the reach of 25% of the U.S. population.

The conclusion I reach when reviewing the recent literature on homelessness is that the principal public policy problems are economic ones, not psychological ones.

Charles A. Kiesler, *American Psychologist*, November 1991.

---

homeless persons targeted for hospitalization by Project Help were ultimately deemed unqualified for involuntary hospitalization. Comments by staff of Project Help are revealing: "Many of the homeless are overtly psychotic, yet have adapted to the life in the streets and are not at significant risk." Similarly, D.A. Snow et al. found that "efforts of the homeless mentally ill to survive on the streets are not as chaotic or as irrational as they appear from a distance." Several well-designed studies have supported these observations, showing that only 5%-7% of single adult homeless persons are in need of acute inpatient care.

Yet there is a grain of truth in the observation that being entitled to stay out of institutions is a real problem for the homeless mentally ill and society. However, unlike those who focus first on mental illness and believe that the homeless mentally ill have too many rights, our focus on homelessness reveals that the mentally ill homeless, like the rest of the homeless, do not have enough rights. Their right to be truly in the community is merely theoretical until they have procured the legal, political, therapeutic, and economic means necessary to construct and maintain a secure niche within the community.

A Wider Net

Emphasizing homelessness challenges the current scope and nature of psychiatric concern and practice with homeless populations. It calls for the profession, along with others, to cast a wider net so as to recognize and address the broad social and psychiatric causes and effects of homelessness and destitution, helping the homeless to solve their problems and to build a new, more humane niche for themselves in society. Among other things, this necessitates a restructuring of clinical encounters with patients so that they are less paternalistic and disease oriented and are more focused on empowering individuals and groups to solve their problems by eliciting sources of health and strength. This perspective recognizes that individual-oriented clinical and social services are not sufficient in themselves. Rather, they must be integrated with a range of social psychiatric interventions that are akin to the strategies used with refugees, displaced persons, and persons experiencing extreme life stressors, such as combat veterans, cancer survivors, and disaster victims. Thus, in addition to clinical attention on the individual level, this entails the kinds of systems-level interventions advocated by mental health professionals in communities that have endured major catastrophes or other forms of social instability. Examples of this work are 1) the establishment of settings that provide permanent independent living with ongoing social supports and 2) an effort by one of us (K.S.T.) and others to establish a therapeutic community in a men's shelter. On a much larger scale, an example of this kind of approach can be found in the report "To Build a Community," produced by the Los Angeles Citizens' Task Force on Central City East, an area of Los Angeles where the homeless congregate. In addition to traditional community mental health services, the report called for large-scale preventive projects to identify at-risk individuals, community development programs including conflict management and consensus building, and close collaboration with universities to develop model service programs.

"Is caring for people too sick to know they need care truly a violation of their freedom?"

The Homeless Mentally Ill Should Be Institutionalized

A.M. Rosenthal and Richard Cohen

A.M. Rosenthal is a columnist for the *New York Times*. In Part I of the following viewpoint, he argues that the problem of the homeless mentally ill is the consequence of the emptying of the state mental hospitals that began in the mid-1950s. He objects to laws that grant seriously mentally ill people the right to refuse treatment and live on the streets. In Part II, Richard Cohen, a columnist for the *Washington Post*, concludes that the homeless mentally ill should be institutionalized for their own safety and for the benefit of society.

As you read, consider the following questions:

1. According to Rosenthal, if society decided to adequately care for the homeless mentally ill, where would the money have to come from?
2. According to Cohen, why would a more effective outreach system not have helped Yetta Adams?

A.M. Rosenthal, "On My Mind: Park Avenue Lady," *The New York Times*, November 23, 1990. Copyright ©1990 by The New York Times Company. Reprinted by permission. Richard Cohen, "Forced Shelter," *The Washington Post Weekly Edition*, December 13-19, 1993, ©1994, The Washington Post Writers Group. Reprinted with permission.

I

On a fine autumn morning in New York, just before Thanksgiving, when the streets were full of handsomely dressed people
off to work, a gray-haired woman about 60 years old stepped off
the curb at Park Avenue and 67th Street, raised her dress, bared
herself, and defecated in the gutter.

I did what everybody else did. I turned my head in disgust
and walked away toward the office. But that morning I found it
a little harder to walk away from the mentally ill of the city.

A demented man was stretched on his back, near Madison
Avenue, eight blocks south of the woman in the Park Avenue gutter, shouting out loud to the demons of his mind. A mile on, a
few steps away from the office, a woman lay in a doorway as she
does every day, in filth of body and pain of mind. She clutched
the bottle of liquor almost never out of hand—the gift of death by
poison that passers-by give to her with their coins. . . .

I have seen the Park Avenue lady and the raw-faced woman in
the doorway in Chicago, San Francisco, Los Angeles, Houston,
Miami. If you travel America, try getting away from the homeless mentally ill—try.

How Did We Get Here?

How did we get to this point, where Americans calmly accept
the fact that we cannot deal decently with scores of thousands
of destitute Americans who suffer so desperately in their minds
that they cry their pain in the streets, where we send them to
live? When and why did this country accept madness in the
streets as part of the city scenery, turn its back on the deeply
disturbed, unless they happened to defecate in front of our deli-
cate eyes? In the mid-50's, there were more than 550,000 patients in American public mental health hospitals. [In 1990
there were] about 100,000.

The public saw the mental hospitals as snake pits. Some were
and some were not, but closing them was supposed to save the
states a nice pile of tax money. A little later, tranquilizer drugs
speeded the emptying of the wards. But on the streets, without
care or attention, the mentally disturbed did not take the drugs,
and regressed rapidly.

The idea was to give the mentally ill post-hospital care in
halfway houses or community centers. Officials and taxpayers
never came up with enough money. When the hospitals closed,
the mentally ill poor went into the street. That helped push at
least a third of them into even more nightmare worlds—alcoholism and drug addiction.

They found friends—organizations and individuals who try to
help them get off the streets. But God help them, they also
found some "advocates" who insist that living on the sidewalk

month in month out, freezing or baking, the prey of human street rats, eating garbage, and refusing treatment or even food and shelter is an acceptable alternative life style. As long as they do not commit a serious crime—not just the misdemeanor of befouling private or public property—they have the right to live in the streets and the right to die there.

Is This Sanity?

Some advocates argue that there is no such thing as mental illness, just another way of looking at reality. Maybe they are right. Is what we have come to accept really sanity—that mental illness is a right to be exercised to the point of suicide rather than a disease demanding medical care for the victim?

The Population of U.S. Public Mental Hospitals

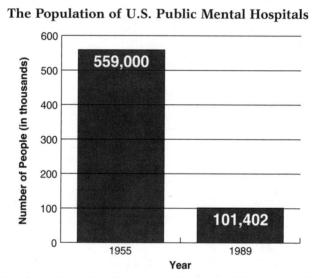

Source: David A. Rochefort, *From Poorhouses to Homelessness: Policy Analysis and Mental Health Care*, 1993.

Is it sanity to say that if you are bleeding from a car accident an ambulance will take you away, but if you are bleeding from the mind you can lie there until you rot?

Is caring for people too sick to know they need care truly a violation of their freedom?

It is a disservice to all the homeless to lump their problems together. That makes homelessness seem unsolvable, when it is not.

The economically destitute homeless need economic help—and can respond to it as members of society, not some murky, psychically troubled, mysterious underclass.

The addicts or mentally disturbed—estimated at 70 percent of the homeless—need a range of treatments if they are to escape the streets into decent housing. Is it beyond the American legal and medical mind to provide that help even to those who do not grasp that they need it?

If we won't put enough taxes—yes, taxes—or attention into doing the job, let's have the honesty not to blame the Governor or Mayor. Let's just shut up, keep on walking away from the lady on Park Avenue, and enjoy our next Thanksgiving.

II

On Monday, Nov. 29, 1993, a homeless woman by the name of Yetta Adams was found dead on a bus shelter bench near the headquarters of the Department of Housing and Urban Development. It is HUD, of course, that is charged with the federal government's program for the homeless, and so the irony of Adams's death was not lost on anyone. She was 43 years old and had succumbed on a cold night

But it was not a freezing night. (The low hit 34). And she was not destitute, because $300 was found on her body. She did not die because of a lack of shelter, because she had been living in one and left only a week before. She was not even alone in Washington. Her family lives here—a brother and three grown children. This was her town.

In many respects, Yetta Adams was the archetypal homeless person, which is to say that her problem was not a lack of shelter. She died not because the city had no bed for her but because she chose not to occupy it. She was, it now seems, a mentally incapacitated person and an alcoholic as well. During the 13 years she lived on and off in shelters, she was occasionally disruptive, refused to follow any rules and from time to time was asked to leave. You or I might call her crazy, hardly a term of any precision, but that's what she was.

An Inappropriate Response

None of the details about Adams would be news to the federal and local officials who deal with the homeless. Yet her death triggered a spasm of guilt, which, while not entirely undeserved, does not really fit the facts of her case. Following Adams's death, HUD Secretary Henry Cisneros convened an emergency meeting and advanced the District of Columbia "several hundred thousand dollars" of the money it was going to get for its homeless program. . . . Cisneros essentially argues that everyone—the city and the federal government—has to do more.

He has a point—but not much of one. Possibly, if the city had a more effective outreach program, Adams would have been found and enticed into a shelter. I say possibly, since she already knew where the shelters were, had stayed in them and, for some reason, refused to go back. The chances are, in fact, that outreach would not have done a bit of good. The woman was deranged, a diagnosis I make on the basis of common sense. When you have a bed to go to, when you have $300 in your pocket, you do not spend the night on the street in cold weather.

But what neither Cisneros nor city officials said—not in their statements nor in their writings—was that the remedy for the problem of the so-called homeless might not be more money, even money more efficiently spent. What they did not say, in other words, was that there might not be a remedy—not as long as society grants the alcoholic, the drug addicted and the addled the civil right to live (and sometimes die) on the streets. None of them questioned the very notion that a population of drug addicts, alcoholics and schizophrenics (up to 85 percent of the homeless) could be treated in any other way but placing them in the sort of institutions where they were once housed.

Making Things Worse?

The law, of course, does not permit the forced incarceration of people who, no matter how deranged they might be, are not a threat to themselves or others. But the law ought to look at the Yetta Adams case and wonder if it is not making things worse instead of better. Clearly crazy, she was permitted to wander off and live, as best she could, on the streets. A child would not be granted those rights. Why treat an adult who acts like a child any differently?

Those of us who can remember the days when mental hospitals were stuffed with people held against their will can also remember the occasional exposes of conditions in those institutions. All of that would happen again. American society has not so radically changed since deinstitutionalization was implemented that mental hospitals and the like would now become radically different institutions, staffed always by gentle and solicitous people. Make no mistake about it, to go back to the ways things were is to go back to how they were bad.

But these mentally ill homeless are suffering anyway. When, on a cold night, I walk around this or any other city and see people lying in doorways on beds of cardboard and under newspaper blankets, I cannot really conclude that they are better off than in an institution. As for the cities themselves, they are worse off—their civic life, if not their civility, soiled by the presence of countless beggars. There is no good solution to the problem of the so-called "homeless." The least bad one, though, is to put them back in institutions. Had that happened, Yetta Adams might still be alive.

"There will be no magic in reinstitutionalizing the homeless mentally ill."

The Homeless Mentally Ill Should Not Be Institutionalized

Joel Blau

In the following viewpoint, Joel Blau disputes the popular belief that deinstitutionalization (the large-scale release of patients from state mental hospitals that began in the 1950s) is responsible for the increase of homelessness that started in the 1980s. Blau argues that American society has never adequately cared for the mentally ill either inside or outside of institutions. He contends that rather than institutionalization, the homeless mentally ill need a comprehensive system of services that includes psychiatric care and supervision tailored to individual need. Blau is an assistant professor at the School of Social Welfare at the State University of New York in Stonybrook and the author of *The Visible Poor*, from which the following viewpoint is excerpted.

As you read, consider the following questions:

1. What two factors account for the cycles in attitudes toward the mentally ill, according to the author?
2. According to Blau, why would reinstitutionalizing the mentally ill be futile?

Excerpted from pp. 85-89 of *The Visible Poor: Homelessness in the United States* by Joel Blau, ©1992 by Oxford University Press, Inc. Reprinted by permission of Oxford University Press, Inc.

It has long been customary to assert that . . . the policy of de-institutionalization [the large-scale release of patients from state mental hospitals that began in the 1950s] . . . must be a primary cause of homelessness. First heard when homelessness proliferated in the early 1980s, this argument got weaker with the passage of time. Sixty-five percent of the decline in the hospital census had already occurred before 1975. Deinstitutionalization therefore cannot explain very much about the spread of homelessness one decade later. Clearly, by the early 1990s, when 40 percent of the homeless consisted of families, and upwards of 100,000 children were without shelter, even federal agencies such as the National Institute of Mental Health were reporting to Congress that deinstitutionalization had played a comparatively small role.

A Texas study attests to its limited impact. Between 1979 and 1984, the institutionalized population in the state declined by 10.5 percent, from 5,508 to 4,928 people. At the same time, however, the number of Salvation Army users jumped from 4,938 to 11,271 people, or 128 percent. Although mental hospitals did set stricter requirements for admission, it would still stretch anyone's powers of argumentation to explain how a five year decline of 580 people yielded a 6,333 person increase in the number of those who turned for help to the Salvation Army.

The passage of time and better current behavior add to the doubts about the relationship between homelessness and previous institutionalization. Although 22 percent of the population had been institutionalized in one Berkeley study, slightly less than half had been released five or more years before. Deinstitutionalization may have made them vulnerable, but it was other events that made them homeless. Similarly, while 29.9 percent of an Ohio study had spent time in an institution, interviewers judged less than 5 percent to be currently in need of hospitalization. The coincidence of homelessness and deinstitutionalization is indisputable, but a causal relationship of real significance is hard to detect.

Deinstitutionalization Overemphasized

What ultimately disproves the hypothesis of deinstitutionalization as an explanation of homelessness are the research data on psychiatric hospitalization. In thirteen studies of the previously institutionalized among the homeless conducted in cities throughout the United States, the proportion of the homeless population ranged from 11.2 to 33.2 percent. The low and high figures—both of which come from New York—encompass a relatively narrow set of results from other cities including Los Angeles, 14.8 percent (1986) and 20 percent (1985); Chicago, 23 percent in 1983 and 1986, and Detroit, 26 percent in 1985. The implications of this data are unequivocal: deinstitutionalization has contributed to homelessness, but since the vast majority of homeless people have never been in a psychiatric institution, most explanations substantially overemphasize it as a cause.

Previous psychiatric hospitalization is, of course, a poor indicator of the prevalence of mental illness within the homeless population. Moreover, one could well argue that fewer people have histories of previous hospitalization precisely because deinstitutionalization has tightened the standards for admission. But this argument would miss the larger point. Even if fewer people carry with them the stigma of a former inpatient, the psychological and the social symptoms of homelessness are hopelessly intertwined. This is not to say that mental illness does not exist among the homeless population, or to deny that in some cases, psychosis has pushed some people toward homelessness. It is, however, to warn against an overly psychological interpretation of a social problem, especially when, despite numerous flaws, that interpretation has been repeatedly deployed to explain the problem away.

The Musical Chairs of Housing

But if deinstitutionalization and, more generally, mental illness do not deserve the prominence they usually receive, the incidence of mental illness among the homeless does highlight the changes in their plight. Most mentally ill people are not homeless; neither, to be sure, are most poor people. In both groups, however, the growth of homelessness suggests that inadequate shelter is what has put them at risk. Though each confronts a shortage of affordable housing, a lack of affordable housing with adequate supportive services compounds this shortage for the mentally ill. A loss of SRO [single-room-occupancy] hotels affects both the poor and the mentally ill; the shortage of community residences leaves the mentally ill trapped in a still tougher game, the housing equivalent of musical chairs.

This is a game for which the players are particularly ill-equipped. While a direct route from an institution to the street is not their usual path to homelessness, they are vulnerable to defeat by any crisis or personal catastrophe, from the public assistance check that fails to arrive to the medical emergency that they cannot handle. Although poor people with greater emotional resiliency might cope successfully with these events, the mentally ill cannot. Increasingly, in the United States, homelessness is the punishment for this failure.

Sweep the Streets Clean?

Deinstitutionalization, then, is not a proximate cause of homelessness. While mental illness bears a closer relationship, it, too,

187

is clouded by its interaction with the social consequences—the hunger, sleeplessness, and anxiety—of lacking a home. For those who believe in the prevalence of mental illness among the homeless, these conclusions create two problems. First, they dilute the power of mental illness to explain homelessness as a public issue, and second, they do not get the most conspicuously mentally ill off the streets. Only reinstitutionalization would do that, and it, according to its most enthusiastic advocates, would virtually sweep the streets clean.

A Step Backward

Reinstitutionalization is a step backward in our commitment to progressive service-support systems. We do not doubt that a small number of the service-dependent will always require a secluded, protected living situation; but there is no need—either economic or therapeutic—for such quarters to be provided in large-scale institutions. The onus should be on the advocates of reinstitutionalization to demonstrate the requirement for "new asylums" and we are frankly pessimistic that such demonstrations can be made.

Michael J. Dear and Jennifer R. Wolch, *Landscapes of Despair: From Deinstitutionalization to Homelessness*, 1988.

Several well-publicized cases have been instrumental in broadening the appeal of reinstitutionalization. In 1978, Angus McFarlane, a resident of Pierce County, Washington, murdered an elderly couple in his neighborhood after he was denied voluntary admission to a state mental hospital. The resulting clamor brought about passage of the 1979 Involuntary Treatment Act, which eased commitment standards. A similar controversy arose in 1986, when Juan Gonzalez, a homeless man who had been staying in the shelter at New York City's Fort Washington Armory, was held briefly in the emergency room of Columbia Presbyterian Medical Center. Crying "Jesus wants me to kill," Gonzalez was so disturbed that four doses of an antipsychotic drug had to be administered to him in the space of ninety minutes. Although Gonzalez actually signed a voluntary commitment form, the hospital released him after forty-eight hours because its psychiatric service was overcrowded. Two days later, Gonzalez used a sword purchased in a Times Square souvenir shop to kill two passengers on the Staten Island ferry. Together with the widespread visibility of the homeless mentally ill, cases like these sensitized the public. As a result, by the time a debate erupted in 1988 about Joyce Brown's [a mentally ill homeless woman] "right" to live on a New York City street, it was mental health, and not merely violence, that had crystallized popular feelings.

Out of the sentiment that deinstitutionalization had gone too far came a campaign to recommit both the dangerous and the seriously disturbed. Acting on this change in public opinion, five states besides Washington—Alaska, North Carolina, Texas, Arizona, and Hawaii—have revised their commitment laws, and a number of other states have [considered] such revisions. As part of the vanguard to reinstitutionalize, the decision of these states suggests that the United States may well be beginning what can only be described as another period of reform.

The Cycles of Treatment

In the United States, attitudes toward the mentally ill have always run in cycles. At one end of the cycle, we attribute the causes of mental illness to the society at large, as we did in the 1830s. At the other end of the cycle, we discharge patients because we see institutions as contributing to mental illness. There are really two issues here. One revolves around changes in public sentiment about who is more at fault—the society outside the institutions or the institutions themselves. But underpinning this issue is a second consideration. Chronic mental illness is an intractable problem for which there is no sure remedy. Imputing the failure to the locus of care, we have consistently oscillated between institutional and noninstitutional modes of treatment. Neither works very well. In the next cycle, we then hope that the other mode of treatment will be more successful, or at least substantially cheaper.

Quality vs. Location

The issue, then, is the quality, rather than the locus, of care. Just a small minority of people are dangerous enough to necessitate commitment to an institution. For everyone else, a high quality of care does not depend on its delivery at a particular site. Good care could be given in a mental hospital; good care could be provided in the community. We might well prefer the latter for civil libertarian reasons, on the principle of the least restrictive environment. Yet a larger problem looms. The problem is that, with some notable exceptions, adequate care in the United States has never really been provided at either site.

The commingling of the poor and the mentally ill has always been the most damning index of this failure. The mentally ill were thrown into almshouses with the poor throughout the nineteenth century. Although reformers periodically tried to separate them, the mentally ill rarely resided in an institution devoted solely to their own needs. When counties transferred aged senile people to the state mental asylums in the early 1900s, they exacerbated the problem. The centralization of power within the state government sanctioned a model of the mental hospital that maintained rather than cared for the patient. Containment of the most disruptive poor was a none too hidden advantage of this custodial arrangement.

No Magic

A history in which long periods of shabby treatment follow closely on the occasional cry of outrage comes equipped with its own warning. There was no magic in deinstitutionalization of mental patients, and there will be no magic in reinstitutionalizing the homeless mentally ill. When Washington enacted the first flexible commitment laws, involuntary commitments doubled within two years. The new patients nevertheless received very little treatment. In effect, a scarcity of resources replicated exactly those conditions that had initially prompted the movement to deinstitutionalize.

Without new resources, the campaign to send the homeless mentally ill back to an institution implies the existence of a quality of care that has yet to be forthcoming. Since history is not very reassuring on this account, reinstitutionalization can be seen for what it is: misdiagnosing the causes of homelessness, it misprescribes the solution. The drive to reinstitutionalize the homeless therefore suffers from a very large credibility gap. Those in the movement with a short historical memory may genuinely believe that the homeless as a group would receive better care in an institution. But overall, it is hard to resist the conclusion that the main goal of the campaign to reinstitutionalize is simply to get the homeless off the streets and out of public view.

A Multitiered Approach

If quality of care is the true objective, reinstitutionalization and the current fragmented system cannot be serious alternatives. For this purpose, the homeless mentally ill need a multitiered approach like that recommended by the 1984 Task Force on the Homeless Mentally Ill of the American Psychiatric Association. Insisting first on the provision of adequate food, shelter, and clothing, the association argued for a comprehensive, integrated model of care. This model would include readily accessible psychiatric services along with a range of supervised community settings appropriate to each individual's needs. To avoid a major pitfall of deinstitutionalization, case managers would be responsible for ensuring that no one fell between the cracks.

Ideally, this system would provide superior services to both the homeless mentally ill and to everyone else who needed help with their emotional problems. It would universalize mental health services and remove the stigma from those seeking assistance. True, in the short run, it would be more expensive. But a large part of these expenses derive from addressing social costs that were previously unacknowledged: the emotional difficulties visible on the street, as well as the emotional difficulties hidden at home. The homeless mentally ill are not the only people who need help. Both for them and for everyone else, a comprehensive multitiered approach would represent the best alternative.

Periodical Bibliography

The following articles have been selected to supplement the diverse views presented in this chapter.

American Psychiatric
Association

"General Directions for Public Policy in Behalf of the Mentally Ill Among the Homeless Population: An Interim Report by the Task Force on the Homeless Mentally Ill of the American Psychiatric Association," Spring 1990. Available from 1400 K St. NW, Washington, DC 20005.

Gabriel Constans

"This Is Madness: Our Failure to Provide Adequate Care for the Mentally Ill," *USA Today*, November 1991.

Albert R. Hunt

"A New Focus to the Homeless Problem," *The Wall Street Journal*, December 9, 1993.

Interagency Council
on the Homeless

"Outcasts on Main Street: Report of the Federal Task Force on Homelessness and Severe Mental Illness," February 1992. Available from the Center for Mental Health Services, Office of Consumer, Family and Public Information, 5600 Fishers Ln., Rm. 15-99, Rockville, MD 20857.

Tamar Jacoby

"Thinking About the Homeless," *Dissent*, Spring 1991.

Charles A. Kiesler

"Homelessness and Public Policy Priorities," *American Psychologist*, November 1991.

H. Richard Lamb and
Doris M. Lamb

"Factors Contributing to Homelessness Among the Chronically and Severely Mentally Ill," *Hospital and Community Psychiatry*, March 1990. Available from the American Psychiatric Association, 1400 K St. NW, Washington, DC 20005.

Elizabeth O'Connor

"Our Rag-Bone Hearts," *The Sun*, September 1993. Available from 107 N. Roberson St., Chapel Hill, NC 27516.

Laurence Schiff

"Would They Be Better Off in a Home?" *National Review*, March 5, 1990.

Anastasia Toufexis

"From the Asylum to Anarchy," *Time*, October 22, 1990.

U.S. Conference
of Mayors

"Mentally Ill and Homeless: A Twenty-two City Survey," November 1991. Available from 1620 I St. NW, Washington, DC 20006.

How Should the Legal System Deal with Mental Illness?

Mental Illness

Chapter Preface

The insanity defense is based on the belief that a person should not be held legally responsible for a crime he commits while suffering from a disabling mental condition. In most of the United States, a defendant can be found legally insane if, at the time of the crime, either he didn't know what he was doing or he couldn't distinguish right from wrong. In some states, the inability to control one's behavior also constitutes legal insanity. The insanity defense drew national attention in 1982, when John W. Hinckley Jr. was acquitted of the attempted assassination of President Ronald Reagan on the grounds of insanity.

Many critics argue that the insanity defense is a charade that allows criminals to evade responsibility for their actions by blaming their behavior on fictional mental disorders. For example, many objected in 1992 when Jeffrey Dahmer pleaded guilty but insane to the grisly murders of fifteen men and boys. Although the jury rejected Dahmer's plea and sentenced him to fifteen consecutive life prison terms, many people used his case to criticize the insanity defense. Thomas Szasz, a leading skeptic of the psychiatric profession, wrote that "Dahmer's trial highlights our deep-seated unwillingness to face the basic facts of human nature and our eagerness instead to conceal the moral agency and personal responsibility of evildoers behind an impenetrable screen of legal fictions and literalized medical metaphors."

Others reject the popular belief that the insanity defense is a ruse staged by criminals trying to escape punishment. They point out that the defense is rarely used; and that when it is employed, it is usually unsuccessful. Eloise Salholz and Susan Miller write in *Newsweek* magazine that "few felons actually 'get off' thanks to the insanity plea." Moreover, according to Lincoln Caplan, the author of *The Insanity Defense and the Trial of John W. Hinckley, Jr.*, most people who plead insanity truly are insane. He cites a study by Policy Research Associates, a private social policy research company, that found that in eight states between 1976 and 1987, "the vast majority of people who used the insanity defense were seriously mentally ill." Therefore, according to Caplan, "The insanity defense shouldn't be misconstrued as an easy out and falsely blamed for crime, irresponsibility or other social ills."

Whether the insanity defense is an "easy out" for criminals or a legitimate legal safeguard, it is an issue of fervent debate. The insanity defense is one of the topics discussed in the following chapter on mental illness and the legal system.

"Being mentally ill does not increase one's civil rights."

Mental Patients' Rights Should Be Limited

Richard W. White Jr.

Since the 1970s, legal advocates have secured extensive legal rights for mental patients—including the right to refuse treatment unless they are a danger to themselves or others. In the following viewpoint, Richard W. White Jr. opposes such advocacy. He argues that because mentally ill individuals are unable to make appropriate decisions, granting them the right to refuse needed treatment merely allows their suffering to continue unabated. White is a research scholar at the Institute for Contemporary Studies, a public policy research group in San Francisco, and the author of *Rude Awakenings: What the Homeless Crisis Tells Us*, from which this viewpoint is excerpted.

As you read, consider the following questions:

1. What is the "patient liberation bar," according to the author?
2. According to White, what was the hidden agenda behind the *Wyatt* v. *Stickney* case?
3. What percentage of all societies is dysfunctional, according to Blake Fleetwood as quoted by the author?

From pp. 30-36, 38-40 of *Rude Awakenings: What the Homeless Crisis Tells Us* by Richard W. White Jr. San Francisco, CA: ICS Press, 1992. Copyright 1992 by Richard W. White Jr. Reprinted with permission.

When the definitive history of America in the late twentieth century is written, I believe that it will lay much blame at the feet of our trial lawyers, particularly those dedicated young attorneys who have forgone high incomes to sue on behalf of what they perceive to be the rights of the poor and powerless. A generation of law school graduates has fought to establish the contradictory principles that various classes of individuals are entitled by right to government benefits and that the rest of society has no right to expect them to do anything in return. In the early 1970s, the mentally ill were identified by these lawyers as an overlooked group of the oppressed—first in need of liberation from mental institutions; then with a right to food, shelter, and treatment; later with a right to live outside in public places if they wished; and then with a right to refuse treatment. Nowhere in all this assertion of rights did anyone consider that the seriously mentally ill often cannot form a reasoned opinion and will suffer and perhaps die in misery unless someone else takes charge. These lawyers give no heed to the role of natural institutions in caring for their members. Instead of the family, friends, or caring professionals deciding with—and, where necessary, for—the patient on issues of treatment or confinement, mental patients themselves would make such decisions. Moreover, lawyers would protect their right to this alleged control over their own lives.

The "Patient Liberation Bar"

In *Madness in the Streets* (1990), Rael Jean Isaac and Virginia C. Armat provide a complete and fascinating narrative of how psychiatry and the law abandoned the mentally ill. Much of their story describes how these devoted attorneys—Isaac and Armat call them the "patient liberation bar"—have striven with great effectiveness and disastrous consequences to protect the rights of the mentally ill from abridgment by the police, psychiatrists, their own parents, and others seen to be acting on behalf of an oppressive system. It serves this bar's ideological biases to believe the writings of Thomas Szasz, Erving Goffman, and academics who either deny the existence of mental illness or see it as caused environmentally—by parents who raise their children badly or by other elements of the system against which they are trying to protect their mentally ill clients.

In 1984, the American Psychiatric Association (APA) published the results of an extensive task force study it had carried out on the homeless mentally ill. The report, *The Homeless Mentally Ill*, shows how pressure from these attorneys has vitiated care for the mentally ill: in fact, the adversary system of our courts has displaced the very cooperation among persons and agencies needed to help these unfortunates. The judiciary, says the report, "values an adversary process, not a collaborative one."

Moreover, "when facing uncertainty about an individual, [the field of] medicine increases its supervisory and observational vigilance, whereas the judiciary tends to free the individual."

This approach would be fine if Szasz were right that mental illness is simply a fiction used in the United States to control deviates. But he is tragically wrong.

In the Interest of No One

According to the APA report, since the late 1970s these lawyers have been increasingly assertive in representing the patients' stated wishes, whether or not their disease enables them to form a reasoned judgment. Citing legal precedents, the APA notes that the law does not require one's attorney to advocate his expressed wishes. In cases of the seriously mentally ill, to do so is frequently in the interest of no one—not the patient, not the people around the patient, and not society at large. While it makes sense for persons with other kinds of disease, for instance, heart patients, to accept or reject treatment, much as this prerogative may frustrate caring medical professionals or family members, it is not the same thing when a mental patient decides. In the words of Isaac and Armat,

> when the diseased organ is the brain, the afflicted individual cannot make the reasoned decisions regarding treatment that a cardiac patient can be expected to make. Nor does heart disease produce the disordered, sometimes dangerous behavior characteristic of mental illness.

Isaac and Armat describe how these lawyers through dedication and skill changed the law, public opinion, and professional practice so that today tens of thousands of mentally ill who otherwise would be in treatment and living lives as normal as possible are instead alienated from families and friends, living in loneliness, fear, and filth and committing violence upon themselves and others. The authors report that studies since deinstitutionalization began show "consistently higher arrest rates for mental patients and higher rates for violent crime." The pattern of findings, they say, "is too consistent for serious challenge." Because of our policies, the rates of violent crime among former patients are several times higher than those for the general population. These problems need not occur, according to E. Fuller Torrey, Isaac and Armat, and many others I have interviewed, if patients were treated in a collaborative system instead of "freed" from coercion in an adversary system. Where appropriate decisions can be made on treatment and confinement and enforced, mental patients need be no more dangerous on the average to themselves or to others than anyone else.

Early on, the goal of the young lawyers was to establish the rights of patients in mental hospitals. A case brought by the

Greater Boston Legal Services (GBLS) ensured the right of patients in these hospitals to refuse treatment. A huge potential
source of revenue to support the movement was uncovered, as
over a million dollars in attorneys' fees was granted to GBLS. One
agency funded by the government (the federal Legal Services
Corporation) sued another agency funded by the government (the
state hospital); the taxpayers paid for both sides of the case and
then also paid the legal fees assessed against the losing side.

Going a step further, the New York Civil Liberties Union
passed a resolution calling involuntary hospitalization incompatible with the principles of a free society. Around this resolution,
attorneys were organized; conferences were held across the
country and lawsuits pursued, some of them successfully. The
arguments presented were often brilliant: time and again it was
demonstrated that psychiatrists were frequently mistaken in
their diagnoses, were poor at predicting dangerous behavior,
and did not know what really caused mental illness. The fact
that families and professionals who care are the only ones who
can help a mentally ill person was lost in a sea of forensic logic.

Thanks to a lawsuit filed by the Milwaukee Legal Services,
moreover, it was found discriminatory to institutionalize only
the mentally ill before actual commission of a crime. In *Lessard*
v. *Schmidt* (1972), the Milwaukee Legal Services convinced the
court that the state's commitment laws were invalid because
they lacked the procedural safeguards of criminal law. What
about the argument that the mentally ill might be dangerous to
themselves? The answer was, normal people smoke cigarettes
without state intervention.

Spurring Deinstitutionalization

The movement rolled on, financed by government grants and
court awards. In *Wyatt* v. *Stickney*, plaintiffs argued that patients,
if they were to be confined to a hospital, had thereby a right to
treatment. Fair enough, but the hidden agenda was to free the patients from confinement. The trick, pulled successfully, was to get
a friendly judge to define the standards for treatment to include
staffing ratios and physical amenities so expensive that hospitals
could not afford to meet them. "Fearing the precedent of costly
improvements that had been set," write Isaac and Armat, "other
states accelerated deinstitutionalization [the large-scale emptying
of the state mental hospitals] after 1972, since it was clearly the
cheapest way to achieve improved staff ratios to patients."

Another suit having a major impact in emptying hospitals was
brought in the name of an involuntarily committed patient in a
Florida state hospital, Kenneth Donaldson. Donaldson, who had
rejected all forms of treatment that doctors at the hospital believed might help him, insisted instead on a combination of oc-

cupational therapy, ground privileges, and psychotherapy. Failure of the hospital to provide these resulted in a jury decision that treatment had been denied and an assessment of $20,000 against two doctors at the hospital. The effect, note Isaac and Armat, after the *Donaldson* and *Stickney* decisions had worked their way through the appeals process and been upheld by the higher courts, was not to establish a right to treatment, but—as the antipsychiatric mental health bar had hoped—to spur deinstitutionalization.

These and the many other lawsuits brought by the mental health liberation bar contributed to the further decline of the patient population of state hospitals that had begun with the exposés [of their abysmal conditions] at the end of World War II and been helped along by the availability of effective neuroleptic drugs [major tranquilizers]. After 1974, the availability of federal Supplemental Security Insurance (SSI) to the mentally disabled, in combination with the lawsuits, according to Isaac and Armat, created "a classic 'push and pull' situation." At the same time that legal actions made it impossible to keep many patients needing institutionalization in the hospitals, SSI enabled states by discharging them to pass along the financial burden for their care to the federal government.

Having confirmed the right to treatment for institutionalized mental patients, the lawyers next went to work to establish the right to refuse treatment. They eventually succeeded in making it so difficult, costly, and time consuming to require treatment for mental patients not wanting it that the release of patients from the hospital to streets or shelters, or leaving patients untreated, became relatively attractive alternatives. In some states, a patient need not even refuse treatment to require a court hearing about it; the simple fact that the patient is seen as too psychotic to make a "competent" decision about his own treatment may require court involvement.

Contributing to the Misery in the World

The only standard of involuntary civil commitment that has survived this legal onslaught is dangerousness: that if the patient is left unconfined or untreated he constitutes a danger to himself or others. Many times this condition would be difficult to prove even if it were not the subject for an adversary proceeding. But as these matters have evolved, it has been made even more difficult. In 1955, the population of our mental hospitals reached its peak at 559,000. About then, as the introduction of neuroleptic drugs became widespread, a long-term decline in the numbers of patients in these hospitals began. By 1970, when the mental patient liberation bar had reached full swing, the number was still 339,000. After ten years of litigation and agitation, the number had fallen to 130,000—a drop proportionately much greater in a much shorter time. The population living in the streets and parks mushroomed: these are the mentally ill individuals whose families and doctors (if any) cannot require them to accept appropriate treatment or hospitalization even when it is available.

> The mental health liberation bar has established a new, cruel system for the mentally ill. The right to treatment has become the right to no treatment, the right to freedom is the right to deteriorate on the streets and die in back alleys. [Isaac and Armat]

These patient advocacy lawyers might be right about the law: the fact that they win so often in court surely raises the presumption that they are. Their efforts, however, have contributed greatly to the misery in the world. Society does not work when it is run on an adversary basis of abstract conceptions of what is right and just; it works only when flesh and blood people can act on their felt, personal commitment to each other and to enduring civilized values.

The Law Must Be Changed

The law must be changed to include a "need for treatment" standard for involuntary commitment. Important precepts of our legal system have been distorted. One, the right to individual self-determination, is now used to block civil commitment of the mentally ill. The other precept, the right of the individual to informed consent, or choice of medical treatment, is used now to thwart treatment, even when someone is ill enough to be committed for treatment involuntarily.

Rael Jean Isaac and Virginia C. Armat, *Reader's Digest*, January 1991.

Mental illness is not necessarily a lifelong condition. According to Torrey and his associates, about a quarter of the individuals with schizophrenia recover from their first or second episode and never get sick again. In many other cases the mentally ill improve spontaneously over time as they get older. Most can be helped to function much better with good psychiatric and rehabilitative services. In a humane system, laws and regulations will be written and interpreted to establish a legal status in between institutional confinement and complete freedom for some classes of patients. Those needing it will be provided medication and other proven therapies, and some will be required to take their medication as a condition of their freedom to live among the rest of us. Hospitalization will be provided when it is needed, and for some this means long-term hospitalization. Such community support services as residential living arrangements and rehabilitative services will also be standard. . . .

A Misguided Policy

Since a 1972 federal court ruling (*Lessard* v. *Schmidt*), decisions concerning involuntary commitment have no longer been based on a determination of "the best interests of the patient" but have required "an extreme likelihood that if the person is not confined he will do immediate harm to himself or others." Most mental health professionals and parent groups believe this policy is a misguided application of civil liberties. According to Elliot Badanes, spokesman for the family-based California Alliance for the Mentally Ill, "There are thousands of people who desperately need help and will not accept it except involuntarily." Family advocates are working to reshape this policy.

The psychiatrist and journalist Charles Krauthammer agrees with them on the issue. For the homeless mentally ill, he asks:

> Why should it be necessary to convince a judge that, left alone, they will die? The vast majority won't. It should be enough to convince a judge that left alone they will suffer.

> What prevents us from doing this is the misguided and pernicious civil libertarian impulse that holds liberty too sacred to be overridden for anything other than the preservation of life. For the severely mentally ill, however, liberty is not just an empty word but a cruel hoax. Free to do what?

> What does freedom mean for a paranoid schizophrenic who is ruled by voices commanded by his persecutors and rattling around in his head?

Some of the opposition to involuntary commitment stems, rightly or misguidedly, from a concern for civil liberties—either for the liberties of the patients themselves or for what might happen unless we "draw the line" firmly where it will protect stigmatized groups. While parent advocacy groups want to change the rules on involuntary commitment, patient groups want to keep the policy strict. Steven Segal, a Berkeley social welfare professor who works closely with patient groups, believes that the "current civil commitment laws are, for the most part, working." Howie Harp, speaking for the California Network of Mental Health Clients, says, "If somebody wants to stay outside and waste away, that's their right." Some do not trust the professional judgment of psychiatrists. Some consider the care system as it now exists in their community inhumane and do not believe it is right to force people into it except perhaps as a last resort.

Others oppose involuntary commitment for reasons other than civil liberties as such: even where the system is adequate, they say, involuntary participation is antitherapeutic. Forcing an angry and alienated psychotic into treatment against his will is likely to make him even angrier and reinforce his feelings of persecution. Leonard Stein argues that to work effectively with patients,

> Staff must believe that the people they are working with are citizens of the community. . . . [and] that patients are indeed free agents able to make decisions and be responsible for their actions. These attitudes influence clinical behavior. Take for example the medication issue. Patients are frequently ambivalent about taking medications. We find we get better compliance if we relate to patients as responsible [individuals] and make them partners in the medication decisions.

In the Dane County, Wisconsin, system where Stein is director of research and training at the community mental health center, a program is run for the mentally ill who refuse to come in for services. The Dane County center, like the Goddard-Riverside Community Center on Manhattan's upper west side, does "assertive outreach." Refusal to come in, says Stein, is considered "part of the illness," so it is treated in the field.

The Rights of the Public

There is another side to this argument. According to columnist Blake Fleetwood, "Public health authorities estimate that between 4 and 8 percent of the population of all societies is dysfunctional because of addiction or mental problems, a percentage that has remained constant throughout recorded history."

Fleetwood is among those who believe that the public has a right to the enjoyment of public spaces set aside and maintained for that purpose. Unrestricted camping, drinking alcohol in public, publicly relieving oneself, aggressive begging, public sex, shouting obscenities, cursing passers-by, lurking threateningly in the bushes, and creating messes are not constitutionally protected. Publicly visible homelessness has increased partly because tolerance of it has increased, argues Fleetwood, and he insists we have a right to enact "quality of life laws" that reasonably regulate behavior in public places. In refusing institutionalization or treatment, the mentally ill have no more right than anyone else, and no less under the equal protection clause of the Fourteenth Amendment, to insist on living on the streets or in the parks.

It is, however, morally questionable, legally dubious, and politically difficult to punish people for having nowhere to live. Practically speaking, the homeless cannot be rounded up and removed unless decent accommodations are available for them. But there is no way to provide pleasant accommodations for the homeless without increasing their numbers: the nicer the accommodations, the more the homeless. Any place so spartan and strict that large numbers of nonhomeless will not be attracted out of their present accommodations will inevitably provoke much complaining by homeless individuals and their advocates that the conditions are inhumane. Still, by providing spartan and strict accommodations to everyone we find living on the street, we could recapture a considerable measure of control over public spaces currently occupied by the severely alienated mentally ill, alcoholics, drug addicts, and persons claiming to be economically homeless. The seriously mentally ill can be offered the same choice of accommodations as everyone else, but they must behave according to the rules wherever they choose to go. No agency is obligated to keep them.

If a mentally ill individual will not or cannot behave in an acceptable manner in any of the places he chooses, then the only logical alternative is commitment. We do not have a legal obligation to let anyone live in the park or anywhere else just because that is what he wants to do. Being mentally ill does not increase one's civil rights, even if under present legal interpretations it does not reduce them.

"Society . . . should not scapegoat the mentally ill in its search for community security."

Mental Patients' Rights Should Remain Broad

John Q. La Fond and Mary L. Durham

John Q. La Fond is a professor of law at the University of Puget Sound School of Law in Tacoma, Washington. Mary L. Durham is an associate professor in the department of health services at the University of Washington in Tacoma.
In the following viewpoint, La Fond and Durham oppose limiting the rights of mentally ill people to refuse treatment. They fear that making it easier to institutionalize the mentally ill against their will would remove the incentive for mental health professionals to provide good care. Furthermore, the authors contend, involuntary hospitalization does not help the mentally ill develop the ability to live in the community.

As you read, consider the following questions:

1. What two major limitations do the authors believe must be placed on the use of coercion on the mentally ill?
2. According to La Fond and Durham, what two conditions justify involuntary hospitalization?
3. Why are most homeless people homeless, according to the authors?

From pp. 160-66, 169-70 of *Back to the Asylum* by John Q. La Fond and Mary L. Durham. Copyright ©1992 by John Q. La Fond and Mary L. Durham. Reprinted by permission of Oxford University Press, Inc.

We accept that mental illness can significantly impair an individual's behavioral controls, endangering the individual or others. Thus, the state will have to use coercion and institutionalization to care for and control some seriously disordered citizens. Nonetheless, since coercion deprives citizens of their constitutionally protected right to freedom, it is an objectionable means that must be justified and limited. We think there are two major limitations that must be placed on the use of state coercion on the mentally ill.

First, state compulsion must lead to acceptable ends. Only if society is willing to actually provide therapeutic and supportive placement and services for the mentally ill should legal compulsion be used. Second, coercion must be subjected to the least restrictive alternative principle. Compulsion should be used only to the extent necessary and only if the mentally ill retain the maximum freedom of action and choice possible. With these two limiting principles in mind, let us examine how the state should care for the seriously mentally ill.

The Primacy of Voluntary Community Care

America desperately needs a mental health system that provides support and care for the chronically mentally ill in the community on a voluntary basis. Most mentally ill citizens are not dangerous and, with assistance, can live on their own. . . .

The community mental health system must serve the clinical and social needs of the chronically mentally ill. But adding these individuals to this system is not enough; programs must be reoriented to address this major public priority. Although the problems of the chronically mentally ill are difficult and unattractive, inattention to their needs is a major failure of the current treatment system. This means we must refocus exclusive attention away from care for the acutely ill and the worried well toward those who have suffered from serious mental illness over a long period of time. A community network must provide easier access, including aggressive outreach, to this group of difficult patients.

In addition, we should not make promises we cannot keep. Treatment resources should be concentrated on methods that have demonstrated success. For example, affective [mood] disorders such as depression can be treated quite effectively and should receive treatment emphasis. Community-based programs that have proven efficacy should be promoted, including those that provide long-term community support and treatment for people who need supervision for their entire lives.

We also need to have realistic aspirations for this system. It is unlikely that significant long-term improvement can be attained in many cases. Maintaining many chronic patients on medications, assisting them in obtaining adequate shelter, and continuing them on government assistance programs may be the best we can hope for. We must also accept the fact that many of the mentally ill will live in extremely modest housing, including single-room-occupancy residences and psychiatric shelters. These are certainly better than cardboard boxes, jail cells, and in many cases, as we shall argue shortly, hospitals.

We should also adopt aggressive incentives for encouraging psychiatrists and other mental health providers to practice in the public health system. America heavily subsidizes the training of thousands of psychiatric residents each year. We deserve a modicum of public service from them in return.

Coercion and institutionalization should not be the cornerstone of our mental health policy. It is a sad commentary that, by and large, only the poor are committed to state mental hospitals. This fact suggests that whether a mentally ill citizen is forcibly hospitalized depends primarily on wealth and status, and not on the illness. Whenever possible, we should assist the mentally ill to maintain independent lives in the community.

The Limits of Involuntary Hospitalization

The mental health system will need to use coercion to provide services, care, and treatment for some seriously mentally ill people. A number of them are so out of touch with reality that they cannot make rational choices. They threaten to harm others or themselves. Or they are simply unable to provide themselves with the basic food, shelter, and clothing necessary to survive. Only a tiny fraction of patients are so disturbed and dangerous that they will be hospitalized for a long time.

Short-term emergency hospitalization is justified to protect some people when serious harm is imminent. It is also acceptable to restore the ability of the seriously impaired to survive. Without involuntary hospitalization, some may literally die, and death inevitably moots philosophic debates about autonomy, freedom, and rights. But the number of such individuals is very small and does not include most street people, even though these homeless individuals live rather stark lives. (Other mentally disturbed citizens who are not imminently dangerous to themselves or others but disturb the community by committing crimes should be controlled through the criminal justice system. . . . Most of these individuals can and should obey the law. This approach, however, will require jails to provide much better psychiatric services than they currently do.)

The public mental health system must also provide follow-up treatment and supportive services for these seriously ill patients once they are released from hospitals. It is unconscionable to simply open the hospital door and expect most of them to successfully find their way back to the community. Many will need assistance finding housing, obtaining government benefits, and integrating into the community mental health system. For too many mentally ill Americans, our mental health system has degenerated into an either/or disaster: Either you are committed to hospitals primarily for short-term therapy or you are released back into the streets without any help at all.

No New Laws

There is a serious risk that the public will demand new, overly inclusive civil commitment laws authorizing mental health professionals to commit mentally disturbed citizens to hospitals simply for treatment or to improve their living conditions. We oppose such laws. If enacted, we fear mental health professionals will use coercion and institutionalization as "therapeutic" instruments of first rather than last resort. Involuntarily committing the mentally ill to hospitals for treatment can be a quick solution to removing the disturbed and the disturbing from public view. Mental health professionals do not have to spend time finding a suitable placement in the community—assuming it is even available—and persuading the individual to accept it. Moreover, hospitalization usually means the immediate administration of fast-acting drugs to subdue and control the patient. But the chronically mentally ill need more than periodic doses of powerful drugs and sporadic sojourns in overcrowded state hospitals. Conscience can too easily yield to the convenience of a hasty but ineffectual solution for a serious, long-term problem.

When expanded therapeutic commitment laws give mental health professionals renewed opportunity to work wonders on a newly "enfranchised" group of patients, the public expects miracles. Tragically, however, the promises of cures for the seriously mentally ill are not well founded. At best, drugs control the symptoms of mental illness, thereby helping restore a patient to more normal functioning, but they do not cure the underlying illness. And the serious irreversible side effects from drugs harm many patients. Not infrequently, staff use drugs to manage patients for their own convenience rather than prescribe them for the patient's benefit.

Any benefits that accrue from receiving a "tune-up" in the hospital must be balanced against the debilitating effects brought on by prolonged institutionalization. Hospitalization may diminish patients' capacity to make decisions on their own and to live outside institutions, because most important decisions are made for them while they are institutionalized. Even short-term involuntary hospitalization can also severely disrupt patients' basic social arrangements. They may lose their apartment, their jobs, social contacts, and sense of routine. In addition, essential financial benefits such as Social Security disability payments terminate when a patient is hospitalized. Reapplication is risky because many claims are denied and many marginally functioning individuals are simply unable to reapply successfully. Delays in restarting these benefits are inevitable.

The Washington State Experience

The Washington State experience with changing its involuntary treatment statute . . . poignantly raised the question of whether involuntary hospitalization helped or harmed the mentally ill. In 1979 Washington State expanded the statutory authority to hospitalize a mentally ill person for treatment. Many patients committed to state hospitals under the new law had never been in hospitals before. When committed, these new patients stayed in hospitals longer than other patients and returned with greater frequency, thereby consuming more and more scarce resources. On the one hand, these individuals may have been in desperate need of the assistance a hospital (among other agencies) can provide—including food, clothing, shelter, and medical care. Thus, the 1979 statute may have given them the aid they required.

For the Good of Society

Forced incarceration, be it involuntary hospitalization or frank imprisonment, can in no way be conceived of as doing its victims a favor; it is done for the good of society exclusively, and any benefit the inmate gets along the way is purely serendipitous. We are a bit more honest with ourselves about this in the case of corrections than we are in the psychiatric field, although I don't see much difference between forcing someone into a cell and forcing him or her into a hospital bed, and neither do the mentally ill.

Ann Braden Johnson, *Out of Bedlam: The Truth About Deinstitutionalization*, 1990.

On the other hand, once they were committed to a hospital, they were likely to return again and again to the hospital for these services. We believe that expanding therapeutic commitment simply sets up a cycle of dependency in which the mentally ill spin in and out of revolving hospital doors. Washington, like other states, had very little to offer them in the community. With the state using an all-or-nothing mentality, the mentally ill received episodic treatment (that could have been provided elsewhere) from the most intensive, expensive resource any mental health system has to offer—the hospital.

We think the Washington study suggests that involuntary hospitalization for treatment may make people *less able* to live in the community. Thus, we are extremely skeptical that forcing even the most seriously ill individuals into hospitals for treatment actually helps them in the long run. Providing them with continuing social services and health care on a voluntary basis or involuntarily in a less expensive, less restrictive environment is far preferable.

Moreover, Washington abandoned patients who sought hospital treatment on a voluntary basis. The 1979 Washington law increased the number of *involuntary* patients so dramatically that *voluntary* patients were pushed out of hospitals. They were left to fend for themselves in the community as best they could.

Intrigued by the results of our Washington study, we did further research to see if there was any persuasive evidence substantiating the claim that involuntary hospital treatment actually helps the mentally ill live independently in the community after their release. To our amazement we could find *no* scientifically sound research supporting this claim. In fact, this major premise of reformers who would expand the therapeutic, coercive power of the state has never been studied rigorously. Thus, there is no reliable evidence establishing that involuntary hospital treatment helps the mentally ill to adjust to living on their own after they are discharged.

In light of our empirical research, we have concluded that coercive hospitalization must be reserved for the dangerous mentally ill and those whose lives are at risk because they cannot provide themselves with the necessities of life. The dominance of the medical model and America's renewed confidence in claims of psychiatric expertise and technological solutions have made society quite willing to hospitalize the mentally ill for their own good even when confronted with powerful contrary evidence that coercive hospitalization might inflict serious, unnecessary harm on many of the patients society is trying to help. Forced hospitalization also encourages the public to continuously short-change the community mental health system.

Thus, we do not support legal changes that would authorize coercive hospitalization on a broadly defined "need-for-treatment" basis. Nor do we think hospitals are the appropriate place for most seriously mentally ill people, although we certainly believe that voluntary hospitalization should be available to those who need and seek it. If our mental health law ignores the evidence provided by objective empirical research, it will do more harm than good.

The Hospital as Asylum

Some experts now claim that many mentally ill people should be involuntarily hospitalized to provide a lifetime of shelter and protection from the harsh vicissitudes of contemporary life. Put simply, the mentally ill do not need treatment, they need asylum. This new justification for coercive hospitalization echoes the nineteenth-century ideology of providing lifetime compassionate care and custody for the disabled in state asylums. But it raises more provocative questions at the close of the twentieth century. Is it in their best interest to provide mentally ill citizens with a caring and humane environment—albeit one they did not choose—to raise their standard of living or to provide them with asylum?

Despite the seductive appeal of this humanitarian plea, the Supreme Court in the *Donaldson* v. *O'Connor* case [a 1974 decision that restricted involuntary hospitalization] clearly indicated the government cannot constitutionally take away a person's liberty for "pure asylum." As Justice Potter Stewart said:

> May the State confine the mentally ill merely to ensure them a living standard superior to that they enjoy in the private community? That the State has a proper interest in providing care and assistance to the unfortunate goes without saying. But the mere presence of mental illness does not disqualify a person from preferring his home to the comforts of an institution. Moreover, while the State may arguably confine a person to save him from harm, incarceration is rarely if ever a necessary condition for raising the living standards of those capable of surviving safely in freedom on their own or with the help of family or friends.

Nonetheless, our long-standing commitment to individual responsibility does not require us to desert those who genuinely need public assistance. Abandoning people who are down and out in America is nothing short of social Darwinism. Many mentally ill citizens require temporary safe havens. But, as mentioned earlier, for all but a few persons, that should only consist of *voluntary* placement in facilities which alleviate stress and provide a supportive and caring environment. Neither coercion nor institutionalization is required to provide a safe haven for most mentally ill citizens.

The Homeless Mentally Ill

Homelessness is a provocative contemporary issue that some reformers would exploit so as to use coercive hospitalization to provide asylum for the mentally ill. The impulse to help the homeless has been a powerful force to expand the net of therapeutic commitment. In our view, the therapeutic state is being distorted to solve the problem of homelessness. To understand why this strategy for coping with homelessness is a catastrophe in the making, we must be more forthright about why people are homeless in America.

Most homeless people are not mentally ill individuals living on the streets because restrictive commitment laws prevent them from receiving desperately needed hospital treatment. The most rigorous research shows that no more than one-third of all homeless Americans can be considered mentally ill. While the fact that many homeless people are mentally ill demonstrates the tragic deficiencies of the mental health system, it does not establish that mental illness causes homelessness.

A Social and Economic Problem

Most people are homeless as a result of socioeconomic factors. Rising rates of mental illness have contributed to homelessness but cannot explain its rapid proliferation. Many mentally ill individuals are homeless because they, too, have exhausted government benefits, cannot obtain employment, have no family or social support, and are generally poor competitors for the increasingly limited resource of low-income housing. Although most homeless mentally ill could benefit from help with their mental disabilities, coercive hospitalization is unwarranted for all but a very few. Most homeless mentally ill need access to low-income housing or financial and social services to help them obtain shelter, as well as other social, economic, and medical assistance.

By involuntarily hospitalizing the mentally ill because they are homeless, we are choosing to medicalize what is primarily a social and economic problem. Blaming homelessness on mental illness is appealing because it locates the fault in the individual rather than in society's social and economic structure. The better solution is to provide realistic assistance to the homeless and to the homeless mentally ill to obtain the essential services for keeping them off the streets. This would, of course, include mental health care for the homeless mentally ill. And it would also require more social services to meet a broad spectrum of needs.

Even for those few mentally ill who cannot secure life-sustaining shelter as a result of their illness, involuntary hospitalization is a fleeting and ultimately unsatisfying solution. Hospitalization may briefly stabilize their condition but provides only temporary respite from the calamity of their social situation. If we do not help these seriously ill people obtain shelter in the community before and after they are hospitalized, coercive hospitalization will, at best, provide an intermittent Band-Aid that will not solve their homelessness or prevent their inevitable recommitment. It will only temporarily reclaim public buildings, parks, and sidewalks for the more privileged.

Outpatient Commitment

Some mentally ill citizens will need to be controlled while living in the community. Coercion through outpatient commitment will be necessary to make certain that they receive the social, economic, and medical support essential to maintain themselves outside of hospitals. This commitment helps ensure that patients' needs are met by the most appropriate service. A match of needs and solutions is both good medicine and good law.

In addition, outpatient commitment appears to be reasonably effective in keeping patients on necessary medication, thus enabling them to live in the community. This control should also help prevent patients from deteriorating, since they frequently stop taking their medication after they are discharged from a hospital. It also minimizes governmental restraint on the patient's liberty, thereby conforming to the least restrictive alternative principle.

The use of outpatient commitment also passes our litmus test for limiting coercive interventions to those that appear to work. Preliminary studies indicate outpatient commitment can be an effective alternative to hospitalization when structured like programs in operation in North Carolina, Hawaii, and Wisconsin. Finally, outpatient commitment may avoid making many mentally ill patients worse off through involuntary hospitalization.

A cautionary note is necessary. The American public has always overestimated the power of the law to control human behavior. Significant resource constraints and limited sanctions for violating the terms of outpatient commitment require that this strategy be used sparingly. . . .

Individual Rights: The Soul of America

Many of the mentally ill in U.S. cities are being forcibly removed from the streets to overcrowded, shabby, and unsafe shelters. Others are being coercively dumped into crowded and understaffed state hospitals. This action strongly suggests that coercive institutionalization is less for the benefit of the mentally ill and more for the public's convenience. Legal reform ostensibly undertaken for humane reasons can quickly be transformed into a powerful instrument of social repression. It is imperative that mental health policy be vigilant to guard against this destructive metamorphosis.

America is at risk of losing touch with its fundamental values. The quest for complete safety in a more threatening world is understandable. Society, however, should not scapegoat the mentally ill in its search for community security. Currently civil liberties do not enjoy the cachet they did in the Liberal Era [the 1960s and 1970s]. But individual rights are more than passing fancies. They are the soul of America. When revising mental health law and policy to ensure adequate protection of the community, we must be careful to be fair to disabled citizens. It is too easy to rearrange fundamental social policy out of fear and anger.

"Jail is not the proper place for those who suffer from a mental illness."

The Mentally Ill Should Not Be Jailed

Chuck O'Reilly

Chuck O'Reilly is the sheriff of Lewis & Clark County in Montana. In the following viewpoint, he argues that across America, mentally ill people are often inaptly jailed, charged with either no crime or with spurious misdemeanor violations to justify keeping them off the streets. According to O'Reilly, these inappropriate incarcerations can be avoided through increased communication and cooperation among various health, government, and law enforcement agencies. He writes that in his county, a cooperative procedure has been developed in which mentally ill people in trouble are taken to the hospital emergency room instead of jail.

As you read, consider the following questions:

1. According to O'Reilly, who paid for the first six months of the Lewis & Clark County procedure?
2. In the Lewis & Clark County program, an incarcerated person who is judged to be mentally ill will be transferred to one of what two places, according to the author?
3. According to O'Reilly, how should a Lewis & Clark County patrol officer respond to a person unable to care for himself?

Chuck O'Reilly, "Mentally Ill—Inaptly Incarcerated," *American Jails*, July/August 1993. Reprinted by permission of the American Jail Association.

In the late 1980s a common buzzphrase within our criminal justice system was that victims of crime were "twice victimized—once by the criminal and once by the system." An even worse scenario is one that exists yet today in your state and mine, and throughout our nation, whereby victims of mental illnesses are inaptly incarcerated in local jails simply because "there is no place else to take them." I am not referring to the criminally mentally ill, but rather to those folks who are the victims of not only our criminal justice system but our society in general. These people enter our system and receive placement in jails and correctional centers without being charged with any crime, or worse yet on a convenient misdemeanor charge simply to justify their incarceration and to get them off the street.

In typically archaic and human fashion, discussions on this topic among the various public and private social service agencies and businesses conveniently lead to finger pointing and great oratorical rationalizations about how it is *your* responsibility, not mine, to deal with this unfortunate situation. Yet in my experience, to a person, everyone agrees that jail is not the proper place for those who suffer from a mental illness.

I don't believe I can begin to comprehend the sheer terror and embarrassment an already stressed out consumer must go through when he is approached by a uniformed officer, handcuffed, placed in a marked police car, and delivered to jail where he oftentimes undergoes the entire regimen of intake procedures including strip searches. The loud clanging of that cell door slamming shut must, I am sure, herald the onset of a loneliness and helplessness far beyond what any of us can begin to understand. How often has this type of scenario been the catalyst that convinced a person suicide was the only answer?

Taking Action

It is a difficult situation, particularly when a community has few known resources to call upon for resolution to the problem. However, with open and direct communication among all of the actors—including consumers—more and greater resources oftentimes will come to the fore, and with proper participation and planning, solutions can be found to everyone's benefit.

All of the abovementioned problems existed in Lewis & Clark County (Montana). In early January 1993 I ordered our Detention Center not to accept persons with mental illness for incarceration unless under court order or if charged with a felony. This was not done without some trepidation as to the possible impacts: nonetheless, my frustration with our situation and its lack of progress necessitated some type of drastic action. For several months previously in 1992, we had undergone a series of planning meetings with numerous participants from various entities within the crim-

214

inal justice, governmental, and mental health systems with the goal of developing a comprehensive plan to keep the mentally ill out of jail. The plan ultimately was written but was replete with excuses and devoid of solutions. In hindsight, perhaps a false start is not all that bad as it allows all to vent their frustrations and yet see the numerous other sides of the problem. At the time, however, we were headed into the future with no workable plan in place and no light at the end of the tunnel. Fortunately, a very able leader and mediator in the form of Deputy County Attorney K. Paul Stahl grabbed the ball, formed a committee, and began a very productive series of regularly scheduled meetings. This group is composed of members from all affected local law enforcement agencies, St. Peter's Hospital and ambulance service, mental health service agencies, AA [Alcoholics Anonymous], the county attorney's office, and a consumer.

A Unified Solution

We soon worked our way through the negativism and finger pointing and began establishing procedures for a unified solution to our problem. These procedures were implemented immediately and subsequent meetings resulted in frank discussions of problems encountered and how best to resolve them. These discussions were not without pain. Turf, lack of money-time-manpower-etc., all were barriers that had to be overcome. One prod that helped keep things moving ahead was recent legislation in our state that mandated each county to develop a crisis intervention program and to provide for alternatives to jail placement. Without give-and-take on everyone's part and especially that of St. Peter's Hospital, which footed the bill for the first six months of our procedure, we could not have succeeded to this point.

As it now stands, persons with mental problems picked up on mental health service orders, complaints by citizens or family members, and/or doctors' requests are taken to the hospital emergency room by ambulance, family member, or responding officer. While enroute to the hospital, the transporting officer will request Dispatch to contact Mental Health Services and advise them of the need for their presence at the emergency room. Our officers will assist in taking the person to the hospital's mental health unit if requested by the emergency room staff. If at some later time the patient becomes violent, the Lewis & Clark County Sheriff's Department will respond and assist the hospital staff in controlling the person if requested.

There are times when an intoxicated person is brought to the detention center and proper mental health assessment by detention center staff is impossible. Our procedure requires mental health personnel to be contacted to respond and assess these folks as soon as they are able to participate. Cases occur whereby a person who has been incarcerated for some time begins exhibiting symptoms of mental illness. Mental health professionals are immediately contacted to respond in these instances. If in the judgment of the mental health professional an illness exists, he will make a recommendation to the county attorney's office who will respond 24 hours a day to begin proceedings to either release the individual to St. Peter's Hospital mental health unit, or seek a commitment order to our state hospital from the courts if the person is unable to voluntarily cooperate in the process and no other avenue exists.

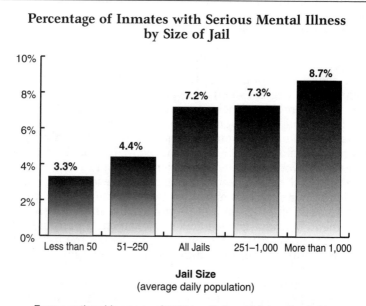

Percentage of Inmates with Serious Mental Illness by Size of Jail

Jail Size
(average daily population)

From a nationwide survey of 1391 local jails, which together hold 62 percent of America's jail inmates.

Source: Public Citizen's Health Research Group and the National Alliance for the Mentally Ill.

In the case of patrol officers coming in contact with a person on the street who appears to be unable to care for himself, the officer is to attempt to locate the individual's residence, family, physician, and/or mental health counselor so the person can be turned over to their care. If the officer cannot obtain this information then the aforementioned process kicks in.

Our Board of County Commissioners and St. Peter's Hospital staff are negotiating an agreement regarding the costs associated with the hospital's caring for the clients they receive. Because of the great cooperation, concern, and support I have witnessed in our latest effort, I am confident an equitable accord will be reached.

Take the Bull by the Horns

While I am not suggesting the process we have established in our area will solve everyone else's problem, I am espousing the virtues of open and honest communication and planning among all agencies, both public and private, who have an interest in, or are affected by, the failure of our current system to effectively and humanely attend to the needs of the mentally ill in our society. Take the bull by the horns and twist a little bit; you may be pleasantly surprised by the results!

"The mentally ill undoubtedly will continue to end up in jail."

Jails Must Accommodate the Mentally Ill

Jane Haddad

Due to a lack of adequate public mental health services, America's jails have become "surrogate mental hospitals," according to Jane Haddad. In the following viewpoint, Haddad argues that jail administrators must adjust their management and treatment practices to accommodate the inevitable presence of increasing numbers of mentally ill inmates. She recommends placing mentally ill inmates in separate mental health units. Haddad is the director of clinical programs for Correctional Medical Systems (CMS), a company that provides correctional health services to prisons and jails.

As you read, consider the following questions:

1. According to Haddad, are the mentally ill more likely than others to exploit one another?
2. What are the three "obvious behavioral signs" of mental illness described by the author?
3. According to the author, what is the purpose of the auditory hallucination exercise she describes?

Jane Haddad, "Managing the Needs of Mentally Ill Inmates," *American Jails*, March/April 1993. Reprinted by permission of the American Jail Association.

A growing concern within our jails today is the increasing number of inmates who are mentally ill. A recent national study supports the existence of this situation and suggests that limited availability of community resources to treat these individuals is a major contributing factor.

This trend, which shows no signs of slowing down, is creating a host of difficulties within our jails that must be addressed immediately and pragmatically by those who administer and work in correctional institutions.

Analyzing the Problem

A 1992 joint report from the National Alliance for the Mentally Ill (NAMI) and the Public Citizen's Health Research Group, *Criminalizing the Seriously Mentally Ill: The Abuse of Jails as Mental Hospitals*, revealed several unsettling statistics, suggesting that jails today have become surrogate mental hospitals that serve to criminalize the seriously mentally ill.

According to the report, more than 30,700 seriously mentally ill individuals serve time in American jails every day. Each year, more than 11 million days are spent by seriously mentally ill individuals in jail. A national survey of 1,391 local jails, which together hold 62 percent of the nation's jail inmates, found that 7.2 percent of jail inmates—more than 1 of every 14 inmates—suffer from serious mental illness.

Many mentally ill inmates are detained in jail—where they may be abused by other inmates or exposed to diseases— on misdemeanor charges such as disorderly conduct, trespassing, or drunkenness. Often, these offenses are simply manifestations of their inability to cope with everyday life due to their mental illnesses. More serious crimes may be a result of mental illness that has been left untreated, typically as a consequence of the breakdown of our public mental health system.

The NAMI report stated that 29 percent of the jails surveyed held seriously mentally ill individuals without any criminal charges against them. Reportedly, they are detained because no other facilities are available to respond to psychiatric emergencies. This policy is legally allowed in only 17 states, although the NAMI survey suggests that the situation also occurs in other states.

From a correctional perspective, jailing the mentally ill can escalate management problems and compromise the jail's overall operation. Mentally ill inmates are generally unpredictable and vulnerable to exploitation. Jailing the mentally ill may also contribute to the overcrowding of jails; thus, it may force judges to reduce sentences for criminals who are genuine threats to society.

Exacerbating the situation, according to the NAMI report, is the fact that of the jails evaluated, more than one in five had no access to mental health services or staff training in mental health issues. Eighty-four percent reported that corrections officers received either no training or less than three hours' training in the special problems of the mentally ill. Forty-six percent of the jails surveyed did not know whether seriously mentally ill inmates received outpatient psychiatric services upon release.

According to the NAMI report, urban and larger jails reported more seriously mentally ill persons, but smaller jails are more likely to house the seriously mentally ill without charges. States with good outpatient programs usually do not rely on jails to hold the seriously mentally ill without criminal charges. This practice occurs in states that do not have laws prohibiting it and is more prevalent in southern, midwestern, and western jails.

Obviously, the increasing incarceration of seriously mentally ill individuals, coupled with the lack of attention given to their treatment in the past, is a critical issue facing professionals in the fields of mental health, corrections, and criminal justice. Jail personnel are, by necessity, finding themselves faced with the responsibility of coping with growing numbers of mentally ill inmates, so they must develop an effective approach to identifying, managing, and treating this population with the goal of ultimately reducing recidivism.

Identifying the Mentally Ill

1. Identification of Mentally Ill Inmates. As a first step, jails must take stronger measures to identify the seriously mentally ill at the time of intake. This can best be accomplished by assigning officers to the booking area who are trained in assessing mental illness through observation and use of structured screening forms with simplified, nonclinical terminology. A brief mental health history also should be taken from inmates as part of the intake process.

Once they have been identified, the seriously mentally ill are best managed by placement in a separate mental health unit or a special area. In this way, they can be more easily treated and monitored to minimize security problems. In addition, there is less risk of their being abused because typically the mentally ill are less likely than others to exploit one another.

It is important to assign officers to the mental health unit who have been specifically trained and who wish to be there. Rotation of these officers should be minimal to increase consistency and efficiency.

Officers often can develop a rapport and sense of accomplishment while they are working in a mental health unit. For example, the Lansing Correctional Facility in Kansas found initially its officers were reluctant to work in the institution's new mental health Extended Care Unit. Those who were coaxed to take on the assignment agreed to a one-year commitment. By the end of the year, most were very positive toward their role and 85 percent wished to remain involved with the unit. In addition, a waiting list of officers interested in working in the unit developed.

2. *Specialized Training for Security Staff.* Proper training for officers in handling mentally ill inmates is vital to the success of mental health programs. All officers in the jail should receive training in mental health issues, with more extensive sessions held for officers stationed in the intake areas and for those working in the mental health unit.

Diversion and Care

Several counties and states have developed model programs and innovative approaches that both divert the mentally ill from the criminal justice system and improve the mental health care of incarcerated M.I.O.s [mentally ill offenders]. . . . Jail diversion programs attempt to identify misdemeanant M.I.O.s when they first arrive at the jail and channel these individuals away from the jail and into community-based treatment facilities. . . . In some of these programs the local judiciary cooperates in dropping the misdemeanant charges against the mentally ill and instead commits them to the state hospital. Several counties in Florida and New York have model programs in which their M.I.O.s in jail receive mental health services from hospitals and agencies in the local community.

Michael J. O'Sullivan, *America*, January 11, 1992.

Mental health professionals should be involved in the training of officers; however, not all mental health staff are equipped for this particular task. Those selected to train jail personnel must be individuals who believe security officers are peers and fellow professionals, and act accordingly. Training can only succeed when it is viewed as a joint venture between mental health professionals and jail personnel.

Understanding Mental Illness

The training program should focus on "nuts and bolts" issues. Correctional officers don't need to know technical clinical terms, "psychobabble," or how to diagnose an illness. What they do require is instruction in general assessment skills and in recognizing more obvious behavioral signs of mental illness, such as darting eyes (a sign of hypervigilance), tangential speech, and backing up nervously against a wall for protection. The officers also need to understand what an auditory hallucination is, and how it can impact one's mental state and behavior. This can be demonstrated by an instructor in a group situation in the following manner:

Select four officers, preferably those who appear least involved in the training process. Send one of the officers out of the room and instruct two of the remaining three to talk about their favorite hobbies, favorite subjects in school, etc., when requested. The remaining officer is instructed to make derogatory comments such as "You are ugly," or "You are bad." The officers are told to converse loudly as instructed all together at a signal from you, after the fourth officer returns.

Bring back the fourth officer and instruct him to respond to what you are saying. While asking this officer straightforward, work-related questions, signal the others to "chime in" simultaneously from behind the target officer. Through this disconcerting exercise, the officers learn how difficult it is to function or communicate in the midst of competing "voices," like those experienced as auditory hallucinations.

The point in this exercise is to assist the officers in gaining a truer understanding of the nature of mental illness. This will help them view the mentally ill with more empathy, and avoid the inappropriate misconception that these inmates are stupid or retarded individuals. It is also helpful during training to encourage the officers to discuss their feelings toward the mentally ill and their own family experiences.

The entire training process can be facilitated through teamwork. Mental health and medical staff professionals should be scheduled with officers for the training. The give-and-take between the groups is very beneficial. The training program will succeed if there is strong commitment and involvement from those in power—the sheriff, the jail officers, or the jail administrators.

Follow-Up and Community Resources

3. Routine Follow-Up to Facilitate Treatment Compliance. While care and treatment of the mentally ill is not the primary mission of jails, the period of incarceration may actually be the only time some mentally ill individuals receive treatment: Left to their own devices, they simply refuse it.

Incarceration, therefore, provides a unique opportunity for an active mental health program to initiate some behavioral change in mentally ill inmates. This can be accomplished through treatment geared toward helping inmates understand their illness and the need to take prescribed medication.

4. Aggressive Approach Toward Accessing Community Resources. Follow-up treatment to assure continued compliance after release from jail is essential to avoid the "revolving door" syndrome, which the mentally ill so often experience.

By taking advantage of community services, such as halfway houses, drug treatment programs, and crisis centers, inmates have a far better chance of continuing to take their medications and staying out of jail. To set up a routine follow-up system, jails must be aggressive in linking up with community resources for mentally ill inmates prior to their release.

The Bottom Line

No one can deny that the mentally ill would be better served in a community treatment program, rather than a jail. However, with the current inadequate level of community resources available, the reality is that the mentally ill undoubtedly will continue to end up in jail.

In view of this, jail administrators should recognize that it is in their own best interests to provide adequate staff, training, and facilities to treat mentally ill inmates. With selection of appropriate mental health professionals and the commitment of jail administrative staff, effective management and treatment programs can be developed for the seriously mentally ill without a significant financial investment.

The alternative is using the same level of a jail's resources *less productively* to simply control the many management problems that this population can create in a traditional jail environment. It is better for all concerned to avoid the problems to begin with.

"The insanity defense is an insanity that should be scrapped."

The Insanity Defense Should Be Eliminated

Joan Ullman

In February 1992, serial killer Jeffrey Dahmer, who reportedly lobotomized, dismembered, cannibalized, and performed sex on the corpses of his victims, pleaded guilty but insane to multiple murder charges. In the following viewpoint, Joan Ullman writes that the insanity plea debased the judicial process in the Dahmer case by allowing so-called experts to engage in absurd and confusing arguments about the definition of insanity rather than acknowledging the obvious barbarity of the defendant's actions. Although Dahmer was found sane and was sentenced to fifteen consecutive life prison terms, Ullman concludes that the insanity defense should be eliminated. Ullman holds an M.A. in clinical psychology from the University of Chicago.

As you read, consider the following questions:

1. According to the author, what motivated the doctors at the Dahmer trial to argue that Dahmer's killings were not sadistic?
2. One psychiatrist at the trial argued that Dahmer was able to "conform his conduct to social norms." What evidence was presented to support this assertion, according to Ullman?
3. According to the author, one psychologist argued at the trial that the "hoarding of heads and genitals" was not psychotic. What alternative explanation did this expert offer?

Milwaukee, Wisconsin—famed for its beer, cheese, chocolate, and sausages—has a Summerfest and a Winterfest. For three weeks in February 1992 I was astonished to find that this predominantly German "great city on a great lake" also had a "Dahmerfest."

The arrest in July 1991 of Jeffrey Dahmer in an apartment crammed with a skeleton, 11 skulls, packages of genitals, and preserved and frozen hearts, muscles, and innards from his 17 slaughtered victims had left me—and most Milwaukeeans—braced for his trial to be a funereal *GotterDahmerung*.

Milwaukee's discovery of a monster in its midst had also ignited smoldering anger and racial tensions in people still unused to seeing their once-tranquil city rent by drugs, murder, and gang wars. Many insisted that if Dahmer had been black and his victims white, the bloodbath would never have gone undetected.

Dahmer pleaded guilty but insane before the trial. The psychiatric experts who would testify also agreed that he knew right from wrong. This left just two questions for Dahmer's jury to decide: Did he have a mental disease and, if so, could he have controlled his conduct and chosen to stop killing?

But from the day I entered the fifth-floor courtroom in the reassuringly named Safety Building, the words I kept hearing from lawyers, spectators, and forensic experts were "healing" and "understanding." The endless talk about Dahmer's profound mental illness, treatment needs, and prognoses made me think of his homicides as almost incidental.

Distance and Distortion

Eventually I developed my own understanding. The euphemistic-sounding words reflected everyone's overwhelming need to deny their revulsion at Dahmer's atrocities and the issues arising from them. They tried to do this by distancing themselves and distorting the reality. Dahmer, for his part, needed to deny that sadism, or hatred of homosexuals and blacks, had motivated him to murder, dismember, and cannibalize so many such victims.

"I carried it too far, that's for sure," Dahmer told police in explaining his frustrated search for a totally compliant, zombie-type sex slave who would always be there for him. In 60-plus hours of confessing, Dahmer had also explained that "I was not into torture. This was not a hate thing. This thing had no racism. This was not a homosexual thing."

The doctors needed to deny their revulsion at Dahmer's deeds, and also their personal and professional inadequacy to explain or deal with an undocumented horror on this scale. Several did so by dwelling on positive traits which they said made Dahmer "a likable guy" and "a forthright historian." Most did so by elaborating on Dahmer's explanations for why his monstrous killings were not sadistic:

"The drugging [was done] to satisfy his sexual need for a not-fully cooperative partner."

"The drilling enterprise . . . was not sadistic . . . it was a realistic attempt to disable, but not to kill. . . ."

"The killing was the unintended consequence of the drilling . . . the taking-of-life issue. . . ."

"Death was an unintended by-product of his efforts to create a zombie."

"Dismembering was a disposal problem. . . ."

"The disemboweling . . . [was] the most efficient way of handling all the remains, which only served an administrative function."

Dahmer's lawyer, Gerald P. Boyle—described as "folksy"—and fervent Milwaukee District Attorney Michael McCann needed to deny their own revulsion and the damage Dahmer's acts had done to their city.

Psychiatric Testimony Compounds the Craziness

Psychiatric testimony at Dahmer's insanity trial compounded the craziness arising from these converging denials. It spewed confusion over semantically similar—but differently defined—legal, psychiatric, and laymen's terms for mental disease and insanity. It also forced the jury to listen to crazy-sounding arguments pushed to logical absurdities by expert witnesses you could only regard as hired goons.

I became convinced that the insanity defense is an insanity that should be scrapped.

I had arrived, like many people, with decidedly mixed emotions about attending. As a psychologist, I was also braced for embarrassment: Dahmer's was the second trial in less than a year in which I would hear the insanity defense argued.

A Perverse Standard

It is absurd to permit the heinousness of a crime to become self-acquitting. That sets up a perverse standard: the more terrible the crime, the crazier, therefore the less culpable the criminal. The man who commits incomprehensible torture is acquitted. The father who steals bread to feed his children is convicted.

Charles Krauthammer, quoted by *National Review*, March 2, 1992.

The first had been a rude awakening to psychiatry's hopelessly inexact nature and dubious value as an aid to distinguishing sanity from insanity. However, I hoped the narrowly defined psychiatric issues in Dahmer's trial would keep to a minimum the confusion introduced by the psychiatric testimony.

I was wrong.

I realized that diagnoses and definitions of psychosis, paranoia, intact thought process, and other concepts I had believed in and studied were shams. For me, one low point came when a psychiatrist said Dahmer had proved his sanity by "remembering to reach for a condom" before copulating with his "dead corpses" or their dissected parts. The psychiatrist testified that Dahmer's capacity to delay gratification and his capacity for impulse control showed he could conform his conduct to social norms.

The doctors' struggles to maintain their images as competent authorities only compounded the lunacy. One referred to "the cannibalism we see in these sorts of cases. . . ." Another said he knew of "other people with a sexual attraction to viscera." A third testified he had "seen hundreds of serial murderers in the last twenty years. . . ."

I kept waiting for someone to say that some of his or her best friends were cannibalistic mass murderers.

An effusive, Italian-born psychiatrist doubted that Dahmer had actually devoured his victims—despite grisly evidence recovered from his freezer. "That would be too much like a vampire. [And] I don't think he was a Dracula," he stated. I asked him whether his European roots might have led him to protect the purity of the Dracula stories from being tainted by Dahmer's grisly acts. He denied it by pointing out that "Hungary isn't that close to Italy."

Struggling for a Diagnosis

In a phrase inapt considering Dahmer's admitted tenderizing, sautéing, and sampling of the hearts, biceps, and thigh muscles of several appealing victims out of "curiosity," another doctor said the killings themselves were "distasteful" to Dahmer. The doctors had also said the killings were "offshoots" of his frustrated quest for the perfect zombie. But most such interpretations were offshoots of the doctors' main struggle to arrive at a diagnosis. The prime one was paraphilia. It was not the only diagnosis.

Along with paraphilia, necrophilia, partialism, and other features, Dahmer was also diagnosed as suffering from alcoholism, a personality disorder "not otherwise specified," and "an antisocial personality disorder with obsessive-compulsive and sadistic components." He was also diagnosed as having a sexual disorder "not otherwise specified." But a psychiatrist explained that Dahmer was not a sexual fetishist "since hoarding was not his main goal.". . .

The expert testimony left me increasingly relieved I wasn't a juror. By now I had no idea how anyone could possibly decide whether Dahmer was sane or insane.

Boyle argued that bodies were piling up so fast in Dahmer's apartment that he was showering with two or three corpses in his tub—which clearly showed he was nuts. "I think it showed that Mr. Dahmer had guts," the prosecution's star psychiatric witness shot back.

Delusional? Psychotic?

Experts also quibbled over whether a bizarre drawing Dahmer made for psychiatrists, depicting a "temple," showed delusional thinking. The drawing showed a black table top, a skeleton, and skulls from his own collection, as well as occult items, including two griffins symbolizing evil and a black leather chair he told them he wanted to buy.

Dahmer had told several of the doctors that when he sat in this chair, he would become like the satanic god in his favorite movie/video, *The Exorcist III*, and would obtain power and wealth from real-estate ventures.

One psychiatrist testified that Dahmer's temple talk suggested "psychotic-like" thinking, but another disagreed. "It was certainly unusual. But it was not delusional," he testified. The doctor added that this was because Dahmer's ideas were "much vaguer than a delusional, or unchanging, belief."

Psychiatrists also clashed over whether Dahmer's ideas about his drawing were "superstitious beliefs" or just signs of "normal stubbornness."

The experts disagreed just as strongly—and confusingly—on whether Dahmer's hoarding of heads and genitals was psychotic.

"It was very, very bizarre behavior," explained a psychologist. But you could also call it "a pretty realistic way to keep trophies."

The psychologist pointed out that hunters display animal-head trophies on walls without being called insane or labeled paraphiliacs. "Paraphilia can lead to pretty unusual stuff . . . occult beliefs," the doctor observed. "Satanic kind of stuff like [in the movie] *Rosemary's Baby*. But this would not necessarily show an impaired mind."

I didn't know about Dahmer's mind. But the numbing mumbo jumbo was certainly impairing *my* mind. . . .

Talk of Healing and Understanding

The verdict, in which the jury found Dahmer sane on all 15 counts of intentional homicide, touched off more talk of healing and understanding. Dahmer himself said he had found God, and had found relief in hearing the doctors testify that he was sick and not evil. Victims' family members said they had found justice, and joined black community leaders in saying it was now time for healing.

Jurors said they had found new understanding of mental illness, which helped them see Dahmer as a person with problems who needed treatment. They said they also found reassurance in realizing that the much-criticized Milwaukee police had not been negligent after all when they had escorted the naked, drugged, Laotian boy back into Dahmer's apartment—only conned by Dahmer, like so many others.

Local and nationally known psychiatrists and attorneys said that the city's gavel-to-gavel coverage of the trial had been cathartic, helping the community to face the horror loosed by Dahmer and to begin to heal. Legal and mental-health organizations were announcing plans to use taped segments of the trial as a teaching device, clarifying issues of mental illnesses and the insanity defense for law and psychiatry students. . . .

The first really sane talk I heard after all this came from the cab driver who drove me to the airport after the verdict was announced. "Those psychiatrists talk a lot, but they don't know what they are talking *about*," he said. "They can't agree on anything. First they should define sanity."

"The insanity defense gives criminal law its moral authority."

The Insanity Defense Should Be Retained

Lincoln Caplan

In the following viewpoint, Lincoln Caplan writes that since the acquittal of John W. Hinckley Jr., who was found not guilty by reason of insanity of attempting to assassinate U.S. president Ronald Reagan in 1982, legal reforms and popular sentiments have opposed the insanity defense. Caplan argues that this opposition is based on the false belief that the insanity defense threatens public safety and provides an "easy out" for criminals. He counters these charges and concludes that the insanity defense should be retained. Caplan is a staff writer for the *New Yorker* magazine and the author of *The Insanity Defense and the Trial of John W. Hinckley, Jr.*

As you read, consider the following questions:

1. What is the "paradoxical importance" of the insanity defense, according to Caplan?
2. According to the author, why did eight states adopt the "guilty but mentally ill" plea after 1982?
3. How does Caplan counter the argument that the insanity defense is an "easy out" for criminals?

Lincoln Caplan, "Not So Nutty," *The New Republic*, March 30, 1992. Reprinted by permission of *The New Republic*, ©1992, The New Republic, Inc.

The insanity defense has a paradoxical importance in the law. By choosing not to hold someone criminally responsible for an illegal act he commits because, as a result of a mental disease or defect, he can't control himself or tell right from wrong, our society indirectly affirms the accountability of the sane. In a sense, the insanity defense gives criminal law its moral authority.

Yet the insanity defense also raises basic questions about the bounds of responsibility that cannot be scientifically established. Since the mid-nineteenth century, insanity pleas have triggered passionate debate about who should be considered bad and who mad. Because of the violence that celebrated defendants have done and the woolliness of some psychiatric evaluations given about them, the defense has been fervently criticized.

That happened when a Milwaukee jury considered acquitting Jeffrey Dahmer on grounds of insanity, before his trial ended in a verdict of guilty on fifteen counts of murder. Focusing on the sensational, the media raised the prospect of a cannibal being let off because of a legal loophole. The precedent usually cited was the case of John W. Hinckley Jr., the would-be assassin of President Ronald Reagan, who in 1982 was found not guilty by reason of insanity. The media often left out any account of how the insanity defense actually works in practice today and, as happened during the Hinckley trial, treated it as a cause and a symbol of various social ills. In reality, the unpopular Hinckley verdict helped weaken the insanity defense considerably. Still, it is a defense we would do well to retain.

Before 1982: Broad Insanity Laws

In the generation and a half before 1982, American insanity laws were widely reformed, with standards broadened to take account of lessons from psychiatry. The most expansive reform, adopted in Washington, D.C., which was a laboratory for the defense, was called the "product" test. It said that an "accused is not criminally responsible if his unlawful conduct was the product of mental disease or mental defect." It was reviewed and rejected by thirty state and five federal courts, and put into law by only two state legislatures.

A majority of states adopted an American Law Institute test that was seen as a moderate solution. It said that a man is not responsible if, because of a mental disease or defect, he "lacks substantial capacity to *appreciate* the wrongfulness of his conduct or to conform his conduct to the requirements of the law" (my italics). As a result, a defendant who knew right from wrong, but lacked emotional appreciation of the difference because his thinking was severely disordered, could be acquitted. The ALI test also broadened the notion that insanity could be a defense for a person if he could tell right from wrong but lost self-control to an "irresistible impulse."

Legal reforms also sought to protect insanity acquittees from being consigned indefinitely to institutions that were worse than prisons, as they had been regularly since the nineteenth century, often for years after they were no longer dangerous to themselves or society. Changes in practices of psychiatry accompanied those in the law, as drug therapy and community care replaced long-term hospitalization in treating the mentally ill. All of these changes amounted to efforts to address the interests of insanity acquittees as well as those of society. Before the Hinckley verdict, Alan Stone of Harvard University observed, "Perhaps for the first time in history, a successful plea of insanity has real bite."

After the Hinckley Acquittal: Narrower Laws

But from the day after the Hinckley acquittal, this judgment became largely moot. Key parts of the insanity defense were significantly altered and, often, limited throughout the country. A new federal insanity defense excluded the notion of insanity for a person who knew right from wrong but lost self-control. (Its practical effect, though, was minimal since only a tiny number of federal defendants pled insanity anyway.)

Thirty-eight states reformed their laws. Eight states adopted a new insanity test, seven of them a narrower one. With these changes, a majority of states now use the old-fashioned "can't tell right from wrong" test of insanity. Eight states added a plea called "guilty but mentally ill" to their criminal laws, to reduce the number of insanity acquittals. Sixteen states shifted the burden of proof in insanity cases, twelve to the defendant. The most common reforms, in twenty-five states, addressed the issue of widest concern: how insanity acquittees are dealt with after trial. All but one state made it easier to commit them immediately to custody, and harder for them to gain release.

A Hallmark of a Civilized Society

Few felons actually "get off" thanks to the insanity defense. Used judiciously, it remains a hallmark of a civilized society.

Eloise Salholz with Susan Miller, *Newsweek*, February 3, 1992.

In 1983 the U.S. Supreme Court approved and encouraged this reversal of direction in the insanity defense. It ruled that a "successful" defendant can be held much longer than he would have been if convicted (in this case, a year for attempted shoplifting).

The Court found that any insanity acquittal is proof of dangerousness and that therefore acquittees are decidedly different from others cleared of criminal charges. As a note in the *Harvard Law Review* stated, the Court judged that "a person who commits a crime is either responsible enough to deserve punishment, or insane enough to deserve commitment." Insanity acquittees were placed in a class of their own—not responsible, yet not beyond blame. The Court's obdurate stand seemed to have broad support.

A Protest Based on Misconceptions

The protest over the Hinckley verdict was based on misconceptions. The primary one was that cracking down on the insanity defense would significantly increase public safety, and shift the balance between what then Attorney General William French Smith called "the forces of law and the forces of lawlessness." There should now be no doubt that this premise was wrong. The rare occasions on which the insanity defense was used—and the rarer occasions on which it was successful—had a negligible impact on broader public safety. The most comprehensive insanity study ever, conducted by Policy Research Associates under the direction of Henry Steadman and reported on in the *Bulletin of the American Academy of Psychiatry and the Law* in 1991, showed that in eight states between 1976 and 1987, the defense was used in less than 1 percent of all criminal cases, and that it succeeded in only about one-quarter of those. Only 7 percent of the acquittals came after contested jury trials. The idea that the insanity defense represents a major threat to public order is simply wrong.

Moreover, the vast majority of insanity defendants are not in the Hinckley-Dahmer category. Only 14 percent of insanity pleas—and 15 percent of the acquittals—in the eight-state study involved murder. Half the pleas involved violent offenses, accounting for 65 percent of the acquittals. The other half of the pleas and 35 percent of the acquittals involved non-violent offenses. Whatever the offenses, probably 90 percent of insanity acquittees spend time in custody after they are judged not guilty. Of those charged with murder, the figure climbs to almost 100 percent. The fact that, on average, they spend somewhat less time there than if they had been convicted of the crimes they were charged with is counterbalanced by the predictability of their commitment. By contrast, in every state each year some people convicted of murder go free. And with the Supreme Court's approval, some acquittees spend much longer in custody than they would have if they had been convicted.

In a book called *Rush to Reform in the Post-Hinckley Era*, Steadman and colleagues hold that the states that do the most effective job are the ones that retain the insanity defense and seek a balance between protecting the civil liberties of acquittees and maintaining the safeguards of society, through careful procedures for commitment and for release.

Wisconsin, where Dahmer was tried, fits the Steadman model. The state didn't weaken its insanity defense after the Hinckley verdict. Still, if Dahmer's defense had succeeded, he would have been placed immediately in custody under the jurisdiction of the criminal court. He would have had chances to prove he was no longer dangerous to himself or society, and that he should be set free, but would have borne the burden of making those proofs. Wisconsin has one of the more liberal approaches to the release of people acquitted by reason of insanity, according to Ingo Keilitz of the National Center for State Courts, and it's fairly restrictive. Dahmer almost certainly would have been kept in custody for life.

Not an Easy Out

It's fashionable to argue that Americans now take less responsibility for their actions than they once did. Insanity defendants are sometimes portrayed as emblematic of the trend, because they are seen as seeking an undeserved dodge. Some critics contend that psychiatry, through the definition of new, expansive mental syndromes and their broad application by experts for hire, makes the problem worse, by excusing behavior it shouldn't.

But the eight-state study dealt directly with that issue. It found that "the vast majority of people who used the insanity defense were seriously mentally ill." Among insanity defendants, 62 percent were diagnosed as suffering from schizophrenia, from some other major mental illness, or from mental retardation, and 72 percent had been hospitalized once or more. Among insanity acquittees, the percentages were 89 and 82. The insanity defense shouldn't be misconstrued as an easy out and falsely blamed for crime, irresponsibility, or other social ills.

When it is made a scapegoat, bad policy can result. That happened in states that adopted the guilty-but-mentally-ill verdict. To the National Center for State Courts, it brought "little change in the manner in which the criminal justice and the mental health systems handle mentally disordered defendants." However, those imprisoned because of it tend to be put away for much longer than those found guilty, and seem to be singled out for unusually harsh punishment. As for abolishing the insanity defense altogether, Steadman and his colleagues report that abolition in Montana didn't make the problem go away. The state still had to deal with defendants who would have pled insanity, usually at hearings where their lawyers argued they were incompetent to stand trial. And it still had to treat them in state facilities.

The insanity defense retains its theoretical place in the law as well as its practical value. The existence of the defense and the very rare cases in which it prevails indicate that American law has kept a traditional, if limited, measure of consistency. The defense isn't likely to gain many vocal supporters, especially when proponents of law and order dominate debate about criminal law, as they have in this country for a generation. But those who claim to seek order in law ought to be among its supporters. In a system rooted in the idea of individual responsibility, the narrow exception of the insanity defense—it is now unquestionably that—strengthens the fundamental rule.

Periodical Bibliography

The following articles have been selected to supplement the diverse views presented in this chapter.

Ray Coleman	"Mentally Ill Youth in the Justice System," *American Jails*, November/December 1993. Available from the American Jail Association, 2053 Day Road, Suite 100, Hagerstown, MD 21740-9795.
CQ Researcher	"The Insanity Defense . . . Fair or Fakery?" August 6, 1993. Available from 1414 22nd St. NW, Washington, DC 20037.
Connie Fortin	"Jail Provides Mental Health and Substance Abuse Services," *Corrections Today*, October 1993.
Rael Jean Isaac and Virginia C. Armat	"Hostages to Madness," *Reader's Digest*, January 1991.
Daniel Kagan	"Cell Check Among the Jailed for 'Crime' of Mental Illness," *Insight*, September 17, 1990. Available from 3600 New York Ave. NE, Washington, DC 20002.
Mark Lopez and Catherine Cheney	"Crowded Prisons and Jails Unable to Meet Needs of Mentally Ill," *National Prison Project Journal*, Summer 1992. Available from the National Prison Project, American Civil Liberties Union Foundation, 1875 Connecticut Ave. NW, Suite 410, Washington, DC 20009.
National Review	"So Guilty They're Innocent," March 2, 1992.
Michael J. O'Sullivan	"Criminalizing the Mentally Ill," *America*, January 4-11, 1992.
Richard M. Restak	"Eliminate Brain Damage Plea from the Courtroom," *USA Today*, January 1991.
Eloise Salholz with Susan Miller	"Insanity: A Defense of Last Resort," *Newsweek*, February 3, 1992.
Thomas Szasz	"Hinckley and Son," *Reason*, July 1991.
Thomas Szasz	"The Socrates Option," *Reason*, May 1992.
Anastasia Toufexis	"Do Mad Acts a Madman Make?" *Time*, February 3, 1992.
James Willwerth	"The Voices Told Him to Kill," *Time*, June 7, 1993.

What Policies Would Benefit the Mentally Ill?

Mental Illness

Chapter Preface

In January 1993, U.S. president Bill Clinton established the White House Task Force on National Health Care Reform, headed by First Lady Hillary Rodham Clinton, to formulate a national health care plan. While most commentators agreed that mental health should be included in the plan, a debate emerged over the extent and nature of treatments to be covered.

Some critics contend that only treatments for severe mental illnesses such as schizophrenia, manic-depressive disorder, and major depression should be covered under a national plan. These critics oppose coverage for what they see as less crucial care, such as substance abuse treatment and psychotherapy for so-called "problems of living." Laurie Flynn, the executive director of the National Alliance for the Mentally Ill (NAMI), a group consisting of family members of people with mental illnesses, argues that "there's a difference between illness and unhappiness." She contends that priority should be given to people with severe "mental illnesses that are diagnosable, treatable, disabling disorders," over people with the "wide range of mental health problems that affect everyone."

Others contend that a national health care plan should include comprehensive mental health benefits, including coverage for substance abuse treatment and psychotherapy. According to Kathryn Pontzer, former director of government relations at the American Association for Marriage and Family Therapy, giving the severely mentally ill priority would establish "a two-tiered system for mental health care, giving the impression that, somehow, certain mental health illnesses are more debilitating and disabling to individuals and their families, and therefore warrant special attention." She concludes that "a continuum of mental health services must be available to all adults and children with mental and emotional disorders." Former first lady Rosalynn Carter agrees: "We must not provide for care based on a hierarchy of pain. We must actively lobby for fair and equitable coverage under any plan of health care reform for everyone who is in need of mental health care."

Like most political issues, the debate over the inclusion of mental health in the nation's health care policy will likely result in some form of compromise that will in turn trigger more argumentation. In the following chapter, various mental health policy proposals are discussed and debated.

"Mental health care represents a significant part of the overall health care system."

Mental Health Should Be Part of General Health Policy

Denis J. Prager and Leslie J. Scallet

In the following viewpoint, Denis J. Prager and Leslie J. Scallet argue that mental health and physical health are interdependent. Consequently, they contend, the traditional barriers between mental and physical health care should be eliminated, and mental health should be included in mainstream health care policy. Prager is director of the health program for the John D. and Catherine T. MacArthur Foundation, a private philanthropic organization in Chicago, Illinois. Scallet is the executive director of the Mental Health Policy Resource Center, a nonprofit research organization in Washington, D.C.

As you read, consider the following questions:

1. According to the authors, whose responsibility is it to develop human potential?
2. Prager and Scallet reject the idea of mental health as two "mutually exclusive categories—mentally well and mentally ill." What conception of mental health do they prefer?
3. According to the authors, what percentage of all hospital days are devoted to mental health care?

From Denis J. Prager and Leslie J. Scallet, "Promoting and Sustaining the Health of the Mind," *Health Affairs*, Fall 1992. Reprinted with the publisher's permission: *Health Affairs*, 7500 Old Georgetown Rd., Ste. 600, Bethesda, MD 20814, 301-656-7401.

In the changing landscape of American domestic politics lies the opportunity for the mental health and well-being of individuals to emerge as a central element of the nation's social agenda. To seize this opportunity, however, our nation must rethink the issues and policy priorities. Despite mental health's relatively low position on the nation's priority list since the early 1980s, much progress has been made, particularly with regard to the most disabling mental disorders. That progress represents a foundation of achievement and experience on which to build for the future.

This viewpoint is a synthesis of views that have emerged from our discussions with leading scientists and policy thinkers. Our purpose has been to develop a working model of the conceptual and strategic elements that are critical to efforts to raise the priority of mental health on the American social agenda and, ultimately, to enhance the mental well-being of individuals. Our hope is that these challenges will suggest a direction for the next decades—guideposts against which we can measure our progress.

Perspective on Mental Health

Our perspective begins with a society that places its highest value on the well-being of the individual. In our view, society's goal should be the realization of every individual's potential, whatever it may be; society thus should assure the conditions under which that potential is developed and expressed. The responsibility to develop human potential is shared among society and individuals. The conditions that promote the development of the individual differ from person to person, and some individuals need more help and support than others.

Inherent in this perspective is recognition of the mind as the core of each individual's being. The mind plays a critical role in the way one learns, thinks, reasons, plans, and makes decisions; the way one relates to others and to the environment, responds to the challenges of living, bounces back from serious life events, and learns from life experiences; and the way one behaves toward oneself, others, and society.

Our future society would value the health of the mind at least as much as it values the health of the body, implementing policies and programs that promote healthy mental development and prevent mental illness, and that provide caring and supportive environments and competent care for individuals with mental, emotional, or behavioral disorders. This will require that society (1) recognize mental health as more than the absence of disease and mental illness as more than categorical disorders defined by standard psychiatric criteria; (2) comprehend the range of mental function and dysfunction; (3) understand mental state to be highly dynamic; and (4) accept the challenge of developing

240

and delivering effective means for sustaining mental health and preventing and treating mental illness.

Defining people as either mentally healthy or mentally ill fails to account for the range of severity of mental dysfunction we routinely lump under the term "mental illness." In reality, one's mental well-being cannot be neatly assigned into one of two mutually exclusive categories—mentally well or mentally ill—any more than one can be described as either physically well or sick.

Just as we routinely view physical health as arrayed along a continuum from poor to excellent, we should conceive of mental health as a continuum of well-being from good health at one end to catastrophic dysfunction and suffering at the other. In between are a number of points, representing greater or lesser degrees of well-being, at which the state of an individual's mental health is a result of the interaction between the nature of his or her disorder—either long-term or transitory—and a range of personal strengths and social or family circumstances.

A Continuum of Intervention Strategies

Treatment Settings Based on Level of Impairment

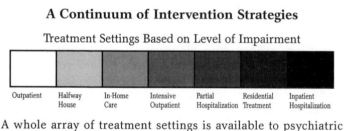

| Outpatient | Halfway House | In-Home Care | Intensive Outpatient | Partial Hospitalization | Residential Treatment | Inpatient Hospitalization |

A whole array of treatment settings is available to psychiatric patients. Increasingly, insurance payers are recognizing the need to provide coverage for all levels on the continuum.

Source: National Association of Psychiatric Health Systems.

This concept should not be misunderstood. It does not imply that every illness has definable stages or could be prevented if caught early enough; nor does it suggest that each definable condition or disorder has its place on a continuum of severity. Rather, we use it to portray an individual's mental condition at a point in time, taking into account all positive and negative factors that apply in a person's life.

Responding effectively to a continuum of mental well-being requires a continuum of intervention strategies. In the more familiar realm of physical disorders, we recognize that treatments range from "sleep, drink fluids, take two aspirin, and call me in the morning," to heroic, lifesaving therapies. Similarly, we should perceive efforts to enhance the health of the mind as arrayed along a continuum, from programs that promote well-being and prevent pathology to crisis intervention.

Since society does not ordinarily categorize people as either always well or always sick, why do we stigmatize individuals with mental disorders and assume that their conditions are permanent, unchanging, and hopeless? Few people with even the most serious mental disorders are ill all of the time. Rather, many long-term conditions are episodic. A person with a severe and long-term mental illness may, with appropriate treatment and support, maintain a relative level of well-being most of the time. A person also may experience a brief but devastating bout of illness that temporarily pushes him or her to catastrophic dysfunction. Many people experience mental conditions at various times that are transitory, treatable, and compatible with a normal, productive existence.

Although society has structured its health policies, programs, professions, and institutions as though there were little relationship between mental and physical health, experience and, increasingly, empirical evidence speak strongly to the contrary. We know from everyday experience that the state of the mind has a profound influence on the state of the body. That influence is deeply embedded in our explanations for ill health, from backaches to cancer. Physicians also know from their experiences that many of the physical symptoms they see in patients are manifestations of mental distress or illness. This base of experiential knowledge is slowly being substantiated by studies documenting the role of mental state in the maintenance and deterioration of good physical health, and in the treatment of and recovery from physical illness.

Health Care Policy

This perspective has significant implications for public policy. . . . One of today's most pressing social issues is the quality, accessibility, and cost of health care. Mental health is considered a basic part of health care when costs are being discussed, otherwise, however, the two are most often treated as distinct. Conceptual and institutional barriers isolate mental health care from the mainstream of health care and sustain the myth that mental and physical health are independent states. The imperative to rein in runaway health costs impedes attempts to break down those barriers.

Mental health care represents a significant part of the overall health care system; more than 20 percent of all hospital days are devoted to mental health care. Health policies that perceive the systems as separate and fail to take into account trends in mental health systems are likely to create perverse and costly distortions in patterns of care. For example, viewing hospitalization for mental illness as the responsibility of the state mental health system belies the reality that expenditures for care in scatter beds in general hospitals now constitute the single largest element of all hospital expenditures for mental disorders.

The health/mental health dichotomy also contradicts the reality of patterns of care. Most people with mental health symptoms—recognized as such or not—are seen first by primary health practitioners. Given the growing reliance on such practitioners for providing the first line of care and for serving as gatekeepers to specialty care, a particular challenge is to develop strategies to increase their capacity to recognize, diagnose, treat, or refer individuals with mental illness. That capacity will be greatly enhanced by diagnostic criteria that are consistent with the realities of the mental conditions that people experience and with the health care system. It also will be enhanced by the development of effective mechanisms for bringing mental health expertise to a range of health care settings. Such advances will assure greater access to competent mental health care without the need for labeling or formal referral.

An integrated approach to health and mental health care also will require that reimbursement [insurance] systems eliminate the current discrimination between interventions for mental and physical conditions. Reimbursement rules [limiting coverage of mental health care] . . . do far more than discourage recognition and appropriate treatment of mental problems. They drive up health costs—often for inappropriate care—masking them under reimbursable diagnoses. Reimbursement systems also discriminate against the use of psychosocial interventions in the treatment of physical illnesses. As we learn more about the relationship of mental state and health, psychosocial interventions proven effective in the treatment of physical conditions should be included in the armamentarium of the health care system and reimbursed accordingly.

Research Policy

One's mental, emotional, and behavioral health at a point in time is determined by a complex set of factors—individual and environmental—that interact to shape the course of human development across the entire life span. Policies capable of enhancing the mental well-being of individuals must be based on sound knowledge of these forces and the ways in which they interact. That knowledge can only derive from research with the capacity to elucidate the genetic, biological, psychological, social, and cultural determinants of health and illness, and to synthesize integrated models of their interactions.

Today's research, hobbled as it is by narrow perspectives, disciplinary boundaries, and institutional compartmentalization, lacks that capacity. The challenge for researchers is to develop intellectual frameworks and models capable of integrating the diverse factors that determine mental well-being and its relationship to physical health, and to translate new knowledge into effective interventions. The challenge for policymakers and administrators is to develop organizational structures, incentives, and funding mechanisms capable of fostering and sustaining intellectual collaboration among those researchers. The challenge for advocates is to promote the broadest, most comprehensive research agenda possible, with the understanding that there are no easy answers. . . .

An important challenge for public policy in the 1990s is to explore how mental health and disorder affect and interrelate with high-priority policy concerns, from homelessness to substance abuse to family preservation. This is not simply a matter of restoring balance to the National Institute of Mental Health (NIMH) [a federal mental health research agency] research portfolio, so that it addresses psychological, behavioral, and social as well as biomedical processes, although this is needed. We must assure that mental health knowledge and perspectives are appropriately incorporated into the nation's conceptualization of and response to critical social problems. . . .

The challenge is to forge a comprehensive concept of mental health capable of linking and integrating the increasingly fragmented elements of policies and programs. Particular attention is needed to assure continuing interaction and dialogue among the research, training, and services communities, to assure that knowledge moves from the laboratory to practice and policy and that questions derived from practice and policy inform research planning.

In a time of extreme pressure on public resources, priorities must be set. If everything is a priority, then nothing can be. However, in setting priorities, we must still recognize the reality of "lesser" needs and the implications of failing to address them. Priorities inevitably will be set through a political process involving disparate groups and interests both within and outside the mental health field.

What is needed is a common set of goals related to enhancing the mental health and well-being of our population. Common goals would provide a positive context for debating specific policy issues and public funding priorities, and a framework within which diverse elements can work to promote their specific interests. They also would point the way to strategies for transcending the barriers that now isolate mental health from health, mental health care from health care, mental health services from social services, and people with mental disorders from other people.

"To the degree that health policy subsumes mental health policy, the latter is doomed to fail."

Mental Health Should Be Independent of General Health Policy

Charles A. Kiesler

Charles A. Kiesler is chancellor of the University of Missouri, Columbia. In the following viewpoint, he argues that mental health policy in the United States is defective because it is dominated by general health policy that supports hospitals and physicians instead of promoting appropriate treatments. By emphasizing acute, inpatient hospital care and surgery, says Kiesler, U.S. health policy fails to meet the mental health needs of most Americans, who would be best treated through prevention, outpatient care, and attention to chronic problems. Kiesler concludes that mental health policy should be developed separately from general health care policy.

As you read, consider the following questions:

1. According to the author, how does the health of Americans rate when compared to other developed countries?
2. Why were prepayment plans originally developed, according to Kiesler?
3. According to the author, how do hospitals and physicians view the problem of indigent care?

From Charles A. Kiesler, "U.S. Mental Health Policy: Doomed to Fail," *American Psychologist*, September 1992. Copyright 1992 by the American Psychological Association. Adapted by permission.

The themes of this viewpoint can be expressed quite simply. Mental health, although historically linked to social welfare policy rather than health policy, has always had nontrivial dependence on federal health policy. Since the early 1980s, this dependence has increased at a rapid rate. The increasing dependence is due in part to changes in federal health policy, which have allowed clever mental health entrepreneurs opportunities in a changing marketplace. However, part of the dependence is also due to the unwitting undercutting or elimination of leadership roles in mental health policy.

The result is a forced mimicry of health services by mental health services under federal health programs in which mental health plays a trivial role. For example, although opportunities for mental health services increasingly exist under Medicare, only 3% of Medicare funding goes for mental health. Because appropriate bodies are not available to articulate mental health policy and services needs, the mental health services most easily reimbursed are those emphasized in health policy, that is, inpatient services, which are demonstrably less effective and more expensive. Lack of articulation of mental health service opportunities and needs, combined with the funding opportunities under health policy, has led to a rapidly increasing dependence of mental health policy on health policy. . . .

The increased absorption of mental health policy under health policy inevitably dooms mental health policy because *U.S. health policy is itself inherently flawed.* Furthermore, the ways in which health policy is flawed have even more negative implications for mental health than for health.

Doomed to Fail

Throughout the 20th century, the cornerstone of U.S. health policy has been the short-term general hospital—the "doctor's workshop"—emphasizing acute care and especially surgery. This fact has led the United States to have the best hospital care in the world but a population that, on average, has only mediocre health compared with other developed countries. This irony is largely determined by the fact that the strengths of U.S. health policy—centered on the short-term, acute-care general hospital—do not match up well with the health needs of the nation. Left underemphasized in U.S. health policy are preventive services needed by the least wealthy 40% of the population; the needed behavioral changes in the population that could lead to healthier practices; and various chronic health problems, especially those experienced by the elderly, children, and youth.

This disparity between service strengths and national needs is exaggerated for mental health policy to the extent that it mimics health policy. In the United States, health care in a short-term acute-care hospital is the best in the world. However, in mental health, care outside a hospital is demonstrably better and less expensive than care in the hospital. Consequently, whatever limitations current health policies have in addressing the health status of the average citizen, the limitations are much more severe for any mental health policy that mimics it. Inevitably, to the degree that health policy subsumes mental health policy, the latter is doomed to fail. . . .

Cornerstone of Health Policy in the United States

One could argue—and effectively—that we do not have any national health policy in the United States. However, to the extent that we do, our health policy is inherently flawed. Current health policy is certainly not an appropriate model for mental health. . . . Numerous articles [have been written] regarding hospital cost containment and health care cost containment in the United States; numerous professional articles on PPS [Prospective Payment System—a capitation scheme (a uniform per-capita fee) introduced by Medicare] and its imitators; and comparisons of health care costs and outcomes with Canada, England, and other industrial nations. A very succinct summary of this literature is that the United States pays more than any other country for health care, has arguably the best hospital care in the world, and as a nation has mediocre health. Over 30 million Americans do not have health insurance at all, and another more than 30 million do not have health insurance sometime during the year.

Rosemary Stevens has described how the United States has found itself in this quandary in her brilliant book *In Sickness and in Wealth: American Hospitals in the Twentieth Century*. Stevens documented the notion that American health policies have always focused on short-term, nonfederal general hospitals, sometimes called voluntary hospitals or community hospitals. These hospitals have always had one primary emphasis—surgery—and one overriding concern—paying patients. Although the terms *voluntary* and *community hospitals* would imply potential treatment for all citizens, this has never really been the case. Historically, capital expenses have come from gifts and investments, but patients have paid for their hospital treatment. In England, the opposite trend could be seen early. In 1911, patients in London provided only 10% of total hospital income. In short, our lack of emphasis on access to health care in the United States is not recent.

Furthermore, a concern with separating doctors' income and hospital income was also always present. In 1904, for example, the Mayo brothers [Charles and William, of the famed Mayo Clinic] and their associates performed more than 3,000 surgical operations. They obviously made a fortune. But their patients stayed in St. Mary's—a Catholic, charitable, nonprofit hospital.

The American Hospital Association (AHA) was formed by hospital administrators in 1899 and was originally called the Association of Hospital Superintendents. In World War I, the enormous success of surgical teams in combat zones (formed largely by groups of surgeons from university hospitals) had a dramatic impact on health policy in the United States then and now. From the 1920s on, hospitals—particularly teaching hospitals—became the cornerstone of the U.S. health care system. They have consistently emphasized short-term acute care, especially surgery, and still do.

The hospital system became big business. By 1930, $2 billion had been invested in general hospitals, making it the fifth largest industry in the nation. By 1923, 23% of the entire nation's medical bill was going directly to hospitals.

The Development of Prepayment

But hospitals were still places for the rich, and the principal question for hospital administrators was how to attract persons of moderate means to inpatient care. In 1929, Baylor University offered services to white school teachers and other groups for a fixed annual fee, collected in monthly installments. The fee depended on whether ultimate care was desired in a ward or in a private room. All standard hospital charges were included in the fees. Stevens emphasized that the primary purpose of this development was not to increase the access of the average citizen to medical care but to stabilize the income of hospitals by providing for a prepayment for potential use.

The American Hospital Association was strongly behind the development of prepayment plans to produce income. Originally, the American Medical Association (AMA) was opposed to any kind of "corporate medicine," including salaries for physicians. Both AHA and AMA opposed the original social security legislation in 1935 for two reasons: They did not want to treat welfare patients, and they saw potential federal control over hospitals and physicians. Throughout the 20th century, despite huge federal contributions to hospital construction, to medical education, and to medical technology, the AMA and the AHA have opposed any strings to the money.

Building on the Baylor Plan, Blue Cross plans were begun to *prepay* hospital expenses, not to provide increased access of the average citizen to care. Of 39 Blue Cross plans surveyed in 1944-1945, hospitals contributed to the starting capital in 22 of them. As Stevens said, "Blue Cross schemes were corporations founded by corporations (hospitals), which responded to the needs of corporations (employers)." Excluded from the Blue Cross plans were mental health, the elderly, the unemployed, the disabled, agricultural and domestic workers, and part-time workers. In general, physicians opposed Blue Cross, and no doctor fees were covered. The opposition was largely on grounds of who would be in control, but negotiations led to increased autonomy for physicians. In the late 1930s Blue Shield was started for similar reasons, to provide income for physicians in hospitals.

Excessive Hospitalization

Not every patient symptomatic with a mental disorder or substance abuse needs the protection or supervision available in 24-hour inpatient care. . . . Many psychiatric patients with acute exacerbations could be treated with day hospitalization to adjust medication, more frequent office visits, domiciliary care, or in other outpatient treatment settings. However, insurers have not traditionally recognized the differences among various outpatients settings, nor have they structured benefits to encourage use of such alternatives. As a result, in-hospital stays are longer than necessary.

Steven S. Sharfstein, Anne M. Stoline, and Howard H. Goldman, *American Journal of Psychiatry*, January 1993.

These themes from the 1930s continue to the present day: (a) Hospitals or medically controlled corporations independently contract for prepayment for services; (b) doctors are independent from hospital control and separately contract for services; (c) both are willing to accept federal funds but not federal control or federal oversight; (d) both hospitals and physicians see indigent care as the government's problem, not the hospital's problem; and (e) both hospitals and physicians' services in them are based on the latest and most expensive technology, which in turn has been mostly paid for by the federal government.

There are two major themes throughout the 20th century regarding U.S. health policy: (a) Short-term, acute-care hospitals are the cornerstone of health care in the United States, and (b) the hospital is regarded as the doctors' workshop—which others pay for but physicians control. The current view of hospitals as effectively conjoining science and treatment is not a new view but one that has been put forth by service providers throughout this century. Stevens argued that discoveries such as sulfa [a bacteria-inhibiting chemical] and penicillin had a much more substantial impact on health care than did hospitals or high technology equipment (and neither was an American discovery).

Nonetheless, the emphasis in the United States now and throughout the 20th century is (was) on hospital care and not health care. Nationally, the emphasis is on quality of care and not access to care. There has never been effective national planning; planning has always more or less been regional in nature, leaving doctors alone and providing them with enhanced hospital and diagnostic facilities.

Hospital Policy, Not Health Policy

My purpose here is not to deprecate either physicians or hospitals but rather to show the following: To the extent we have a health policy in the United States, it is to support general hospitals (rather than health) and the physicians who use them, along with the expensive technology they desire. Our national policy supports *acute care* and technology, along with providing all capital expenses. Hospitals remain the doctors' workshop, and they heavily emphasize surgery.

On the other hand, our health needs as a nation do not match up well with a de facto policy that emphasizes acute care and surgery. In particular, the needs of the elderly, children and youth, families, the uninsured or underinsured—meaning the majority of the citizens of the country—take two forms: prevention and addressing chronic problems. Even partial solutions to both these problems require easy access to general medical care but not necessarily specialized care.

National health policy is flawed at its core: It represents national general hospital policy, not health policy. Mental health—even though traditionally seen as a state and welfare problem—has always been dominated by health policy. However, mental health policy has lost its traditional roots—state hospitals and the CMHC [Community Mental Health Center] system [a federally funded program to establish community-based mental health centers nationwide], and very flawed roots they were—and increasingly comes unwittingly under de facto health policy through Medicaid, Medicare, Blue Cross/Blue Shield, and other commercial insurance.

This increasing domination of mental health by health policy allows us to understand better a number of trends: (a) Although policy analysts have consistently concluded we need to decrease children's hospitalization for mental disorders, it is increasing. Indeed, children's mental hospitalization is increasing dramatically in hospitals without specialized units, in RTCs [residential treatment centers], and in private psychiatric hospitals—all of which represent unknowns regarding treatment effectiveness. (b) Although we conclude that the problems of the elderly are disproportionately chronic, 12% of Medicare eligibles had surgery in 1979, and the total population of Medicare eligibles spent 4.1 days on average per year per person in general hospitals (six times as many as the rest of the population). It appears that acute problems are being emphasized rather than the chronic problems that exist. (c) We conclude in mental health that outpatient care works better than inpatient care, but inpatient care continues to increase, and outpatient care is difficult to fund. (d) In spite of data to the contrary, there are consistent incentives in public and private insurance programs in mental health that favor inpatient care.

Independent Mental Health Policies Needed

In conclusion, our national health policy supports hospital care, not health care. Mental health treatment data are clearly inconsistent with and indeed contradict the bias toward inpatient care. Even though there is improvement in the linkage between mental health policy and data, there are severe limitations of how far we can go in those otherwise encouraging trends, working under an umbrella health policy that favors inpatient acute care.

Some have argued that health and mental health practice and policy should come closer. One could make a good argument for that point of view because of the obvious overlap regarding health and mental health problems in individuals. However, when health policy is flawed and when the cornerstone of health policy is acute inpatient care, the more mental health policy is subsumed under health policy, the more expensive and inappropriate mental health care will become.

Perhaps the best outcome data in either health or mental health are those that demonstrate that psychiatric care of serious mental disorders is more effectively and less expensively treated outside hospitals than in them. I emphasize that the inpatient care in those studies represents perhaps the best psychiatric inpatient care available. The psychiatric inpatient sites that have recently substantially increased their episodes of care—private psychiatric hospitals, RTCs, and quasi-units [organized services and personnel within general hospitals that do not meet the formal legal requirements of a psychiatric unit]—provide demonstratively less intensive care than psychiatric units, and their treatment effectiveness up to now is completely unassessed.

These notions pragmatically dictate a clear conclusion: Mental health policy analysts and advocates need to articulate mental health service needs and treatment data more clearly and to work to develop public federal and state policies that are specific to those needs but independent of health policy.

"Costs associated with the lack of adequate health care coverage for people with severe mental illnesses far exceed the costs associated with providing treatment services."

National Health Care Should Include Mental Health Benefits

National Alliance for the Mentally Ill

The National Alliance for the Mentally Ill (NAMI) is a consumer advocacy organization consisting of families of people with severe mental illnesses such as schizophrenia, depression, and manic-depressive disorder. In the following viewpoint, NAMI argues that treatments for severe mental illnesses should be covered under the nation's health care reform efforts because providing such treatments is cheaper than paying the social service costs created by the untreated mentally ill.

As you read, consider the following questions:

1. What are the "underpinnings" of severe mental illnesses, according to NAMI?
2. According to NAMI, why do many young mentally ill persons "find themselves in limbo" concerning insurance?
3. What is the estimated cost per month of covering biologically based mental illnesses for residents in the state of Maryland, according to the authors?

National Alliance for the Mentally Ill, "Paper for the White House Health Care Task Force: Health Insurance Reform," February 14, 1993. Reprinted with permission.

NAMI [National Alliance for the Mentally Ill] is a national self-help organization of families of persons of all ages with severe mental illnesses, i.e. schizophrenia, affective [mood] disorders, bipolar disorder [manic-depression] etc.; families, who next to the consumers [patients], have suffered the most emotionally and financially through their personal involvement and support of a son or a daughter, a sibling or a spouse, or even a parent afflicted with these devastating brain diseases; dedicated families who continue as volunteers to support NAMI's mission to improve the quality of life for all persons with severe mental illnesses and ultimately to eradicate these tragic brain diseases. NAMI's membership totals over 140,000 persons consisting of families of persons with severe mental illnesses, as well as recovering consumers themselves. . . .

NAMI members subscribe to the prevailing scientific judgement that severe mental illnesses—including depression, manic-depression, and schizophrenia—are complex disorders with biological, neurological and possibly genetic underpinnings. Today, there are no known causes or cures for these brain disorders, although in most cases symptoms can be managed through the appropriate combinations of medication, supportive housing and community-based rehabilitative services.

Principles for Reform

In August 1991 NAMI's Board of Directors developed and promulgated the following principles against which health care reform legislative proposals are evaluated:

I. Access to affordable third-party coverage for all Americans with reasonable individual cost-sharing.

II. Coverage of disorders of the brain equal in scope and duration to coverage of other physical disorders.

III. Elimination of arbitrary lifetime limitations on benefits payable for the treatment of these illnesses.

IV. Coverage of all proven-effective modes of treatment: inpatient, outpatient, pharmacologic [drug], case management, rehabilitation, and others appropriate to the individual's needs.

V. For persons dependent on the public sector, coverage of mental illness at least as comprehensive as presently available through Medicaid and Medicare.

Our nation's investment in mental illness research has been paying outstanding dividends. New medications and psychosocial treatments resulting from this investment will more than pay for their development costs by offsetting the tremendous burden now borne by society. For example, the 1969 introduction of lithium to treat manic-depressive illness resulted in average yearly savings in treatment costs of $290 million in the United

States. In this, the "Decade of the Brain" [as declared by George Bush in 1990], research supported by the federal National Institute of Mental Health (NIMH)—now part of the world-renowned National Institutes of Health (NIH)—has spawned revolutionary breakthroughs in treatment so that millions of Americans can be helped to lead more productive, less painful lives. The 1990 introduction of clozapine to the U.S. market has permitted thousands of previously treatment-resistant persons with schizophrenia to regain social and economic productivity. While the causes of mental illnesses remain unknown, data from several major studies illuminate the role of biological factors in schizophrenia, bipolar disorder, major depression, obsessive-compulsive disorder and panic disorder.

The Cost of Not Providing Care

Untreated or under-treated mental illness results in enormous costs to society, including lost work, reduced productivity, and prison recidivism. The number of persons with mental illness among the homeless is estimated to be between 200,000 and 350,000. There is a shockingly high rate of suicide among persons with severe mental illnesses on our nation's streets, and in its shelters and jails.

The 1992 federal Interagency Task Force Report on Homelessness and Severe Mental Illness "Outcasts on Main Street" vividly depicts the personal and societal consequences of this failed commitment to a vulnerable class of citizens. In September 1992, NAMI and Public Citizen Health Research Group released a national study, *Criminalizing the Seriously Mentally Ill: The Abuse of Jails as Mental Hospitals*, revealing that over 37,000 mentally ill individuals are now in jails, most charged with simple misdemeanors such as loitering or trespassing. Nearly one-third of these persons have not been charged with any crime; they have been arrested on "mercy bookings" because access to mental health care is restricted or denied.

A pervasive public stigma against persons with mental illnesses manifests itself in countless ways, only one of which is in insurance coverage. Third-party [insurance] payers typically cover the costs of treatment for non-psychiatric or physical illnesses in full, or with minimum patient contribution, while excluding or limiting coverage of the treatment of mental (or psychiatric) illnesses. Schizophrenia and severe depressive illness are essentially viewed by private industry and government as second-class illnesses in this country. Often private coverage is limited to $1000 a year for outpatient care and 30 days of annual hospitalization with a $25,000 lifetime maximum, while similar limitations do not exist for the treatment of cancer, diabetes or heart disease. These misguided restrictions often force families to deplete their lifetime savings, liquidate their homes and personal belongings, and ultimately rely upon an under-funded and overburdened public system. For persons fortunate to be enrolled in a minimally acceptable employer-provided insurance program, the irony is that professional mobility is restricted because of industry-wide "pre-existing condition" clauses. Persons with severe mental illnesses are particularly impacted by these restrictions, as mental illness often strikes during the late teen years and early adulthood. Many young persons find themselves in limbo—too old to continue coverage under their parents' policy and too young to be in the workforce where insurance is generally purchased. And most persons diagnosed as mentally ill are unable to qualify for *any* form of health insurance.

Insurance for Mental Illness Is Feasible

The debate over national health care reveals a concern that insurance cannot support endless psychotherapy for "problems of living" that affect the so-called "worried well." NAMI agrees that such non-medical interventions are not vital to the needs of persons who suffer severe mental illnesses. We do assert that advances in diagnosis and treatment for specific, biologically based, severe psychiatric disorders make them relatively inexpensive additions to private coverage. The cost of caring for persons with mental illnesses in the community in the PACT [Program for Assertive Community Treatment] Program of Dane County, Wisconsin, has reduced costs by two-thirds. This model program [which assists patients in the community] . . . is widely acknowledged to offer state of the art treatment and support for persons with severe mental illness.

In the 102nd Congress, a bipartisan group of twenty-one U.S. Senators, led by Senator Pete V. Domenici and including then Senator Albert Gore, Jr., co-sponsored legislation which would [have] establish[ed] a comprehensive federal policy with respect to provision of the health care coverage and services to persons with severe mental illnesses. [The legislation has since died.] Several state legislatures have either enacted or considered proposed legislation covering the more severe mental illnesses, once presented with the relevant data outlining the incidence of these illnesses and the modest medical treatment costs associated with their management. Actuarial data on the costs/benefits associated with coverage of the most severe mental illnesses have been instrumental in convincing policy-makers across the country that these illnesses can be included in insurance coverage at only a small additional premium cost when set against a large pool of insured persons. For example, the added cost of covering the biologically based mental illnesses on the same basis as other physical illnesses for residents of the State of Maryland is estimated at approximately $1.00 per covered person per month. A Coopers and Lybrand [a large accounting firm] study of residents of the State of California yielded a $0.78 increase in premium cost. . . .

In order to keep total costs within tolerable limits the Domenici sponsors and certain state legislatures have recognized the need to draw some distinctions between the severe and persistent illnesses and emotional distress associated with life events. The costs of treatment of severe brain disorders are not excessive as studies have proven, if the patient has available, and adheres to, an integrated regime of treatment with pharmacological agents, medical monitoring, and some supportive services.

An Appropriate Intuition

There is a strong intuition that society should give the highest priority to treating the sickest or most disabled patients. This "hierarchy of pain" criterion is seen clearly in the strong human proclivity to respond to the worst-off victims of illness or accident. . . . In certain cases the intuition seems appropriate. Take for example the case of a minor mental dysfunction that causes little harm, is limited to the individual, and has no real impact on the smooth functioning of the society; our intuition that this sort of case ought not to be a high public priority is probably correct.

Philip Boyle and Daniel Callahan, *Hastings Center Report*, September/October 1993.

President Bill Clinton has repeatedly stated his belief that government must first serve those in our society who are most vulnerable. NAMI supports this position and believes that the direct and indirect costs associated with the lack of adequate health care coverage for people with severe mental illnesses far exceed the costs associated with providing treatment services. NAMI believes that mandating health insurance coverage for the severe mental illnesses could slow the explosive growth of Medicaid, SSI [supplemental security income] and SSDI [Social Security Disability Income] since persons with mental illnesses are the largest single group among those now covered. Over time, more equitable coverage of persons with severe mental illnesses will also stem the tide of persons with mental illnesses in crisis now pouring into jails, emergency rooms, and shelters. People with severe mental illnesses are a growing burden on public hospitals which face rapid escalation in the cost of uncompensated care. By shifting those specific costs to the private sector and treating severe mental illnesses like any other major illness such as cancer, diabetes and heart disease, an entire group of vulnerable disabled people can avoid descent into poverty, which typically occurs when psychiatric benefits are exhausted but the illness continues.

Managed Care and Managed Competition

Given the dismal failure of our present fee-for-service third-party reimbursement system, NAMI members view with cautious optimism the new emphasis on organized systems of health care delivery. The emphasis within these delivery systems on the total care management ["managed care"] for the individual seeking treatment services could well mitigate the problems associated with the fragmented funding and delivery system which currently exists for persons with severe mental illnesses and allow for a continuum of medically necessary and appropriate services. In addition, the large health insurance purchasing groups [to be created by proposed reforms] should certainly have the economic clout to negotiate more comprehensive coverage of benefits than is presently available for small employers and individuals, thereby assuring greater consumer access to coverage. . . . NAMI strongly calls for a role for consumers and family members in the governance of these new health insuring structures as well as in ongoing monitoring to assure high quality clinical services in both hospital and outpatient settings.

At the same time, NAMI members join with our colleagues throughout the disability community in wishing to reserve judgement until a new delivery system is operational and fully evaluated by consumers and their family members. Our primary concern at this time is whether specialty care services—such as those provided by a psychiatrist to an individual with a severe mental illness—can be integrated into the core benefit package [guaranteed services] likely to be required in any accountable health plan. The range of treatment needs for persons disabled by illness is presently provided through the state Medicaid program through several optional benefits. Should Medicaid be repealed [as some reformers propose], the discussion must immediately center on how best to ensure access to rehabilitation, pharmaceuticals, case management and other support services within the framework of the managed care model. The acute care insurance model with its emphasis on physician and hospital services is critical to this population, but not nearly sufficient. The services provided through the public sector of government (Medicaid and the state hospital system) must continue to be provided, either through direct inclusion in the basic benefits package or perhaps through contracts or other affiliations with existing public providers. For the longer term services needed for full consumer functioning in society, such as housing supports and vocational rehabilitation services, NAMI insists that government continue to support them categorically and with sufficient funding.

Continuous and timely access to specialized treatment and rehabilitative services must be assured if in fact these services are mandated within the managed care model. . . . NAMI feels that for those individuals in need of more than primary care services, consideration [should] be given to assigning a psychiatrist as the primary care gatekeeper who would then be responsible for managing that individual's treatment planning. All too often, our members report, general medical professionals are poorly trained in the management of psychiatric illness and lacking the continuing education to stay abreast of modern effective treatment interventions.

While severe mental illnesses cannot be prevented with the current state of medical science, specific, recurring episodes of psychosis, mania, depression and other aspects of the illnesses can be prevented by early identification and early initiation of good treatment regimens. Innovative programs such as those in Madison, Wisconsin, and Waterloo, Iowa, feature a central authority, like the managed care "gatekeeper," which is responsible for all aspects of treatment and services provision. In these example areas, the cost of treatment was reduced by more than two-thirds in the years following implementation. Important to the success of these integrated services models is the continuous treatment, team concept which integrates and links medical and social support services.

Given the broad agreement that coverage of severe mental illness reduces societal costs in terms of homelessness, reliance on the criminal justice system, and other social and welfare programs, the following summarize NAMI policy objectives in health care reform efforts:

- Distinction between severe, disabling brain disorders and emotional distress associated with problems of living in order to keep program costs within reasonable limits.
- Attention and resources must be devoted to the needs of persons with chronic and disabling illnesses in any acute care model.
- Integration of medical, rehabilitative and social support services in the delivery system.
- Attention to the needs of special populations, e.g., veterans, children and ethnic minorities.
- Attention to maintaining and equalizing guaranteed access to long-term rehabilitation services when and if Medicaid support is phased out.
- Emphasis on treatment guidelines and treatment outcomes to create accountability.
- Consumer and family involvement in evaluation of program effectiveness.

*"We apparently were healthier as a people . . .
when we spent less trying to let everyone feel
just right."*

National Health Care Should Not Include Mental Health Benefits

The Wall Street Journal

In 1993, the Clinton administration proposed a plan to reform the nation's health care system. In the following viewpoint, written shortly after the plan was unveiled, the *Wall Street Journal* questions the feasibility of the plan's inclusion of mental health and substance abuse treatments. The *Journal* maintains that the definitions of mental illness have become too broad, and that the costs of treating millions of people for vaguely defined conditions such as "anxiety disorder" and "functional impairment" would be excessive. The *Journal* concludes that rather than extensive mental health treatment, the nation's troubled citizens need "a stabilized social order" based on traditional families and values.

As you read, consider the following questions:

1. According to Tipper Gore, cited by the *Journal*, what percentage of Americans suffer from mental problems in any given year?
2. What does the *Journal* suspect is another label for "oppositional defiant disorder"?
3. What does the *Journal* believe that "the worst of wretches" on the nation's streets may need?

Is the U.S. destined to be a therapeutic state in which all deficiencies of body and mind are the proper concern of Washington and its 50 state adjuncts?

To date, medical attention has been financed publicly for the poorest and oldest and sickest among us—an increasingly loose and unaffordable distinction, granted, but at least an attempt to draw some lines. Bill and Hillary Clinton's proposal [to reform the nation's health care system] is all about erasing lines, and nowhere is this more portentous than in mental health and "substance-abuse" treatment.

To grasp this, just listen to Tipper Gore, the inside crusader for more generous coverage in this area. The Vice President's wife has argued that in any given year, 28% of all Americans suffer from mental problems, including drug and alcohol addictions. At a Cleveland, Ohio, forum, she referred to 50 million mentally ill, including 14 million children, being consigned to a care "ghetto" or receiving no help at all in the U.S.

These are staggering numbers. As Mrs. Gore acknowledged, they include afflictions ranging from "severe schizophrenia to more mild bouts of depression." The most common condition among those included in this group is "anxiety disorder." That ought to give us pause.

Demand Is Determined by Supply

Who does not suffer from anxieties? When do they become a clinical disorder? Despite the work of psychiatrists to define the illnesses they treat, the history of government entitlements suggests there will be no definable limit to such complaint. The number of sufferers is likely to expand or contract based on the tenderness of the helping hand available and the hourly rate it charges. How might we know this? Consider the experience of many residential college campuses, whose student health programs function as laboratories of the Clinton model.

At least 10% of these college students receive psychological help, and the number may be double that at some campuses. According to Robert Gallagher, director of the University of Pittsburgh's counseling center and knowledgeable about the situation nationwide, the effective limit is the budget for professionals handling the load. "If you doubled the staff, you could probably double the number coming in," he says.

As it is, despite tightened belts in academia, there's been a gradual increase in patient demand, he reports, and the number of sessions per counseled student is increasing. A further note on this front is a report in *Lear's* magazine, anecdotal and rather dramatized, of the college health center becoming a prime dispensary of Prozac and other antidepressant drugs.

The subject of a best-selling book [*Listening to Prozac*, by Peter

D. Kramer], Prozac has become a kind of metaphor for the therapeutic state. Without doubt, this kind of drug has helped many in genuine need of their restorative powers. Yet as Prozac's sales zoomed to more than $1 billion within five years of introduction, it seemingly appealed to large numbers of Americans who are simply dissatisfied with their personalities and desire a surer ticket to happiness and social success.

An Expanding Category

Given the nebulous behavioral criteria for psychiatric diagnosis, there is really no scientifically sound way to confirm or disconfirm a diagnosis. Nearly any patient could be diagnosed as suffering from "adjustment disorder," for example—a catch-all mental disorder defined by psychiatry's diagnostic manual as "a maladaptive reaction to an identifiable psychosocial stressor." Unlike real physical illnesses, "mental illnesses" have no measurable pathology specific to their diagnoses, and for more than 95% of Americans, there is not even a serious claim of physically caused psychiatric disorder. . . .

Mental illness, unlike physical illness, is an infinitely expandable category; we cannot afford the costs of allowing all of humankind's problems in living to be transmogrified into "diseases."

Richard E. Vatz and Lee S. Weinberg, *Los Angeles Times*, December 13, 1993.

How many of these people are among those lumped under "anxiety disorder" is hard to know, though presumably they have graduated beyond routine therapy to an M.D. (ideally a psychiatrist) to gain their prescriptions. What the Clinton plan, with its expanded psychopharmacological benefits, would add to the Prozac craze is hard to fathom.

Disorder-Seeking and Blame-Shifting

In a more specialized vein, the state of Wisconsin (and perhaps others) has seen a rise in youngsters classified as having "oppositional defiant disorder" under the SSI [Supplemental Security Income] arm of Social Security. This temperament flaw, which sounds suspiciously as if it could encompass what once earned the label "brat," entitles a parent to increased state support.

Within the field of treatment for alcohol and drug addictions, great shifts are occurring as companies and their insurers pull back from the runaway costs that these endeavors piled up in the 1980s. So, too, are the Clintonites being scared off (for now), but the basic fright seems to be about how long these patients reside in a facility, and not who all they consist of. As "substance abuse" has emerged as a disability under the law, what was a taint can turn into a totem for those who want to game the system.

An addict is an addict, it might be said, but do we really know? Some put the number of alcoholics in the U.S. as high as 30 million. And what about all the "enablers" and "co-dependents"? Should they receive tax-paid treatment, too? And what addictions shall we stop at? Tobacco? Sex? Who knows what psychological odyssey lies beyond Ira Magaziner's 2001?

(Actually, in mental health the answer may come down to the phrase "functional impairment," which is to be the threshold used by the 50 state medical directorates in deciding—each according to its own lights—whose bills to pay.)

America is engulfed by a wave of disorder-seeking and blame-shifting. It is somebody else's or some other thing's fault when individuals are messed up, and the diagnoses are adaptive to the circumstances. The National Institute of Mental Health reported that by 1990, $69 billion was being spent in the U.S. in this area. Mrs. Gore maintains that the problem, including substance abuse, is costing the economy $270 billion a year, which then probably becomes the ceiling price for dealing with it.

An Absence of Societal Will?

But cost is not the only great risk in the extensive ambitions of the therapeutic state. Another is the likelihood that as nearly everybody is "helped," fewer of those who undeniably ought to have it will get it, or enough of it. The dispute over paying for anything more than short-burst detox for addicts is part of this concern. Maybe, for the worst of wretches on our nation's streets, a longer confinement—somewhere—is the only answer.

The lame truth is that while the U.S. remains on a tear to insure everyone for everything from hangnails to heartaches, its public spaces and prisons teem with lost souls who in many cases could be helped with drugs and therapies that medicine has developed. In that respect, Mrs. Gore and her lobby, which includes Rosalynn Carter and Republicans such as Alan Simpson and Pete Domenici, are so right: Intelligent and caring application of mental-health resources has the potential to curb all kinds of antisocial behavior. But we have to wonder, in how many of those awful instances was the absence of a treatment facility the difference, as opposed to the societal will to see that its wayward elements go and stay where they might get attention?

A Stabilized Social Order Is Needed

From that core pathological constituency, it is a series of distinguishable steps up through the underclass to the dysfunctional fallouts from the middle class and finally to those still affluent but alienated from the world around them. At each of these levels there surely exist the clinically ill. But there is other, better attention we can give them first.

That other is a stabilized social order that helps the distracted to maintain some purpose in their lives, that prevents them from crashing off the roadway in the first place. It starts with having a parent tend to a child, with having a father stay with a mother, with having the television and the CDs turned off long enough to relate once a day and with having the whole bunch trundle off to church or some such place where they might regularly reflect on love and other values that used to hold families and individuals together in stressful times.

If we had to isolate one set of shortcomings that have led Americans to where they are today, with Tipper Gore estimating that more than a quarter of us are in need of special help, it would be those addressed in that prescription. We suspect Mrs. Gore wouldn't disagree with our analysis, as far as it goes, but would hold out nevertheless for a vast new taxpayer-supported entitlement to deal with matters she thinks have gotten beyond hearth and home.

That brings us to the fundamental divide in U.S. politics, which is where, in addition to the pure economic considerations of the Clintons' medicine show, the legislative battle needs to be fought out. We apparently were healthier as a people, psychologically and in many cases physically, when we spent less trying to let everyone feel just right. That is a paradox that those who demand that we spend so very much more must first explain. Otherwise the wild fiscal currents will leave them eventually with nothing to stand on.

"Solutions to the mental-health mess are possible
if government has the will to implement them."

Government Policy Reforms Would Benefit the Mentally Ill

E. Fuller Torrey

Since the 1960s, according to E. Fuller Torrey, a series of mistakes made by the U.S. government and society has led to a "social disaster," with increasing numbers of untreated mentally ill people living on the streets, landing in jails and prisons, and committing violence. In the following viewpoint, Torrey, a clinical and research psychiatrist in Washington, D.C., proposes six steps that government should take to solve the "mental-health mess." For example, he argues that fiscal responsibility for the mentally ill should be shifted from the federal government to the states, and that state laws should be changed to make it easier to involuntarily hospitalize patients.

As you read, consider the following questions:

1. According to Torrey, what percentage of Community Mental Health Centers has provided good services?
2. Why did the states try to empty their psychiatric hospitals when the mentally ill were made eligible for federal programs, according to the author?
3. According to Torrey, where do most mental health professionals work?

E. Fuller Torrey, "The Mental-Health Mess," *National Review*, December 28, 1992, ©1992 by National Review, Inc., 150 E. 35th St., New York, NY 10016. Reprinted by permission.

Providing care for people with serious mental illnesses has been seen as a legitimate function of state government since before there was a United States. In 1766 Governor Francis Fauquier went before the Virginia House of Burgesses and asked for funds to open the first public psychiatric hospital. Fauquier was concerned about the increasing number of the seriously mentally ill—people we would diagnose today as having schizophrenia and manic-depressive psychosis—who were accumulating on the streets and in the jails of Williamsburg and other Virginia towns. Fauquier's efforts led to the opening of what would become Eastern State Hospital. For the next two hundred years state governments accepted full responsibility for these people, housing them in state-operated asylums because there was no effective treatment for their illnesses.

Social Disaster

Since the early 1960s this situation has changed dramatically. First, medications became available to control many of the psychiatric symptoms—medications such as Prolixin, Haldol, and Navane, which control the voices and delusional thinking of schizophrenia, and lithium, which controls the mania of manic-depressive psychosis.

Next, we began emptying the state psychiatric hospitals, reducing their overall population from 559,000 in 1955 to just over 100,000 in 1992. Most of the people thus released *could* live in the community *if* they continued to receive medication and other aftercare. But we have not provided this aftercare, for reasons that will be explained below. The consequence has been the largest social disaster in late-twentieth-century America.

The dimensions of the disaster are obvious to anyone who has been downtown in any American city since the early 1980s. The seriously mentally ill, who make up one-third of the total homeless population, can be seen on streetcorners chatting amiably with or responding angrily to voices in their heads. These individuals are suffering from schizophrenia and manic-depressive illness. At the time they were discharged from state psychiatric hospitals almost all of them were taking their medication and were clinically in reasonable condition. But that was months or years ago; they failed to receive aftercare, and so they became sick again and eventually homeless.

A study in Massachusetts showed that 27 per cent of those discharged from state psychiatric hospitals became homeless within six months; a similar study in Ohio found the figure to be 36 per cent. These people joined other mentally ill homeless people in cities like New York and San Francisco.

Another measure of the mental-health mess is the increasing number of mentally ill people in jails and prisons. One survey found that, on any given day, there are approximately 30,700 persons with schizophrenia or manic-depressive illness among the 426,000 inmates in the nation's local jails. Many of these mentally ill inmates *have no charges whatsoever against them* but are merely being held in jail awaiting transportation to, or the availability of a bed in, a state psychiatric hospital. In 17 states it is still legal to hold such mentally ill people in jail without any charges. Another large segment of the mentally ill in jails are there on minor charges, such as "dine-and-dash" (ordering a restaurant meal they cannot pay for). Sometimes police charge the mentally ill with minor crimes just to get them off the streets, a practice commonly known as "mercy bookings." In the jail survey 69 per cent of the respondents said that the number of seriously mentally ill inmates has increased since the early 1980s.

Studies in state prisons corroborate these findings. A summary of these studies by Dr. Ron Jemelka and his colleagues at the University of Washington concluded that 10 to 15 per cent of the 771,000 inmates in state prisons are seriously mentally ill. This would be approximately 100,000 inmates. When this number is combined with the 30,700 seriously mentally ill in local jails and the 116,000 in the homeless population, it becomes evident that, on any given day, approximately 250,000 seriously mentally ill people—a quarter of a million—are living on the streets, in public shelters, in jails, and in prisons.

Public and Family Violence

Another measure of the mental-health mess is the increasing episodes of public violence by the *untreated* mentally ill. (It is important to emphasize the word "untreated," because studies have shown that *treated* individuals with serious mental illness are *not* more dangerous than the general population.) Such cases include Juan Gonzalez, who killed two people with a sword on New York's Staten Island ferry; Sylvia Seegrist, who shot ten people in a shopping center near Philadelphia; Laurie Dann, who shot six children in an elementary school near Chicago; Herbert Mullin, who randomly killed thirteen people near San Francisco; and James Brady, who shot five people in a shopping mall in Atlanta. All of these people had been identified as seriously mentally ill and were in need of treatment but were not receiving it. A study of people who push strangers in front of subway trains in New York City showed that more than half of them had a diagnosis of schizophrenia but apparently were receiving no treatment.

Such cases are merely the visible tip of an iceberg of violence. A study of families of the seriously mentally ill, carried out by the National Alliance for the Mentally Ill, reported that in 11 per cent of these families the person who was mentally ill had physically attacked a family member or someone else within the past year. In most instances the mentally ill person was not receiving treatment at the time.

The mental-health mess is all the sadder because we *know* how to organize good services for those with serious mental illnesses. Furthermore, approximately $25 billion is being spent each year by federal, state, and local governments on public mental-health services, a remarkably large amount of money, given the mediocre product being delivered. It is neither lack of knowledge nor lack of funds, then, that has produced the mental-health mess. Rather it is the consequences of six mistakes that have been made over the years. Three of these mistakes were made by the federal government, one by both federal and state government, and one by state government alone; the sixth mistake was made by everyone.

Misdirected Funds and Shifted Costs

1. *Federal funds were misdirected.* In the early 1960s, when the discharge of hundreds of thousands of the seriously mentally ill from state psychiatric hospitals was just getting under way, President John F. Kennedy proposed using federal funds as seed money to help start Community Mental-Health Centers (CMHCs) to treat the mentally ill closer to home. In congressional hearings it was explicitly stated that the proposed CMHCs would provide care for patients discharged from state hospitals.

From day one the CMHC program was an abysmal failure. Federal officials bypassed state mental-health authorities in funding local programs, thereby earning the permanent enmity of the states. The National Institute of Mental Health (NIMH) provided vague guidelines and virtually no oversight, so that some CMHCs used federal funds to build swimming pools and tennis courts, even hiring swimming instructors on federal staffing grants. A total of 789 CMHCs were eventually given more than $3 billion in federal funds. Follow-up studies of the CMHCs suggest that about 5 per cent of them have provided reasonably good services for the people targeted by the original legislation. The other 95 per cent have simply ignored those people.

2. *Costs were shifted from states to the federal government.* Up until the early 1960s, the federal government provided only 2 per cent of the total cost of care for those with serious mental illnesses. When the federal government began funding CMHCs, however, it also decided to make the seriously mentally ill eligible for emerging federal programs such as Medicare, Medicaid, Supplemental Security Income (SSI), Social Security Disability Income (SSDI), food stamps, and federal housing subsidies.

As a result, states have tried to empty their psychiatric hospitals, for which they pay virtually all the costs, and let the patients become eligible for the various federal subsidies instead. Once the patients have been discharged, the states close down those beds. If the patients need re-admission, the states direct them to the psychiatric wards of general hospitals, where federal Medicaid funds will cover much of the cost.

Raeside/Cartoonists & Writers Syndicate. Reprinted with permission.

Furthermore, the states, having discharged patients, have no incentive to provide aftercare. The discharged patients can end up homeless or in jail and often do; from a purely fiscal point of view, this costs state mental-health authorities nothing, since shelters and jails are mostly run with local (county and city) funds. The single most important function of state mental-health authorities today is to find additional ways to shift costs to other levels of government.

Research Neglected

3. *The federal government failed to support research.* Research on diseases is a function of government that has been most effectively funded at the federal level. The primary purpose of the National Institute of Mental Health, created in 1946 as a part of the National Institutes of Health, was to do research on "the cause, diagnosis, and treatment of psychiatric disorders." Al-

lowance was also made for "training personnel in matters relating to mental health" and for "developing and assisting states" with treatment programs, but research was to be the cornerstone of the Institute.

The NIMH's cornerstone was more like a pebble. Research occupied an increasingly small share of its annual budget, and, within that budget, an increasingly large share of funds was devoted to research on social problems such as violence, racism, and sexism. In 1969 the NIMH left the National Institutes of Health altogether, no longer wishing to be viewed as a research institute. One consequence was neglect of research on schizophrenia and manic-depressive illness. By 1985 the federal government was spending the same amount of research money on schizophrenia as it was on tooth decay. Per-patient total research expenditures were 8 times higher for multiple sclerosis than for schizophrenia, 15 times higher for cancer, and 50 times higher for muscular dystrophy.

Insufficient Public-Sector Manpower

4. *Federal and state governments failed to ensure adequate manpower in public-sector psychiatric jobs.* In 1940 there were approximately 9,000 psychiatrists, psychologists, and psychiatric social workers in the United States. In 1990 there were over 200,000, a 22-fold increase during a period when the population did not quite double. The training of such professionals had traditionally been a function of state government until the 1950s; over the following thirty years more than 2.1 billion federal dollars were spent on training.

The problem was that neither the federal nor state governments made any effort to ensure that the professionals, once trained, would be available for public-sector jobs. During the 1945 congressional hearings creating the NIMH, Representative Clarence J. Brown of Ohio explicitly asked Department of Health, Education, and Welfare officials whether they planned to include some arrangement "whereby a man who gets a subsidy from the federal government must pay back or in some way compensate the government" with a period of public service. Dr. Robert Felix, representing HEW, replied that there was such a plan: "I would think that a reasonable requirement of these men would be that they would spend at least one year in public service for every year they spent in training at public [federal] or state expense." Despite such assurances, a payback was never implemented federally until 1981, by which time training funds had been markedly reduced because of the program's failure.

The consequence is that many state mental hospitals and mental-health centers find it virtually impossible to recruit competent staff. In 1985 Wyoming State Hospital went almost a year *with no psychiatrist whatsoever* on its staff; five mental-health centers in South Dakota must share a single psychiatrist (each gets him one day a week); and many centers in rural areas have no psychiatric professionals whatsoever.

Where did all the mental-health professionals go? Most of them went directly into private practice in wealthy neighborhoods. For example, affluent Princeton, New Jersey, has one psychiatrist for every 250 residents, while poorer Jersey City has one for every 13,000. Psychologists and psychiatric social workers are similarly distributed.

Reforms and Misconceptions

5. *States changed their laws to make involuntary hospitalization and treatment more difficult to impose.* A major contributor to the mental-health mess has been lawyers—especially those connected with the American Civil Liberties Union and the Mental Health Law Project—who, with more idealism than common sense, persuaded the majority of state legislatures to change these laws. It would be a great thing if all individuals with schizophrenia and manic-depressive illness could think clearly and understand their need for treatment. Unfortunately the organ they use for thinking, the brain, is the one that is affected by these diseases. Hence approximately half of all those with serious mental illnesses have little or no insight into their own condition or need for treatment.

6. *Until recently, many people misunderstood the nature of serious mental illnesses.* Of all the mistakes that were made, this was the most understandable. In the 1960s, when the foundation for the current problems was being laid, much less was known about the causes of serious mental illnesses. Followers of Sigmund Freud said the illnesses were caused by bad mothering; Dr. Ronald Laing called them a sane response to an insane world; novelist Ken Kesey described the hospitalized mentally ill as being politically oppressed; Dr. Thomas Szasz claimed that the illnesses did not really exist at all. Looking back, such opinions now seem more thought-disordered than the opinions of the mentally ill.

It is now known that schizophrenia and manic-depressive illness are brain diseases, with structural and functional brain changes, just as multiple sclerosis, Parkinson's disease, and Alzheimer's disease are. As with these other diseases we do not yet know the precise neurochemical, neuropathological, and genetic sequence of causal events, but it *is* clear that these events are biological in nature. Thus, whereas thirty years ago well-meaning advocates might open the gates of mental hospitals and hope the released inmates would, by themselves, live happily ever after, as in the movie *King of Hearts*, today we should fully realize that, in order to do so, such individuals will need medication, aftercare, housing, and rehabilitation.

Fix Responsibility at the State Level

Getting out of the mental-health mess will depend upon correcting the mistakes that got us into it. The following steps must take place.

1. *Clarify responsibility and funding.* The effort to shift fiscal responsibility from one level of government to another is the single biggest cause of the problem.

One can make a theoretical argument that complete fiscal responsibility for these services should be assigned to the federal government. Personally I would disagree, because that fixes responsibility at a level too remote from where the services must be delivered.

State government is a more logical level. Some states, especially larger states, may wish to pass this responsibility down one more level to counties, as California and Wisconsin now do, or to local service boards, as Ohio does. The main point is that fiscal authority must accompany responsibility or the system will not work.

The most logical way to end the current division of both responsibility and fiscal authority is to block-grant to the states all federal funds for the mentally ill. This will be easier to do for programs like Medicaid and Medicare and more difficult for entitlement programs such as SSI and SSDI, but it must be done.

Fixing responsibility and fiscal authority at the level of state government would make single-source funding possible. This means that decisions regarding how many hospital beds are needed, how to reduce rehospitalization rates, how to develop better housing for the mentally ill, how to develop jobs programs for them, etc., could be made depending on clinical needs, not on what will be reimbursed by federal programs. Single-source funding is the main reason why a Canadian province such as British Columbia offers better services for people with serious mental illnesses than any U.S. state, although British Columbia spends less money on these services than do most states.

Set a New Course

2. *Establish priorities.* Mental-health centers in most states try to be all things to all people. They function as counseling centers for marital problems, existential crises, adolescent turmoil, and general unhappiness. Many mental-health centers spend so much staff time on these problems that little time remains for people with serious mental illnesses. Since states are funding these centers, the states can establish priorities any time they wish simply by reimbursing for some conditions (e.g., schizo-

phrenia) but not others (e.g., marital strife).

3. *Encourage innovation.* Present attempts at innovation are severely restricted by the reimbursement formulas of the various federal funding sources. Privatization is one avenue to explore, although the few efforts at privatization so far have resulted in widely varying outcomes. Some ventures (e.g., Northwest Mental Health Services in Seattle) have been highly praised; others (e.g., Brooklyn Psychosocial Rehabilitation Institute in New York) have been accused of offering poor services and of corruption.

4. *Ensure professional manpower for public-sector jobs.* This problem can be solved simply by having an automatic one-year-for-one-year payback obligation attached to all state-funded training programs. Another way to alleviate the shortage of psychiatrists, especially in rural areas, is to provide a special training program for psychologists, physician assistants, and nurse practitioners and then give them the jobs the psychiatrists refuse to take.

Change Laws and Ensure Research Funds

5. *Change state laws.* Any state that wishes to do so can change its laws back again, to make it easier to involuntarily hospitalize and treat the seriously mentally ill. A few (e.g., Washington) have already begun.

6. *Ensure adequate research funds.* Since the late 1980s there has been a marked increase in federal research funds. Much of the leadership on this issue has come from Senator Pete Domenici (R., N.M.). Legislation also returned the NIMH to the National Institutes of Health. Finally, private foundations have begun supporting such research; a noteworthy example is the Theodore and Vada Stanley Foundation, which in 1992 alone donated almost $2 million to research on schizophrenia and manic-depressive illness. Such public and private investments of research funds may well pay as rich dividends as they did in the prevention of polio.

A Bipartisan Solution

In summary, solutions to the mental-health mess are possible if government has the will to implement them. The leadership issue is further complicated by the fact that mental-health issues have traditionally been politicized. Advocates for the mentally ill have been strongly identified with liberal causes and Democratic politics, whereas opponents of mental-health causes have been identified with right-wing organizations (and particularly with the John Birch Society in the 1950s and 1960s). It is time to move beyond this traditional dichotomy. The mess has now been presided over by three Democratic and four Republican Presidents. Serious mental illnesses are not respecters of political boundaries. The mental-health mess is truly bipartisan in origin and must be bipartisan in solution.

"Chronic patients need our assurance that all of the things [they need] . . . will be available to them for as long as they need them."

Appropriate Programs and Services Would Benefit the Mentally Ill

Ann Braden Johnson

Ann Braden Johnson is a social worker who works primarily with the chronically mentally ill in community treatment settings. In the following viewpoint, she contends that in order to be successful, America's public mental health programs and services must be tailored to meet the needs of the chronically mentally ill population. These needs include tolerance of their peculiar habits, ongoing access to care, behavioral training, work, and treatment free of condescension. Johnson is the author of *Out of Bedlam: The Truth About Deinstitutionalization*, from which the following viewpoint is excerpted.

As you read, consider the following questions:

1. What three factors make chronically mentally ill people "poor candidates for infrequent individual clinic treatment," according to the author?
2. According to Johnson, why is it inappropriate to gauge therapeutic success for chronically mentally ill patients based on the length of time they remain outside a hospital?
3. In the Cuban treatment system Johnson describes, what is the incentive for patients to get better?

Excerpts of pp. 179-80, 184-90 of *Out of Bedlam: The Truth About Deinstitutionalization* by Ann Braden Johnson. Copyright ©1990 by Basic Books. Reprinted by permission of Basic Books, a division of HarperCollins Publishers, Inc.

If mental health experts from another planet were to visit the United States, they would almost certainly be struck by the vast array of programs and services available, most of them highly specialized and articulated to identify precisely the specific sub-group of the population that they serve. The visitors would also notice, however, that while virtually all of the U.S. programs accept public funds, few of them actually treat the public case-load; and none of the programs is well integrated with any of the others. In short, these experts would see a big, chaotic system, uncoordinated and incoherent, one that utterly fails to fulfill its mission, which is the ongoing care and treatment of the mentally ill.

Except on paper. There, we have an accountable, coordinated, integrated, unified, cost-effective, and comprehensive system of care available to all who seek it at a cost they can afford, tailored to their individual needs. We have hospitals, day hospitals, clinics, clubs, socialization programs, vocational programs, drop-in centers, crisis centers, lounges, outreach services, hot lines, and prevention programs—and still, it isn't enough. Despite the vast array of services and programs, and despite all the money we spend on these, there are seriously mentally ill people all over the country who have been left to manage on their own, without visible assistance from the rich panoply of treatment programs. After all these years, we still seem to be at square one, paralyzed by the sheer size of the problem of a huge and growing caseload of seriously impaired mental patients no one seems to want and no one apparently knows what to do with. After all this time, money, and effort, says one critic of the system,

> The bewildering distribution of responsibility among different levels of government and such varying providers as those of medical care, housing, and disability assistance almost guarantees significant gaps in service and a lack of accountability. The severely disabled inevitably depend on public services, but the public sector is too disorganized and demoralized to respond appropriately to the challenge.

Dismal as this picture is, it is also very deceptive. In fact, we know—and have known for years—what to do with the chronically mentally ill, we know how to treat them, and we know what they need. . . .

A Place to Loosen Up

The first thing the mentally ill need, like the rest of us, is a place to live. No one living on the street has any hope of recovering from any illness, regardless of its nature. Besides that, though, the mentally ill need to be able to live in a place where they can belong, where their peculiarities will be tolerated and even better, understood. This point may seem elemental, but it really is not:

even people who know better than to try to force chronic patients into appearing normal go ahead and do so anyway, whether out of anxiety (rationalized along the lines of "If the patients look crazy, the neighbors will complain and they'll shut the program down") or simple meanness (I knew an old man in an adult home who used to mutter constantly to himself about what God would say when He came to earth, so the staff of his adult home derived great amusement from faking occasional telephone calls to the old man in which they pretended to be God).

Like anyone else, the mentally ill need a home that is a refuge, a haven, a place where they can loosen up a little, even if in their case, "loosening up" means stockpiling thousands of recipes they'll never cook or writing undecipherable documents to Congressmen to whom they have decided they are related. Interestingly enough, a review of all research comparing the outcome of institutional versus alternative care for the mentally ill noted that it mattered less *where* patients lived than it did what the place was like to live in: a tolerant and accepting custodial institution was better than a hostile community residence.

Aggressive Outreach

The next thing we know mentally ill patients require is aggressive outreach. It is amazing to me how slow mental health professionals have been to figure out this elemental lesson, but we still haven't fully caught on. The fact that chronic mental patients are notorious for failing to get to their outpatient clinic appointments at all, let alone on time, is invariably attributed by clinic workers to the patients' resistance or their negativism, and there the matter is left until the patient falls apart and needs rehospitalization. Collectively, the chronic population has largely been written off as "inappropriate" for clinic treatment, whereupon a self-fulfilling prophecy takes over at the bottom line of every treatment plan: chronic patients drop out of treatment because they are expected to. One would think that clinic directors should realize that if whole portions of the clientele avoid using their services, then maybe something is wrong with those services; however, in my experience it is the rare mental health program that tailors its services to the requirements and limited abilities of its chronic patients.

What we know, but are rarely willing to incorporate into our treatment facilities, is that severely mentally ill people often do not have a good sense of time, do not always do what they are supposed to, and are used to being able to blame their own failures on their illness—all of which, put together, makes them very poor candidates for infrequent individual clinic treatment. Aggressive outreach, as it is called, means aftercare staff have to call the errant patients up or even go visit them when they do not show up; it also means therapists may have to squeeze them in unexpectedly if they do show up on the wrong day or at the wrong time. Having supervised therapists for many years, I know how unpopular these ideas are with most professional staff, but let's face it: such approaches are what all chronic patients need—and not just the homeless ones.

Ready Access to Hospitals

Another thing the chronically mentally ill need is permission to regress occasionally in the course of treatment and the ability to be rehospitalized at once when they need it. The notion that community-based treatment *had* to be adequate to the task of keeping even the chronically mentally ill out of the hospital forever has been extraordinarily slow to give way to overwhelming evidence that it cannot be done. This does not mean the chronically mentally ill cannot live in the community; it means that they cannot be guaranteed never to need brief, intermittent rehospitalizations. The goal of keeping each and every patient out of the hospital indefinitely is so pervasive as a measure of therapeutic success that for practitioners, each rehospitalization of one of their patients can feel like a devastating personal failure.

Nevertheless, all existing outcome research related to the chronic population has as its primary index of treatment success the length of time patients remain outside a hospital—even though it has long since been established that what they suffer from in the first place are disorders defined, in part, by a perpetual need for intermittent, intensive treatment of a sort traditionally available only in a hospital. Abbott S. Weinstein, for example, says that the number of mental patients readmitted to state facilities has remained constant over the years, as have the percentages of those patients readmitted frequently (three or more times in one year) or rapidly (within three months of discharge). His goal was to correct the widespread, but inaccurate, belief that readmissions to state mental hospitals reflected accelerated returns of prematurely discharged patients. Even though everyone recognizes that the chronic mentally ill require the occasional readmission—practitioners, from direct observation; researchers, from their own and colleagues' findings; policymakers, from hospital census figures—we still seek program perfection in an impossible clinical goal. One potentially damaging distortion of the reality of severe mental illness and its remedy can be found in the denunciations of community-based care by those who use the fact of patients' inevitable brief rehospitalizations to justify their call for a return to the total institutions of the past, which they, knowing no history, have decided are the only suitable setting for the population. Such a simplistic and insupportable conclusion shows just how easy it is to politicize clinical data in defiance of demonstrated patient need.

The chronically mentally ill need something that in the literature is sometimes called "treatment" and other times "rehabilitation." I have always thought of it as training in the art of acting normal, but whatever it is, the nature of the work is to reeducate the mentally ill in the myriad skills of interpersonal life. Included in such a catchall category are such things as personal hygiene and grooming, shopping, budgeting, traveling, social skills, and polite discourse—all the little skills of civilized behavior that we take for granted. A special task for the severely mentally ill is learning a kind of symptom management: to get along in the world, schizophrenics, for example, need to learn that it is not all right to talk openly to one's "voices" (auditory hallucinations) on a bus or in a store, nor is it okay to menace strangers with dire warnings and threats, however important it may seem at the time to communicate the information. The distinction I try to make in practice, one that seems very important to patients, is that learning to act like normal people does not mean they have to give up their voices or their peculiar thoughts—something they would find a terrifying, even impossible, challenge. The biggest problem with this necessary therapeutic activity is that most psychotherapists much prefer, understandably, to practice a highly verbal psychotherapy rather than to communicate the simplest skills of daily life to people whose tendency is first, to communicate through action rather than speech, if at all possible, and second, to use speech that is almost entirely metaphorical.

The Importance of Work

Next, the mentally ill need work to do. Most mental patients have nothing to do all day. They had nothing to do all day in the hospital, unless you count the occasional "current events" group or "community meeting" as something to do (I, for one, do not), and they have nothing important or even very real to do out in the world. In my neighborhood there is a large public library with a surprisingly inexpensive snack bar; and since I spend a fair bit of time in the library myself, I have come to recognize a substantial population of discharged mental patients whose daily life is centered there, especially in the snack bar. While it is possible that they are all doing profound and significant research, it seems far more likely that they are in the library because they have nowhere else to spend the day. There is no excuse for this.

Discharged mental patients are never going to learn to live in the real world as long as they are living in the same kind of unreal half-life of empty inactivity that characterized the custodial hospitals. Besides, if normal people work for a living, why shouldn't they? The chronically mentally ill need to be able to work, at real jobs; furthermore, there is no reason why they can't work. In one interesting study, for example, the researcher [R. Jay Turner] found that over 80 percent of a group of patients who had been diagnosed schizophrenic and discharged after a single hospitalization went right back to work. The researcher noticed that all the previous studies of work performance among schizophrenics had used hospitalized patients exclusively, a sampling bias that resulted in overstating the relationship between work failure and mental illness. To the contrary, he concluded that "the capacity to perform the work role cannot be wholly or even largely accounted for on the basis of the presence or degree of manifest psychopathology." We must face the fact that we cannot seriously expect the mentally ill to live out their whole lives wasting time—no one, perceiving that to be his future, could seriously want to go on with it. No wonder even a mental hospital comes to look like a better bet.

At the Community's Mercy

Despite enlightened thought on the therapeutic needs of the mentally ill, very little has changed in the public's response to insanity. In fact, the treatment of the mentally ill today might almost be called genocide, except that it occurs on such an unconscious level, and so slowly and subtly, as to be unrecognizable. Too few see the seriously mentally ill as sick and helpless people utterly dependent on the mercy of the community.

Elizabeth O'Connor, *The Sun*, September 1993.

Cuba has devised a fascinating solution to this problem. The Cubans have identified a series of five or so levels of mental impairment, each keyed to a treatment setting; as patients' mental status improves, they move from hospital to community in a series of graduated steps. Every step, even the lowest, requires each patient to work at a job, and the jobs pay better as the patient gets better and moves to successively less restricted settings. There is thus a built-in incentive to continue to get better—it pays to get well, literally—and there is no "free ride" for the dependent patient, no secondary gain in staying in the hospital.

Tolerate Smoking and Provide Coffee

One of the most important considerations for anyone who is thinking of working with the chronic mentally ill is generally overlooked by mental health professionals: that mental patients nearly all smoke, all seem to drink gallons of coffee, and all love junk food. These days, of course, most mental health professionals abhor smoke and prohibit it whenever and wherever they can. Without challenging professionals' right to spend the day in a smoke-free environment and without endorsing nicotine addiction, it nevertheless should be obvious to anyone trying to develop a program for a population that smokes so heavily that, for example, rules against smoking on the premises may drive patients away. Surely it is wiser to face the inevitable and design smoking areas with the best possible ventilation as standard equipment in the program's physical plant. By the same token, coffee is so clearly viewed as a necessity by the population that surely it is worth a few dollars and a little of someone's time to have a pot available in the waiting room.

In my experience, though, most clinics aren't set up to attract chronic patients, and their waiting rooms are often devoid of ashtrays, while phonily polite signs prohibit the consumption of food or beverage altogether. The excuse generally given is that to allow chronic patients to "hang out" in the waiting room—which they would certainly do if there were free coffee, according to the party line—is to allow "chronics" to drive off the more desirable, middle-class population, who won't want to share a waiting room with crazies. The crazies get the message and drop out of treatment—but that's understood and written off, because everyone knows how resistant they are. Genuine outreach to people who differ from the norm means that services and the manner in which they are delivered have to differ from the norm if they are to be accepted by the target population, even if that means creating a smokers' lounge and providing free coffee.

Treatment Free of Condescension

Above all else, I have noticed, the chronically mentally ill are thoroughly schooled by life on the margins of society in the detection of hypocrisy and condescension, and one of their treatment needs is to be able to have some say about the therapists they will work with. Susan Sheehan's wonderful book about "Sylvia Frumkin," *Is There No Place on Earth for Me?*, includes a telling illustration of how important being able to choose one's therapist is, even to psychotic patients, who are all too often written off as "too out of it to notice."

In Sylvia's earliest days as a psychotherapy patient, at her first regular session after the intake interview, she met her assigned therapist for the first time. Since she could read upside down, Sylvia saw that the intake report on the therapist's desk began with an unflattering comment on her appearance. In what she remembered as a deliberate test of the therapist's truthfulness, Sylvia asked her to read the first page out loud. The therapist complied, but she changed the content so it would be less unflattering. Sylvia decided from then on that the therapist was neither trustworthy nor helpful, although she continued in treatment for a year, pretending everything was all right. When in the course of treatment the patient and the therapist completely disagreed about whether she should be hospitalized, Sylvia asked for and got a new therapist, whom she promptly put to the same test. The second therapist passed the test with flying colors by reading the report as written. Sylvia not only decided she could trust this new therapist but went on to develop so strong an attachment to the second therapist that twenty years and countless successors later, Sylvia still remembered her as "the only therapist with whom she would ever try to work out her problems . . . 'something just clicked . . . [she] was my fairy godmother.' "

Two things strike me as important about this illustration: First, seriously mentally ill people are fully capable of making shrewd and lasting assessments about other people even though they often appear out of it and totally indifferent to interactions, which suggests that many of us who work with them are seriously underestimating their abilities to assess *us*. Second, patients probably choose their own therapists whether we permit them to or not. In any case, the need for patients to feel free to make their own decisions about the mental health professionals whom they can trust and therefore work with is rarely acknowledged, much less acted upon. What they *do not* need, any more than the rest of us do, is to be patronized and shut out of all decision making that directly affects their own lives.

Long-Term Illness, Long-Term Access

Finally, chronic patients need our assurance that all of the things described thus far—homes, coffee, cigarettes, rapid hospitalizations, real jobs, and real treatment with therapists they feel they can trust—will be available to them for as long as they need them, even if that means forever. No one likes feeling insecure about the future availability of what he needs, and mental patients are no exception, even if they cannot or will not say so. The odds are that most severely mentally ill people are well aware that they have a lifetime disability, and the concept of "short-term" or "time-limited" treatment must strike them as ridiculously inapposite in the face of that lifelong illness. Nevertheless, many programs and entitlements stress from the outset how very limited they intend their services to be, not because time-limited service is what the population requires, but because policymakers and auditors think they are saving money by preventing long-term dependency.

Even worse, in a way, is the misguided practice of punishing mentally ill people for breaking the rules of a program by kicking them out, or threatening to do so. When people are as anxious and uncertain as chronic mental patients are, this practice can only undermine what little self-assurance they have been able to develop, and it is hard to see how that can be called treatment. Consider the comments of the Joint Commission on Mental Illness and Health, made nearly thirty years ago:

> The mental patient is *not* unconscious of how he is handled, but is usually hypersensitive, quick to resent injustice, and apt to interpret harsh and punitive handling as substantiation of his own sense of guilt or persecution, of being "no good," or of feeling that everyone is against him.

It is crucial that chronic patients be able to feel they belong and fit in somewhere, that their odd behavior and peculiar ways can be tolerated by someone, and that their particular needs will be understood and addressed in some fashion. A program that takes back membership at will, that uses it as a tool or even a weapon to ensure compliance, is providing none of those and can hardly be considered therapeutic. It is not enough simply to dream up and enforce rules among a population whose social skills are as limited as those of the chronically mentally ill, if only because they may not even know how to comply. Although it is admittedly much more difficult to design, the program chronic patients will take to is one that considers their potential need to stay there forever: even if they do in fact move on, the important thing is that they can count on the program to be there to go back to when and if they need it. Not surprisingly, crazy people need a safe place, a family, to be able to turn to, and the odds are that they need it a lot more than the rest of us do.

"Helping people to join the market and to compete is an important part of their rehabilitation and genuine social integration."

Social Enterprise Programs Would Benefit the Mentally Ill

Ota De Leonardis and Diana Mauri

Ota De Leonardis is an associate professor of sociology at the University of Milan in Italy. Diana Mauri is research coordinator of the Centro Studi della Regione Fruili Venezia Giulia, also in Italy. In the following viewpoint, which was translated from the Italian by Adrian Hamilton, the authors describe the "social enterprise," a type of social program developed in Italy that unites mental health patients and workers, along with other interested individuals, in an endeavor to produce goods and conduct business. The authors conclude that the social enterprise enhances people's capabilities, provides practical therapy, and promotes social integration.

As you read, consider the following questions:

1. What two features of deinstitutionalization in Italy do the authors cite?
2. Why is it therapeutic to bear risk, according to De Leonardis and Mauri?
3. According to the authors, how is the social enterprise different from the welfare state's services?

Ota De Leonardis and Diana Mauri, "From Deinstitutionalization to the Social Enterprise," *Social Policy*, Fall/Winter 1992, published by Social Policy Corporation, New York, NY 10036. Copyright 1993 by Social Policy Corporation.

Mention the word "deinstitutionalization" in the United States and you invoke images of the government's abandoning vast numbers of people with serious psychiatric disorders and waves of homeless, helpless people flooding city streets. Few people remember that deinstitutionalization, when it was initially proposed, was conceived as a liberal proposal for *empowerment* of patients in mental hospitals.

In the US the policy turned out horrifically, not least because deinstitutionalization at the hospitals was not accompanied by any meaningful follow-up to insure housing, treatment, and social services for former patients in the community.

It didn't have to be that way. Our experience in Italy has shown that deinstitutionalization, when thoughtfully carried out, can truly be a way of mobilizing the resources of both the individual clients and the local communities they live in.

The Meaning of "Deinstitutionalization"

From the outset we should stress that the term "deinstitutionalization" has a different meaning in the context of Italian mental health care policy than it has come to have in the United States. In Italy, the term does not imply a radical political perspective that is against all institutions, nor is it synonymous with the administrative measure of de-hospitalization. Rather, the main impetus behind deinstitutionalization in Italy was a strategy to transform the legal, organizational, and material framework of the relationship between service providers and their clients. The measure had two specific features: 1) it was produced by institutional actors (mainly professionals in the mental health field) through a long process of deconstructing and transforming the institutions they worked in from the bottom up; 2) its prime therapeutic target was to enrich the total existence of mental patients so that, however ill they might be, patients were no longer passive objects of treatment, but could become active (and also conflictual) actors in their relationships with the services.

Deinstitutionalization can be conceived of as a homeopathic process that deconstructs the institution in order to mobilize its inner energies. Institutions, in this process, are transformed from within by working on already existing facilities—by reorganizing the same physical spaces, the same personnel, the same patients, the same material and human resources, but changing the system of interaction of which every element is a part.

The deconstruction process begins with the mental hospital, then converts and reorganizes the inner resources released to build new structures rooted in the community. The reshaped administration of local public mental health resources becomes oriented toward investing resources in patients' everyday life rather than in bureaucracies and institutions. Health workers are brought to patients in their social context, not the other way around. More resources are managed directly by patients. Resources are invested in meaningful activities and jobs for patients. And self-help and community organizations are encouraged to participate in the therapeutic environment.

Leading Productive Lives

Numerous demonstration programs attest that the mentally disturbed can lead safe, productive and happy lives outside institutions. . . .

One of the most successful programs is New York City's Fountain House, which began in the late 1940s as a meeting place for former mental patients. . . .

The core of Fountain House is its work program. Members perform almost all the chores at the complex, from tending the gardens to keeping the books. Those who do well are placed in part-time entry-level jobs at some 31 companies, including banks, law firms and ad agencies.

Anastasia Toufexis, *Time*, October 22, 1990.

In Italy, a rich and diverse community has evolved around these programs that includes mental patients and health workers, volunteers and young people with occupational difficulties, dropouts, drug addicts, and their relatives, and many others. The cooperative effort mobilizes and combines resources provided by the public, the market, the local community, and the people involved. In short, managing public health resources in this way promotes and supports people's autonomous choices and their capabilities, skills, and intelligence. The issue is not just one of rights: a crucial reason this process works is that allowing recipients of health resources to enhance their own capabilities is in turn productive of resources—in other words, it increases effectiveness.

Investing in People

Individual capabilities, under this model of deinstitutionalization, are considered human capital that must not be wasted, but instead must be invested productively. Several experiments based on this principal are currently being conducted as part of local health and welfare policies in Italy: the *Consorzio delle cooperative* of the Department of Mental Health in Trieste; the *Castello dei diritti* set up by the local administration in Parma; the *"Improsa"*

project launched jointly in Primavalle, Rome, by a private association for vocational training (ENAIP) and the local health department; the *Agenzia Sociale* organized in Sesto S. Giovanni, Milan,
by the cooperative *Lotta contro l'emarginazione*. These experiments differ from one another in many specifics, but they all
have the following objectives in common.

- They break with the prevailing principal of fragmentation
  and specialization in professions and services, and they promote intersectoral programs with new partnerships and
  coalitions among different public and private agencies.
- They address the combined problems of marginality in the
  local community as a whole: drug abuse, mental health
  problems, disabilities, youth unemployment.
- They activate a mix of market, government, and social resources.
- They promote participation in projects by the services' consumers and enable them to make use of their resources,
  skills, and capabilities usually wasted.
- They invest these resources in productive activities, so that
  both consumers of health services and health service providers become producers and indeed entrepreneurs.

A Social Enterprise

The aim of these experiments can be summed up in the idea
of constructing a "social enterprise." What is a social enterprise?
The Trieste project, which pioneered this concept, has given the
most complete expression of the process.

The social enterprise in Trieste was begun in 1987 with financing provided by the Social Fund of the European Economic
Community for the vocational training and job integration of
young people considered "at risk." The funding was put to innovative use, and its conventional rehabilitative rationale was radically redefined. It financed, in fact, the construction of a productive social enterprise that provides training and jobs (and therefore also rehabilitation). The enterprise consists of a consortium
of five cooperatives with around 250 member-workers, of whom
100 are apprentices, and a total annual fees invoiced of about
1.5 billion lire. Each cooperative has a number of small production units operating in a variety of sectors: production of wooden
design objects and furniture; a publishing house that also issues
a magazine and a newspaper; video, computer, and radio work-
shops; graphic design and bookbinders' studios; a theater company that also runs a school; three cleaning, transport, and
catering firms; a bar, a restaurant, and a hotel; a jewelery bou-
tique; a beauty salon, a firm that rents bicycles, and others.

In the social enterprise, priority is given to the talents, skills,
and vocational choices of individual participants. Participants

include not only patients and mental health workers in the strict sense, but also the wider circle of mental health service consumers—young people at risk, drug addicts, the patients' relatives, and so on, in addition to members of the local community who have decided for whatever reason to invest their money, time, or know-how in the enterprise: banks, companies, professionals, artists, scientists, and businesspeople. Economic interest here blends with solidarity.

Business as Therapy

The driving force behind the social enterprise is a commitment to increasing the individual and institutional, material and cultural resources available to people in their everyday social life. This is not merely a matter of creating add-on opportunities for work or social activities; it is a profound change in the very ways that therapy, care, and help are defined and delivered. For example, as mental health workers and patients strive together to accomplish concrete tasks, they struggle with problems jointly and decide together on purposeful action. Therapy is no longer based on a strictly symbolic and relational interaction; it is anchored in a practical and real enterprise. In this context, working and earning are not merely yardsticks by which to measure "improvements" achieved by therapy; rather, they are a precondition for these improvements. Finally, an underlying principle is that bearing part of the enterprise's risk produces therapeutic effects because it is therapeutic to be able to make mistakes, to learn by trial and error, to run the risk of change.

The social enterprise is thus a business in the real sense—it has very little in common with occupational therapy, or with the sheltered workshop where patients "kill time" by doing whatever they want (usually producing shoddy handicrafts to be sold for charity). Helping people to join the market and to compete is an important part of their rehabilitation and genuine social integration.

High product quality is a priority. The decision to emphasize products with a cultural meaning and to strive for a high quality and variety of products and jobs creates a loosely coupled organization and relatively transitive power relationships. It encourages people to diversify their activities, and it rewards their creativity.

The abundance and variety of resources released by the mix of personal, private, and public contributions make the social enterprise very different from the welfare state's traditional services, with their current frugality, meager resources, and cost-cutting efforts. This abundance also has a fundamentally therapeutic value—it enables people to achieve, produce, and risk.

The social enterprise is a business that protects, produces, and enhances people's basic capabilities. This approach is focused on a productive social justice, *producing* and not only redistributing wealth. It considers not just what is given *to each*, but also what is given *by each*, according to his or her capabilities.

An Open Bet

The development from deinstitutionalization to social enterprise being worked out in Italy is still an open bet, and it could easily fail. It stands on the borderline between state and market, and hence has to cope with the constraints and rigidities of public institutions on the one hand, and with the material and cultural limitations of the market on the other. However, if it succeeds, it represents a powerful model not only for how to deal effectively with mental health care, but also for the many other social institutions in which the relations between service providers and clients need to be dramatically transformed.

Periodical Bibliography

The following articles have been selected to supplement the diverse views presented in this chapter.

Bernard S. Arons et al.
"Mental Health and Substance Abuse Coverage Under Health Reform," *Health Affairs*, Spring 1994. Available from PO Box 8015, Syracuse, NY 13217.

Philip J. Boyle and Daniel Callahan
"Minds and Hearts: Priorities in Mental Health Services," *Hastings Center Report* (special supplement), September/October 1993.

Janice Castro
"What Price Mental Health?" *Time*, May 31, 1993.

CQ Researcher
"Mental Illness," August 6, 1993. Available from 1414 22nd St. NW, Washington, DC 20037.

Daniel Goleman
"Mental Health Therapists Worry over Change," *The New York Times*, May 10, 1993.

Tipper Gore
"The High Social Cost of Mental Illness" (letter), *The Wall Street Journal*, January 12, 1994.

Health Affairs
Entire issue on mental health policy, Fall 1992.

National Advisory Mental Health Council
"Health Care Reform for Americans with Severe Mental Illnesses, *American Journal of Psychiatry*, October 1993. Available from 1400 K St. NW, Washington, DC 20005.

National Forum
Entire issue on mental illness and national policy, Winter 1993. Available from PO Box 16000, Louisiana State University, Baton Rouge, LA 70893.

Steven S. Sharfstein, Anne M. Stoline, and Howard H. Goldman
"Psychiatric Care and Health Insurance Reform," *American Journal of Psychiatry*, January 1993.

Karen Shore
"Mental Health in the Clinton Plan: Corporate Dictatorship in Therapy," *Health/PAC Bulletin*, Fall 1993. Available from 853 Broadway, Suite 1607, New York, NY 10003.

Gary R. VandenBos
"U.S. Mental Health Policy: Proactive Evolution in the Midst of Health Care Reform," *American Psychologist*, March 1993.

Glossary

civil commitment   A legal term for the involuntary hospitalization of mentally ill people who pose a danger to themselves or others and who refuse voluntary treatment.

CMHC   Community Mental Health Centers Act; federal legislation enacted in 1963 to transfer care of the mentally ill from state hospitals to neighborhood community mental health centers (CMHCs). The CMHC program is often at the center of the debate over the causes of homelessness among the mentally ill.

deinstitutionalization   The nationwide release of mental patients from state hospitals that began in the 1950s. Deinstitutionalization resulted from a variety of social forces, including the belief that state institutions were inhumane and that patients would be better served in community treatment settings.

***Diagnostic and Statistical Manual of Mental Disorders* (DSM)**   A publication, periodically revised, of the American Psychiatric Association that describes and classifies mental disorders on the basis of their symptoms. It defines what the psychiatric profession considers to be a mental disorder. Consequently, it is often a target of criticism and the center of debate over the definition of mental illness.

etiology   Also *aetiology*. The cause of a disease. It also refers to the branch of knowledge concerned with the causation of diseases.

major depressive disorder   Also called *clinical depression, depressive illness*, or *depression*. A severe state of depression characterized by persistent sadness; loss of interest in activities formerly enjoyed; loss of energy; feelings of worthlessness, hopelessness, and guilt; inability to concentrate; indecisiveness; and thoughts of suicide.

manic-depressive disorder   Also called *bipolar disorder*. A condition in which sufferers alternate between extremes of excitement (mania) and despair (depression). Symptoms of mania include irritability, euphoria, increased energy, racing thoughts, and unrealistic self-confidence. Symptoms of depression are the same as those for *major depressive disorder*. Manic-depressive disorder is frequently treated with lithium and other medications.

NIMH   National Institute of Mental Health; a federal agency that plans and conducts research into the causes, prevention, diagnosis, and treatment of mental illnesses.

obsessive-compulsive disorder   A form of anxiety induced by obsessions, which are unwanted thoughts that repeatedly intrude on the mind. In extreme cases, obsessions can lead to compulsions—involuntary ritual behaviors repeated over and over for extended periods of time. Common compulsions include cleaning, counting, and hoarding.

post-traumatic stress disorder (PTSD)   A condition that affects survivors of traumatic experiences such as war, disaster, and abuse. Symptoms include flashbacks, recurrent nightmares, and avoidance of reminders of the event.

psychopharmacology   The use of drugs to treat mental disorders and affect behavior.

schizophrenia   Also called *dementia praecox*. A chronic mental disorder that usually sets in during adolescence or young adulthood. Symptoms include delusions, hallucinations, and thought disorders. There is no known cure for the disorder, but its symptoms are often controlled with medications.

For Further Discussion

Chapter 1

1. Erica E. Goode believes that labeling increasing numbers of conditions "mental illness" threatens to reduce human personality to "a collection of syndromes and disorders." Do you agree? Why or why not? What conditions do you think qualify as mental illnesses?

2. Thomas Szasz suggests that psychiatry enables people to evade personal responsibility by blaming their actions and conditions on fictional "mental illnesses." Sheldon H. Preskorn contends that psychiatry promotes personal responsibility by expecting mental patients to be "active participants in their treatment." Whose argument is more convincing? Explain your answer.

Chapter 2

1. Irving I. Gottesman uses information pooled from forty family studies to conclude that genes contribute more than environment to the risk of acquiring schizophrenia. Peter R. Breggin argues that since families share environment as well as genes, such studies do not prove that genes cause schizophrenia. Which viewpoint do you find more persuasive? Why?

2. Eadbhard O'Callaghan and colleagues use data from public records to assert that exposure to influenza in the womb increases the risk of developing schizophrenia later in life. Timothy J. Crow and D. John Done present data from public records to argue the opposite. How do you account for the fact that these authors reached contradictory conclusions based on information of a similar nature and source?

Chapter 3

1. James Hillman argues that psychotherapy's emphasis on resolving internal conflicts harms society because it encourages people to neglect the external social and political conditions that require their attention. Do you agree? Why or why not? Do you agree with Hillman that "there are parts of the psyche that are changeless"? If so, what aspects of your own personality do you consider to be changeless?

2. David Calof contends that patients often "recover" repressed memories of childhood sexual abuse while in therapy. Martin Gardner argues that memories of sexual abuse usually cannot be repressed and that these "recovered" memories are

fantasies implanted by therapists. Whose argument do you find more compelling? Why? Does the fact that Calof is a therapist influence your assessment of his viewpoint? Explain your answer.

3. Richard S. Schwartz fears that psychopharmacology (the use of drugs for psychiatric purposes) may harm society by inducing conformity to cultural norms. Peter D. Kramer is less concerned about psychopharmacology's potential to encourage conformity. Which author do you agree with? Why? Do you believe that it would be ethical to take a drug that made you feel good all the time even though you suffered from no psychiatric disorder? Explain your answer.

Chapter 4

1. H. Richard Lamb argues that the mentally ill become homeless due to the symptoms of their disorders. Carl I. Cohen and Kenneth S. Thompson contend that social, political, and economic factors are more important causes of homelessness among the mentally ill. Which argument is more convincing? Why?

2. Richard Cohen argues that the mentally ill homeless should be involuntarily institutionalized because they are unable to take care of themselves. Do you agree? Why or why not?

Chapter 5

1. Based on your reading of Richard W. White Jr., John Q. La Fond, and Mary L. Durham, do you think a mentally ill person should have the right to refuse psychiatric treatment? Why or why not? Under what conditions, if any, should that right be revoked?

2. Joan Ullman uses a farcical tone to describe the trial of serial killer Jeffrey Dahmer in order to make her point that the insanity defense is an absurdity. Lincoln Caplan uses historical and statistical information to defend the credibility of the insanity defense. Which technique do you find more persuasive? Why? Do you think the insanity defense is legitimate? Explain your answer.

Chapter 6

1. Denis J. Prager and Leslie J. Scallet argue that mental health care is usually thought of as separate from general health care. Charles A. Kiesler contends that mental health care is increasingly viewed in the same terms as general health care. Which argument do you find more persuasive? Why?

2. Based on the viewpoints by the National Alliance for the Mentally Ill and the *Wall Street Journal*, do you think insurance should cover treatments for only severe mental illnesses, all mental disorders, or no mental problems? Explain your answer.

3. Based on the recommendations of Ann Braden Johnson, plan a program for the mentally ill people in your community that provides housing assistance, coordinates mental health treatment, and administrates rehabilitative services. Determine the location, the types of facilities, and the number of personnel you will need to perform these functions. Account for the fact that some of the mentally ill are homeless and that many of them are resistant to treatment.

Organizations to Contact

The editors have compiled the following list of organizations concerned with the issues debated in this book. The descriptions are derived from materials provided by the organizations. All have publications or information available for interested readers. The list was compiled on the date of publication of the present volume; names, addresses, and phone numbers may change. Be aware that many organizations take several weeks or longer to respond to inquiries, so allow as much time as possible.

American Association of Suicidology
2459 S. Ash
Denver, CO 80222
(303) 692-0985

The association is one of the largest suicide prevention organizations in the nation. It believes that suicidal thoughts are almost always a symptom of depression and that suicide is almost never a rational decision. The association provides referrals to regional crisis centers in the United States and Canada and helps those grieving the death of a loved one to suicide. It publishes numerous pamphlets and reports.

American Psychiatric Association (APA)
1400 K St. NW, Suite 501
Washington, DC 20005
(202) 682-6220

An organization of psychiatrists dedicated to studying the nature, treatment, and prevention of mental disorders, the APA helps create mental health policies, distributes information about psychiatry, and promotes psychiatric research and education. It publishes the *American Journal of Psychiatry* and *Hospital and Community Psychiatry* monthly. For a free packet of brochures on mental disorders, write to the above address, "Division of Public Affairs, Code GP."

American Psychological Association (APA)
750 First St. NE
Washington, DC 20002-4242
(202) 336-5000

This society of psychologists aims to "advance psychology as a science, as a profession, and as a means of promoting human welfare." It produces numerous publications, including the monthly journal *American Psychologist*, the monthly newspaper *APA Monitor*, and the quarterly *Journal of Abnormal Psychology*.

Committee for Truth in Psychiatry (CTIP)
PO Box 76925
Washington, DC 20013
(703) 979-5398

The committee consists of former recipients of electroconvulsive therapy (ECT). It believes ECT causes brain damage and that patients should be adequately informed about its adverse effects prior to consenting to the treatment. CTIP seeks to maintain the Food and Drug Administration's classification of ECT as a high-risk procedure. The committee publishes a monthly newsletter.

False Memory Syndrome Foundation
3401 Market St., Suite 130
Philadelphia, PA 19104-3315
(215) 387-1865
fax: (215) 387-1917

The foundation was established to combat False Memory Syndrome (FMS), a condition in which patients are led by their therapists to "remember" traumatic incidents—usually childhood sexual abuses—that never actually occurred. The foundation seeks to study, prevent, and assist the victims of FMS through publicity, counseling, and research. It publishes the *FMS Foundation Newsletter* and distributes information and articles on FMS.

Father Flanagan's Boys' Home
Town Hall
Boys Town, NE 68010
(402) 498-1830
national hotline: (800) 448-3000

Father Flanagan's Boys' Home was established in 1917 as a home for troubled or orphaned boys. Since then, it has grown in size and in the scope of its mission, which now includes providing counseling to troubled and suicidal teens. The home maintains a national crisis hotline and provides the public with pamphlets and other materials concerning teen crises and suicide.

The Foundation for Depression and Manic Depression (FDMD)
7 E. 67th St.
New York, NY 10021
(212) 772-3400

The foundation is a nonprofit treatment and research center specializing in mood disorders such as depression, manic-depressive illness, and anxiety. It subscribes to the theory that these disorders are biologically caused and can be successfully treated with both medication and psychotherapy. The foundation publishes a periodic newsletter and assorted educational brochures.

International Society for the Study of Multiple Personality and Dissociation (ISSMPD)
5700 Old Orchard Rd., 1st Fl.
Skokie, IL 60077-1024
(708) 966-4322
fax: (708) 966-9418

The society's membership comprises mental health professionals and students interested in multiple personality and dissociation. It conducts research and promotes improved understanding of these conditions. It publishes the quarterly journal *Dissociation* and a quarterly newsletter.

National Alliance for the Mentally Ill (NAMI)
2101 Wilson Blvd., Suite 302
Arlington, VA 22201
(703) 524-7600
fax: (703) 524-9094

NAMI is a consumer advocacy and support organization composed largely of family members of people with severe mental illnesses such as schizophrenia, manic-depressive illness, and depression. The alliance adheres to the position that severe mental illnesses are biological brain diseases and that mentally ill people should not be blamed or stigmatized for their condition. NAMI favors increased government funding for research, treatment, and community services for the mentally ill. Its publications include the bimonthly newsletter *NAMI Advocate*, and various brochures, handbooks, and policy recommendations.

National Alliance for Research on Schizophrenia and Depression (NARSAD)
60 Cutter Mill Rd., Suite 200
Great Neck, NY 11021
(516) 829-0091
fax: (516) 487-6930

The alliance is a nonprofit coalition of citizens groups that raises funds for research into the causes, treatments, cures, and prevention of severe mental illnesses. Funded by families, organizations, foundations, and corporations, NARSAD awards prizes and grants to researchers. It publishes *NARSAD Research*, a quarterly newsletter.

National Association of Psychiatric Health Systems (NAPHS)
1319 F St. NW, Suite 1000
Washington, DC 20004-1154
(202) 393-6700
fax: (202) 783-6041

The association represents the interests of private psychiatric hospitals, residential treatment centers, and programs partially consisting of hospital care. It provides a forum for ideas concerning the administration, care, and treatment of the mentally ill. It publishes various fact sheets and policy recommendations, including *How You Can Help Reform Mental Health: A Grassroots Guide to Political Action*.

National Association of Psychiatric Survivors (NAPS)
PO Box 618
Sioux Falls, SD 57101
(605) 334-4067

The association consists of current and previous mental patients and their supporters. NAPS opposes involuntary psychiatric procedures such as civil commitment and forced treatment. Instead, it advocates the rights of mental patients to choose their own treatments and to refuse unwanted treatments. It publishes the quarterly newsletter *NAPS/News* as well as a brochure, a reading list, and a list of state protection and advocacy agencies.

National Association for Rural Mental Health (NARMH)
PO Box 570
Wood River, IL 62095
(618) 251-0589

The association consists of mental health professionals, administrators, and other people dedicated to improving mental health services in rural areas. It provides training to mental health practitioners, and it promotes the use of mental health services by those living in rural communities. NARMH publishes the quarterly *Rural Community Health Newsletter* and distributes occasional position statements.

National Depressive and Manic Depressive Association (NDMDA)
730 N. Franklin St., Suite 501
Chicago, IL 60610
(312) 642-0049
fax: (312) 642-7243

The association provides support and advocacy for patients with depression and manic-depressive illness. It seeks to persuade the public that these disorders are biochemical in nature and to end the stigmatization of people who suffer from them. It publishes the quarterly *NDMDA Newsletter* and various books and pamphlets.

National Foundation for Depressive Illness (NAFDI)
PO Box 2257
New York, NY 10116
(212) 268-4260
recorded message: (800) 248-4344
fax: (212) 268-4434

NAFDI seeks to inform the public, health care providers, and corporations about depression and manic-depressive illness. It promotes the view that these disorders are physical illnesses treatable with medication, and it believes that such medication should be made readily available to those who need it. The foundation maintains several toll-free telephone lines and distributes brochures, bibliographies, and literature on the symptoms of and treatments for depression and manic-depressive illness. It also publishes the quarterly newsletter *NAFDI News*.

National Institute of Mental Health (NIMH)
Information Resources and Inquiry
5600 Fishers Ln., Room 7C-02
Rockville, MD 20857

NIMH is the federal agency concerned with mental health research. It plans and conducts a comprehensive program of research relating to the causes, prevention, diagnosis, and treatment of mental illnesses. It produces various informational publications on mental disorders and their treatment.

National Mental Health Association (NMHA)
1021 Prince St.
Alexandria, VA 22314-2971
(703) 684-7722
fax: (703) 684-5968

The association is a consumer advocacy organization concerned with combating mental illness and improving mental health. It promotes research into the treatment and prevention of mental illness, monitors the quality of care provided to the mentally ill, and provides educational materials on mental illness and mental health. It publishes the tabloid *NMHA Focus* four times a year and various leaflets, pamphlets, and reports.

National Mental Health Consumer Self-Help Clearinghouse (NMHCSHC)
311 S. Juniper St., Suite 1000
Philadelphia, PA 19107
(215) 735-6082
fax: (215) 735-0275

The clearinghouse helps develop self-help and consumer advocacy groups by providing information to and encouraging cooperation and networking among self-help groups and consumer advocates across the nation. It maintains a library of reprinted materials and publishes numerous pamphlets and manuals relating to self-help groups and consumer advocacy.

National Resource Center on Homelessness and Mental Illness (NRCHMI)
Policy Research Associates, Inc.
262 Delaware Ave.
Delmar, NY 12054
(800) 444-7415
fax: (518) 439-7612

The center provides information and technical assistance to various agencies concerned with the housing and other needs of the homeless mentally ill. It publishes *Access*, a quarterly newsletter that provides information on research, programs, and initiatives affecting the homeless mentally ill. It also provides free information packets on request.

Obsessive Compulsive Foundation (OCF)
PO Box 70
Milford, CT 06460
(203) 878-5669
fax: (203) 874-2826

The foundation consists of individuals with obsessive-compulsive disorders (OCDs), their friends and families, and the professionals who treat them. It seeks to increase public awareness of and discover a cure for obsessive-compulsive disorders. It publishes the bimonthly *OCD Newsletter* and brochures and educational materials on OCDs.

Project Overcome (PO)
50 Fourth Ave. N., Apt. 32A
Minneapolis, MN 55401
(612) 340-0165

Project Overcome is a group of recovered and recovering mental patients concerned with eliminating the stigma associated with mental illness. It publishes the quarterly newsletter *Voices* and educational materials on mental health.

World Federation for Mental Health (WFMH)
1021 Prince St.
Alexandria, VA 22314
(703) 838-7543
fax: (703) 684-5968

The federation consists of individuals and associations dedicated to improving public mental health worldwide. It strives to coordinate mental health organizations in an effort to enhance mental health care in developing countries. It publishes a newsletter four times a year.

Bibliography of Books

Richard Abrams — *Electroconvulsive Therapy.* 2nd ed. New York: Oxford University Press, 1992.

Nancy C. Andreasen — *The Broken Brain: The Biological Revolution in Psychiatry.* New York: Harper and Row, 1984.

Louise Armstrong — *And They Call It Help: The Psychiatric Policing of America's Children.* Reading, MA: Addison-Wesley, 1992.

Alice S. Baum and Donald W. Burnes — *A Nation in Denial: The Truth About Homelessness.* Boulder, CO: Westview Press, 1993.

Allen E. Bergin and Sol L. Garfield, eds. — *Handbook of Psychotherapy and Behavior Change: An Empirical Analysis.* 4th ed. New York: John Wiley & Sons, 1994.

Peter R. Breggin — *Electroshock: Its Brain Disabling Effects.* New York: Springer, 1979.

Tom Campbell and Chris Heginbotham — *Mental Illness: Prejudice, Discrimination, and the Law.* Brookfield, VT: Dartmouth, 1991.

Lincoln Caplan — *The Insanity Defense and the Trial of John W. Hinckley, Jr.* Boston: D.R. Godine, 1984.

Neal L. Cohen, ed. — *Psychiatry Takes to the Streets: Outreach and Crisis Intervention for the Mentally Ill.* New York: Guilford Press, 1990.

Dorothea Dix — *On Behalf of the Insane Poor: Selected Reports.* New York: Arno Press and The New York Times, 1971.

Colette Dowling — *You Mean I Don't Have to Feel This Way?* New York: Charles Scribner & Sons, 1991.

William W. Dressler — *Stress and Adaptation in the Context of Culture: Depression in a Southern Black Community.* Albany: State University of New York Press, 1991.

Patty Duke and Gloria Hochman — *A Brilliant Madness: Living with Manic-Depressive Illness.* New York: Bantam Books, 1992.

Matthew P. Dumont — *Treating the Poor: A Personal Sojourn Through the Rise and Fall of Community Mental Health.* Belmont, MA: Dymphna Press, 1992.

Norman Endler and Emanuel Persad — *Electroconvulsive Therapy: The Myths and the Realities.* Toronto: Hans Huber, 1988.

Seth Farber — *Madness, Heresy, and the Rumor of Angels: The Revolt Against the Mental Health System.* Peru, IL: Open Court, 1993.

Suman Fernando	*Mental Health, Race, and Culture*. New York: St. Martin's Press, 1991.
Seymour Fisher and Roger Greenberg, eds.	*The Limits of Biological Treatments for Psychological Distress: Comparisons with Psychotherapy and Placebo*. Hillsdale, NJ: Lawrence Erlbaum Associates, 1989.
Michel Foucault	*Madness and Civilization: A History of Insanity in the Age of Reason*. New York: Vintage Books, 1965.
Richard G. Frank and Willard G. Manning Jr., eds.	*Economics and Mental Health*. Baltimore: Johns Hopkins University Press, 1992.
Sigmund Freud	*The Essentials of Psychoanalysis*. Translated by James Strachey. London: Hogarth Press, 1986.
Sigmund Freud	*The Psychopathology of Everyday Life*. New York: Macmillan, 1917.
Albert C. Gaw, ed.	*Culture, Ethnicity, and Mental Illness*. Washington, DC: American Psychiatric Press, 1993.
Frederick K. Goodwin and Kay Redfield Jamison	*Manic-Depressive Illness*. New York: Oxford University Press, 1990.
Irving I. Gottesman and James Shields	*Schizophrenia and Genetics: A Twin Study Vantage Point*. New York: Academic Press, 1972.
Gerald N. Grob	*From Asylum to Community: Mental Health Policy in Modern America*. Princeton, NJ: Princeton University Press, 1991.
Gerald N. Grob	*Mental Illness and American Society, 1875-1940*. Princeton, NJ: Princeton University Press, 1983.
Agnes B. Hatfield and Harriet P. Lefley	*Surviving Mental Illness: Stress, Coping, and Adaptation*. New York: Guilford Press, 1993.
D. Jaklow Hershman and Julian Lieb	*The Key to Genius: Manic Depression and the Creative Life*. Buffalo: Prometheus Books, 1988.
Leonard L. Hoeston	*Mending Minds: A Guide to the New Psychiatry of Depression, Anxiety, and Other Serious Mental Disorders*. New York: W.H. Freeman, 1992.
bell hooks	*Sisters of the Yam: Black Women and Self-Recovery*. Boston: South End Press, 1993.
Christopher G. Hudson and Arthur J. Cox, eds.	*Dimensions of State Mental Health Policy*. New York: Praeger, 1991.
Dana Crowley Jack	*Silencing the Self: Women and Depression*. Cambridge, MA: Harvard University Press, 1991.

Kay Redfield Jamison   *Touched with Fire: Manic-Depressive Illness and the Artistic Temperament*. New York: Free Press, 1993.

Karen Johnson and Tom Ferguson   *Trusting Ourselves: The Sourcebook on Psychology for Women*. New York: Atlantic Monthly Press, 1990.

Susanna Kaysen   *Girl, Interrupted*. New York: Turtle Bay Books, 1993.

Ken Kesey   *One Flew over the Cuckoo's Nest*. New York: Viking, 1962.

Donald F. Klein and Paul H. Wender   *Understanding Depression: A Complete Guide to Its Diagnosis and Treatment*. New York: Oxford University Press, 1993.

R.D. Laing   *The Divided Self*. New York: Pantheon Books, 1969.

R.D. Laing   *The Politics of Experience*. New York: Pantheon Books, 1967.

Ronald Leifer   *In the Name of Psychiatry: The Social Functions of Psychiatry*. New York: Science House, 1969.

Murray Levine and Adeline Levine   *Helping Children: A Social History*. New York: Oxford University Press, 1992.

R.C. Lewontin, Steven Rose, and Leon Kamin   *Not in Our Genes*. New York: Pantheon Books, 1984.

Mario Maj, Fabrizio Starace, and Norman Sartorius   *Mental Disorders in HIV-1 Infection and AIDS*. Seattle: Hogrefe & Huber, 1993.

David Mechanic   *Mental Health and Social Policy*. 3rd ed. Englewood Cliffs, NJ: Prentice Hall, 1989.

Karl Menninger   *The Vital Balance*. New York: Viking, 1963.

Kent S. Miller and Michael L. Radelet   *Executing the Mentally Ill: The Criminal Justice System and the Case of Alvin Ford*. Newbury Park, CA: Sage Publications, 1993.

Jeffrey Moussaieff Masson   *Against Therapy: Emotional Tyranny and the Myth of Psychological Healing*. New York: Atheneum, 1988.

Jeffrey Moussaieff Masson   *Final Analysis: The Making and Unmaking of a Psychoanalyst*. New York: Addison-Wesley, 1990.

Carol S. North   *Welcome Silence: My Triumph over Schizophrenia*. New York: Simon and Schuster, 1987.

Daniel Offer and Melvin Sabshin, eds.   *The Diversity of Normal Behavior: Further Contributions to Normatology*. New York: Basic Books, 1991.

Roy Porter	*A Social History of Madness—The World Through the Eyes of the Insane*. New York: Weidenfeld & Nicolson, 1987.
Dorothy S. Ruiz, ed.	*Handbook of Mental Health and Mental Disorder Among Black Americans*. New York: Greenwood Press, 1990.
Wilbur J. Scott	*The Politics of Readjustment: Vietnam Veterans Since the War*. New York: Aldine de Gruyter, 1993.
Susan Sheehan	*Is There No Place on Earth for Me?* Boston: Houghton Mifflin, 1982.
John F. Shumaker, ed.	*Religion and Mental Health*. New York: Oxford University Press, 1992.
Charles Silverstein, ed.	*Gays, Lesbians, and Their Therapists: Studies in Psychotherapy*. New York: Norton, 1991.
Zahava Solomon	*Combat Stress Reaction: The Enduring Toll of War*. New York: Plenum Press, 1993.
William Styron	*Darkness Visible: A Memoir of Madness*. New York: Random House, 1990.
Thomas Szasz	*Ideology and Insanity: Essays on the Psychiatric Dehumanization of Man*. Syracuse, NY: Syracuse University Press, 1991.
Thomas Szasz	*The Myth of Mental Illness*. New York: Harper and Row, 1961.
E. Fuller Torrey	*The Freudian Fraud: The Malignant Effect of Freud's Theory on American Thought and Culture*. New York: HarperCollins, 1992.
E. Fuller Torrey	*Nowhere to Go: The Tragic Odyssey of the Homeless Mentally Ill*. New York: Harper and Row, 1988.
E. Fuller Torrey	*Surviving Schizophrenia: A Family Manual*. New York: Harper and Row, 1983.
E. Fuller Torrey et al.	*Criminalizing the Seriously Mentally Ill: The Abuse of Jails as Mental Hospitals*. Arlington, VA: National Alliance for the Mentally Ill, 1992.
U.S. Congress, Office of Technology Assessment	*The Biology of Mental Disorders*. Washington, DC: U.S. Government Printing Office, 1992.
Jane M. Ussher and Paula Nicholson, eds.	*Gender Issues in Clinical Psychology*. New York: Routledge, 1992.
William Vega and John W. Murphy	*Culture and the Restructuring of Community Mental Health*. New York: Greenwood Press, 1990.
Mary Jane Ward	*The Snake Pit*. New York: Random House, 1946.

Index

303